HOW TO RECOGNIZE AND REFINISH A FOR PLEASURE AND PROFIT

Fifth Edition

PRAISE FOR PREVIOUS EDITIONS:

"The author, an avid collector, writes with enthusiasm."
—*New York Times*

"Practical advice to the novice collector on looking for bargains
and restoring the damaged furniture that others may not buy."
—*Antiques Review*

"Filled with sound advice . . . a useful reference."
—*Decorating* magazine

"Helpful to antique enthusiasts and those considering
marketing their restorations."
—Harris Publications, Inc.

HOW TO
RECOGNIZE
AND REFINISH
ANTIQUES
FOR PLEASURE AND PROFIT

FIFTH EDITION

BOB BROOKE

The Globe Pequot Press

GUILFORD, CONNECTICUT

To buy books in quantity for corporate use or incentives, call **(800) 962–0973,** or e-mail **premiums@GlobePequot.com.**

Text design by Nancy Freeborn
Photographs by Bob Brooke
Illustrations by Todd Telander

Library of Congress Cataloging-in-Publication Data is available.
ISBN-13: 978-0-7627-4022-2
ISBN-10: 0-7627-4022-1

Manufactured in the United States of America
Fifth Edition/First Printing

CONTENTS

INTRODUCTION

Twenty some years ago, I went through some changes in my life—divorce, relocation, starting a new career. Financially, I wasn't in the position to furnish an apartment, but a friend showed me how I could do just that and not spend a lot of money as long as I had some time available.

He had been collecting antiques for some time, and to look at his place, you'd have thought he had spent a fortune. But he assured me that each piece had been purchased at garage sales and flea markets and lovingly restored over the years. In the early 1980s, people were still throwing out or giving away what they called "old" furniture. A lot of it ended up in secondhand shops, so this is where my friend and I started my search for furnishings for my new apartment.

When he told me I could find some good antique pieces, I wondered how that could be. At the time, my only connection to antiques was the ones owned by a rich uncle and his wife. I never figured I could afford to own anything like that, but my friend showed me I was wrong.

I soon learned the real story behind today's antiques market. Yes, many of the really fine antiques—those in pristine condition and of rare value—are in museums and elegant private homes. However, men and women with an eye for good pieces buy hundreds of antique chairs, tables, dressers, cabinets, beds, and bookcases for rock-bottom prices, often paying as little as one-tenth of their retail value.

These people buy antiques that are in such poor condition, no self-respecting fine shop owner would even consider selling them. They buy neglected or damaged antiques, then, with lots of effort and love, restore them to objects of genuine beauty and value. These are the same people, like my friend and myself, who sift through the junk in a secondhand store, looking for just the right piece. They're the same ones who sit through long auctions hoping to get a few press-back side chairs that need new seats.

They're the people who rise at dawn on Saturday to check out a promising garage sale.

These are the adventurers in the world of antiques. And if you're the type who welcomes a challenge—who thrives on the satisfaction of creating beauty through your own effort and ingenuity—then you can be one of these adventurers.

Today, both men and women take up refinishing their antique finds every year. Current refinishing materials and tools make it easy to achieve great results without a complete home workshop and years of experience.

This book explains how you can have a lot of fun and tap into potential profit as you go about refinishing furniture and some accessories. Perhaps you'll even turn this hobby into a profitable sideline.

The rationale behind all this is twofold. First, restoring damaged pieces to good condition gives lovers of fine furniture, like myself, the chance to furnish a home with high-quality furniture at a fraction of the cost of new pieces. Smart young adults are picking up antiques, one at a time, and restoring them to furnish their first homes or apartments. Their parents are discovering that this is a way to add distinction to their home in a manner impossible with today's mass-produced furniture and accessories. And because makers of antique furniture took personal pride in their work, its basic construction is often far superior to that of the merchandise coming from factories today. An antique can still have excellent woods and good design regardless of the amount of dirt and wrinkled varnish on its surface. Second, antiques constantly appreciate in value. So instead of becoming merely "used" the moment after purchase, as is the case with contemporary furniture, an antique becomes more valuable the longer it is owned. Antiques are a recognized investment and a hedge against inflation.

Investment counselors list four major areas in which wary purchasers can be virtually guaranteed a reliable and large return on their money: real estate, top-quality art, investment-grade diamonds—and good antiques. The first three investments normally require substantial amounts of capital. Good antiques do, too, if bought at retail prices in better shops. Prices on antiques in need of restoration, however, are within the means of anyone willing to do some hunting to find them. After adding some effort to achieve the transformation, it's possible to quickly multiply an initial small investment many times over.

I stumbled on a solid walnut, marble-topped Victorian Eastlake dresser as I searched through secondhand shops looking for pieces for my apartment. Selling for $75, it was in fair condition but needed some surface refinishing. But the mirror normally attached to its back was missing. After careful cleaning and revarnishing and some marble cleaning, the piece was ready to hold my clothes. That seemed easy enough, but where to find a mirror to go with it? After much searching, I discovered the *exact* mirror for this piece in a nonprofit shop selling architectural antiques. It wasn't in as good a shape as my dresser, but with some loving care and polishing, I was able to attach it to the back of my dresser to complete the ensemble. As a complete piece, its value is now close to $800. Not bad for a few hours' work.

Most people start on this hobby quite by accident or out of necessity as I did. They inherit a family heirloom or are given a small piece in need of repairs. A little glue or varnish remover, a couple of screws, or some gentle sanding later, and they've managed to put it in pretty decent shape. They're thrilled with their own success. Then, they spot another piece at a garage sale that just begs, "Take me home and fix me up!" One or two more such incidents, and they're soon a confirmed restorer, one whose confidence and expertise build with each succeeding venture.

Pretty soon, though, all those small victories begin to crowd the house. I can attest to that. So I began selling or "trading up." Unfortunately, too many people never reach this stage, being satisfied with what they have. To make any antiques collection better, it's necessary to sell off or trade some of the lesser pieces to be able to afford to buy better ones. This is when they realize the profit potential in this interesting hobby.

Trading up is simply trading two or three minor pieces for one of higher value. An older woman friend bought two Victorian side chairs at a monthly flea market, paying $10 each. Neither had usable caned seats, and both had been painted gold and were a bit loose. In spite of how ugly they looked, she knew that their basic designs were excellent.

She went through the renovation procedures described in various chapters of this book and ended up with two beautiful rosewood side chairs, for which she gets many compliments. As time went on, she acquired other chairs and soon had more than she could use. So she located an antiques shop in town in the window of which stood a small Victorian marble-top table, just what she needed next to the easy chair

in her living room. It was priced at $175. She brought her chairs into the owner's back room and asked, "Would you trade me that table for these chairs?" The result was an immediate deal, one that benefited both the dealer and the refinisher. The dealer could easily sell each chair for $125, so his profit margin would be larger than that on the sale of the table alone. And the smart trader had upgraded an original $20 purchase, plus some work and refinishing materials, into a $175 table. So everyone came out ahead.

While not all dealers will trade equally one piece for another, or even several pieces for one, some sort of deal can usually be worked out involving some trade and cash. Obviously, the person who works out such a deal immediately starts thinking ahead to other such deals. From then on, the sky's the limit—whether in trading or selling—for anyone who would like to take basic restoration skills and turn them into a satisfying sideline for pleasure or extra income.

This book was written to help you do the same. With the information in the following chapters, you can furnish your home with fine antiques at affordable prices and/or join the ranks of those happy entrepreneurs whose income is limited only by their ingenuity.

I'll show you how to avoid mistakes and how to make your time and money most productive. The information will, I hope, save you the heartache of irreparably damaging a nice antique simply because you didn't know the proper refinishing techniques.

Many philosophies exist regarding the proper method of restoring antiques. One involves complete renovation, including stripping to the bare wood and taking every member apart. This is restoration. Another says only absolutely necessary repairs should be made, and the original finish should be preserved whenever possible. This is preservation. I'll discuss both.

This book will show you the restoration methods you can safely tackle yourself and those that are beyond the realm of the average do-it-yourselfer. One chapter will show you where to find the best buys in antiques in need of work, and another will discuss ways to detect them under layers of grime, paint, or varnish.

One chapter gives complete information on reseating chairs, and another discusses an easy way to replace missing carving on a picture or mirror frame.

The final two chapters will be for those of you who would like to capitalize on this knowledge to increase your income. They tell you how you can best sell your restored antiques to individuals, how to place work on consignment with antiques dealers, and how to start and manage your own shop if you so desire. You'll also find information on the various legal and financial issues of selling antiques for profit.

At the end of the book you'll find a glossary of terms used in the text. This will help you understand some words and phrases that may be new to you at first.

Lifestyles are changing, and not everyone who reads this book will be a homeowner with full basement, complete workshop, and unlimited space. So, most of what is described here can, with a little care, be completed in the average city apartment or condominium with only a basic knowledge of tools.

Nostalgia is in. People are discovering that acquiring and using the fine furniture and accessories of generations past is one way to establish a link with their treasured heritage. The soft patina of old wood, the delicate carvings that mirror a craftsman's love of his trade, the pride of possessing a one-of-a-kind beauty—these are some of the joys of owning fine antiques.

You're embarking on a genuinely satisfying craft when you start restoring neglected antiques to their rightful beauty—a craft that can occupy you for a lifetime.

CHAPTER 1

WHERE ARE THE BARGAINS IN ANTIQUES?

Half the fun of building a collection of fine antiques can be in finding them in the first place. Antiques lovers are detectives at heart. The greatest thrill is suddenly to discover a gem of a china cabinet, a delicate little Bible table, or a lovely old oval frame hidden away in some unlikely place. After quickly paying for their purchase, they haul it home. Like prospectors, antiques collectors dig and sift through tons of useless junk, always confident that just around the next corner or in the next room is the very piece they need or want to fill out a collection.

It's no problem, of course, to visit fine shops in search of antiques. If you buy in one of these usual outlets, however, you'll pay the going retail prices, and it could be several years before that initial investment increases substantially. You'll be paying for someone else's ingenuity in ferreting the antiques out of their hiding places, perhaps refinishing them, and then providing a showcase while waiting for the owner to come along. Since this book is all about helping you increase your investment in antique furniture from minimal to substantial, it will show you some *better* places to buy your treasures. This information is useful whether you're furnishing your own home or buying for resale.

Since all of these sources are "cash and carry," you'll find a station wagon or small pickup truck ideal for transporting your purchases. Some hatchbacks offer an amazing amount of interior room, but most conventional automobiles will carry only small pieces of furniture, and even then it is awkward to jockey them into a trunk or backseat. If you do own a conventional sedan or coupe, you might team up with a friend who owns a larger vehicle and go scrounging together. Offer to pay for the gas in exchange for the use of that extra cargo space.

You should take along a few tools of the trade, too. You'll need either a yardstick or a retractable tape measure. This will help you decide whether or not a charming hall tree you want to bid on at an auction will fit into your tiny foyer. A sharp knife is useful for flicking off layers of paint to see if a tabletop is actually solid oak. Soft rags and well-capped containers of soapy water and solvent come in handy for cutting through generations of grime and old wax. And you may find one of the better antiques price guides available in bookstores a valuable asset. These give you the current retail prices of antiques so you know whether or not the asking price for that marble-topped fern stand really is a bargain.

The four most likely places to find antiques in need of restoration and at reasonable prices are auctions, garage sales, flea markets, and secondhand stores.

AUCTIONS

"Do I hear twenty-five? Twenty-five? Twenty-five? Sold to the gentleman in the second row for twenty!" The auctioneer's trained voice signals another purchase by an eager buyer. And if the fellow did his homework, he probably went home with a real bargain.

Auction buffs have been acquiring bargains at these lively sales for years. Auctions are, in fact, one of the oldest recorded means of large-scale public sales. Roman conquerors auctioned off war booty in the marketplaces of their sprawling empire two thousand years ago. In the Middle Ages residents of London and other large English cities regularly bought at auction the luscious fruit imported from Italy and Spain. Later, colonists brought the custom with them to these shores, and we have a record of an auction being held in New Amsterdam as early as 1662.

The auction procedures employed today evolved from a variety of now-abandoned customs. It was once common practice for auction-goers to bid against one another as they watched a candle burn. When the candle had burned down a specified distance, usually an inch, or had burned out, the bidding was over, and the last person to enter a bid was the successful one. An hour glass was sometimes used in the same way, the winner of the merchandise being the one to shout a bid just as the last grain of sand dropped into the lower half of the glass.

Procedures may have changed, but auctions are still one of the most exciting places to buy goods of any kind—especially antiques! Antiques are auctioned off in four ways.

Prestigious Auction Houses

The most glamorous auctions are those conducted by world-famous houses such as Sotheby's of London and New York. Here, fine antiques are sold for very large sums to wealthy collectors and/or dealers whose clients are the members of the international social set. Few antiques collectors have the bank accounts to qualify as legitimate customers at one of these glittering affairs! But these auctions, generally held in large metropolitan areas, *are* an important part of the novice's education.

If you live in or near a big city, try to attend auctions at one of these prestigious establishments. You'll quickly learn how valuable fine antiques can be. You'll see knowledgeable men and women bidding thousands upon thousands of dollars for an eighteenth-century French dressing table or a massive mirror that once graced the walls of a Spanish don's mansion. Conduct a discreet survey of your own as to what those same pieces might have sold for ten years ago. Any antiques dealer can give you these figures, or you can check out some old copies of antiques-related magazines at the library. You'll find that the *percentage increase* for those antiques is greater than that of virtually any other commodity available, including stocks, bonds, and real estate. With that knowledge as an incentive, you can then investigate the other categories of auctions, those where *you* can begin to build your own estate by judiciously bidding for antiques.

Now, it's highly unlikely that you will find an eighteenth-century treasure lurking undetected at any other auctions discussed here. What you will discover are mainly nineteenth-century Victorian and turn-of-the-twentieth-century pieces. These won't bring the prices that flirt with five and six figures, no matter how expertly you refinish them. But you can easily double, triple, or even quadruple your original modest investment by buying carefully at these auctions.

Local Established Auction Houses

Many areas, from rural communities to large cities, have permanent auction houses that sell everything from appliances to boxes of freight-damaged merchandise. These houses may devote one evening a month to antiques. The offerings on that night may be an accumulation from many different sources. Individuals who want to sell off an entire household of antiques will commission the auction house to handle the sale. Antiques dealers frequently bring in truckloads of merchandise that hasn't moved out of their shops quickly enough. Managers or owners of the auction house itself may scour the countryside searching for items to add interest to "antiques night." The result is usually a good selection of both average and fine-quality antique furniture.

Some permanent auction houses handle *only* antiques. Their selection is usually made up from estates and dealers' input. The quality of the antiques is often quite a bit higher than that of the auction house that only occasionally offers antiques, and so are the bids. Even so, you can find excellent buys at these houses once you develop a bit of know-how. Some houses have a back room where the auctioneers put the furniture they feel is not in good enough condition to go on the floor with the beautifully refinished items. I've seen china cabinets with glass missing from the doors, bureaus with drawers that wouldn't close properly, tables with loose veneer, and chairs with frayed cane seats. Almost all were prime candidates for refinishing. Each was marked with a set price—no bidding necessary to get them. You might check to see if such a "back room" exists in the better auction houses in your area.

Estate Auctions or Sales

You can frequently find bargains at the so-called estate auctions held at private homes. Conducted by professional auctioneers, these sales offer only the possessions of the family living in that home. Estate sales are often held in conjunction with the sale of a house or the death of the owner. You'll find them advertised in the classified section of the local newspaper.

Often you have to wait through the bidding on second-rate furniture, boxes of plastic kitchenware, and even a doghouse or two before anything you find interesting is offered for bids. You rarely have a place to sit, either, during these auctions, so I often take along a small folding camp stool.

Unlike sales in established auction houses, these sales may start at any time of the day or evening. The newspaper ad will give you the starting time. As with any auction, you should plan to arrive at least a few minutes early to have time to view and examine the furniture to be offered.

Many estate sales will begin in the morning and go right on through the day until everything is sold. This means there's no break for lunch. In such a case, you should take along something to eat and drink. Then you won't mind waiting until the auctioneer gets to the big old walnut bed you're determined to have!

An antiques auction offers plenty of opportunities to buy finer antiques in need of restoration.

Country Auctions

If you live in or near a rural community, you should keep up with the country or farm auctions. The advantage of these sales is that they're so far from the "big city" that casual auctiongoers seldom attend. Good pieces frequently go for much less than they would at the more heavily attended city auctions. Country auctions are not always advertised in the larger newspapers. You can get announcement flyers sent to you through the mail, though, by finding out the names of rural auction companies and asking to be put on their mailing lists. These are the most informal auctions of all and are great fun to attend.

Now, in order to increase the investment you make in the antiques you buy at auctions—no matter which kind you attend—you must maintain a professional attitude. To develop this attitude, emulate the antiques dealers you admire.

If you attend local auctions regularly, you begin to recognize local dealers. The enterprising ones never miss a good auction, always looking for bargains to stock their shops. You learn a great deal about buying at auction, for investment, by watching the dealers.

Let's look at the way an astute dealer—I'll call him Paul—would act at an average auction in an average American city.

Paul arrives at the auction at least a half hour before the scheduled starting time. He immediately goes to the clerk and asks for a bidding card. In an established house, the clerk can usually be found at a counter near the door. At estate auctions and country auctions, the clerk is often found in the front seat of the auctioneer's automobile. The clerk gives Paul a bidding card, a large cardboard card that has a number printed on one side in bold figures. This is the card Paul will hold up to enter a bid. The clerk records Paul's name and address along with the number on his card. This is how the clerk keeps track of what Paul buys during the course of the auction.

The back of this card is blank. It affords an ideal place for Paul to record both the amount he is willing to bid for any item and also his winning bid. There's no charge for the card, so you should always ask for one. No one can enter a bid without a bidding card.

Since Paul is attending an auction in an auction house where seats can be reserved, he has brought along a piece of paper and some cellophane tape. He writes his name on the paper and tapes it to the back of a chair near the front of the house, close to the auctioneer's stand. This informal maneuver reserves that chair for him.

Paul now spends the next half hour inspecting the items that will be put up for bids. All are on display, and each is tagged with a lot number for identification. Paul sees three pieces of furniture that he would like to buy. One is an Eastlake-style bed, another a rocker upholstered in red velvet, the third a small marble-topped table, one of a pair. Paul knows that the bed's retail value at this time is around $800, so he's willing to go as high as $400 for it since it's in fine condition and will need no refinishing. The lot number on the bed is #34.

The rocker is a good example of turn-of-the-twentieth-century oak furniture, but the upholstery is in bad condition, and the wood is obscured with many layers of grimy varnish. It's going to take some work to get this in top con-

The auction house staff gives each item or grouping of items in an auction a lot number. For this piece, it's on the label at the upper left.

dition. The retail value of this rocker—once reconditioned—is around $275. Taking into consideration the time and expense he'll have to put in, Paul decides his top bid on this piece, lot #51, will be $75.

Even though the small table is one of a pair, Paul doesn't want its mate. Close inspection reveals both a long, deep crack running the full length of the pedestal and cracked marble in one table. The other table is in good condition and is worth at least $225, so Paul decides he'll be willing to bid as high as $125 for it, lot #21. Now, if Paul had not examined these tables prior to the sale and noted

down the lot numbers, he might not know the difference between the two when the auctioneer held them up for bids. Some auctioneers will make a point of mentioning any defects in an antique, others will not. It's always good insurance to inspect any piece that interests you.

Paul turns his bidding card over and writes:

#34 — $400
#51 — $75
#21 — $125

By this time the auction is ready to start and everyone must take a seat. Only at very informal country auctions and some estate auctions are customers allowed to ramble through the merchandise after the auction starts. Without a prior inspection and lot numbers to guide them, latecomers must bid blindly.

The auction starts, and before long the bed comes up. Paul enters his bids by holding up his card when the auctioneer calls "Do I hear $400?" "Do I hear $425?" and "Do I hear $450?" Holding up the bidding card is a bidder's silent assent to the amount asked by the auctioneer. Since no one tops his bid of $400, Paul gets the bed. The clerk notes his card number and the price of $400.

Several people are bidding against Paul when the rocker is offered. The bidding is lively and soon reaches the $75 limit Paul decided was his top bid. As much as he wanted that rocker, Paul does not go over his $75 limit. Paul allows the other party to go higher and win the bid. Remember that Paul wrote down his top bid on the back of the bidding card. This actually serves two purposes. First, it helps him remember both the lot number of the rocker he wanted and the amount he was willing to pay for it. Second, it's psychologically more difficult to go over a planned bid if you have the predetermined figure you'll be willing to pay *written down*. This is good insurance against auction fever, the disease that makes people bid higher and higher for a coveted item. It's easy to get caught up in the excitement of bidding and end up paying far more for a piece than you should.

The pair of tables does not come up until late afternoon. Paul, along with everyone else, is getting tired by then. The auctioneer places the tables in front of the audience, mentions the lot number of each, and calls for bids. Paul knows which one to bid on, even though from his seat in the third row they look identical. He's the successful bidder for #21 at $100. Someone else ends up bidding the same amount for the second table, a mistake that could have been avoided by careful examination before the auction started.

Since this is all Paul intended to bid on, he goes to the clerk's desk, pays his bill, and arranges to pick up the furniture.

Now, every rule has its exception. And the one about not going over a prearranged top bid is one you can occasionally break, but only when you know that you're bidding against a dealer, not a collector. Collectors will often pay almost anything for an especially desirable piece of furniture. Dealers won't. They know what the reasonable price is for that item and won't bid over that figure, usually one-third to one-half of its retail price. They're professional enough to set a specific figure and stick with it. They don't become emotionally involved in the bidding, as collectors often do.

If you find something at an auction that you really want and discover you're bidding *only* against a dealer, you may adjust your top bid. An auction buyer named Bill was able to buy a solid-walnut dining table once for just $5.00 over a dealer's limit by doing this. An elderly woman had sold her home and arranged for the local auctioneer to sell off her furniture and household goods at an estate auction in her backyard. As usual, the auctioneer ran quickly through dozens upon dozens of items of little value. The only thing he really wanted was that table. It was beautiful, and Bill knew it would be a good investment if he could get it at a reasonable price. Dining tables are nearly always in great demand. He decided his top bid would be $300.

Several other people were interested in the table, including a woman Bill recognized as a dealer from a town some 50 miles away. The bidding started at $50 and went up rapidly in increments of $10. One by one the other bidders dropped out until only the dealer and Bill were left. At $280 it was her bid. Bill countered with $290. She hesitated then, and offered $300. Bill's instinct, pretty well tuned from years of this sort of thing, told him she had set $300 as her limit for that table. The auctioneer turned to Bill and asked for $310. Bill indicated he wouldn't go $310 but would bid $305. The auctioneer accepted that bid and turned back to the dealer, asking for $310. Very unhappily, she shook her head, and Bill got the table.

This woman was a professional. She knew what she could charge for antiques in her shop and what she must pay for them to make a reasonable profit. She set her limits and stuck with them. In your case, though, where you don't have the overhead costs of running a shop or may be buying for long-term investment, you can use a dealer's professionalism to your advantage as Bill did. If you find yourself bidding against someone you know is a dealer, be willing to go *one step* higher than the limit you think he or she has set. It can pay off in some excellent buys. After some minor refinishing, that table increased in value more than twice what Bill paid for it.

This ploy doesn't always work, of course, especially if you're bidding against a collector.

Many individuals who become enamored of a piece of antique furniture at auction will be willing to bid it right up to the current retail value and even beyond. That is their privilege, of course, but it isn't the way to make a substantial return on your investment in antiques.

One last word about antiques auctions: Bad weather can work in your favor. Casual and non-professional buyers are often discouraged from attending a scheduled auction if a storm makes driving there difficult or cold weather makes staying home by the fire more inviting. This can be your chance to pick up some real bargains. The dealers will nearly always show up, regardless of rain, sleet, snow, or high water, but remember, they set wholesale price limits on themselves. For a few dollars more, you just might be able to bid your way to some fine antique furniture.

GARAGE SALES

Many people find it hard to believe that you can still find bargain antiques, especially those in need of much TLC, at garage sales. "You're joking!" they almost always reply. But with a little care and effort, you'll be able to restore frames and mirrors for your walls, or a delicate hall tree with a round mirror, or perhaps an exquisite English mahogany desk for your home. All of these can look as though they came from fine antiques shops, yet each most likely found its way into your home by way of one garage sale or another.

Never discount the lowly garage sale as a source of antiques to renovate! This is frequently where you'll find your biggest and best bargains. To make your hunt successful, though, you must develop a good strategy and be persistent.

Garage sales are the market entry point for many salvageable antiques.

Your strategy begins by studying the classified listings under "Garage Sales" in your local paper the night before you plan to go out—usually on Friday night, since most garage sales are held on weekends. Look through all the listings, circling any that have the word *antiques* somewhere in the ad. Also, look especially for any that say the person giving the sale is cleaning out "forty years' accumulation of junk" or some such wording. Every once in a while, you'll come upon a little gem at one of these sales. They can be especially productive if the ads give addresses in older, middle-class neighborhoods. These will be people who have lived in their homes for many, many years, and these homes have the big attics and full basements that are conducive to holding onto possessions. Most residents of suburbia move too frequently to accumulate much, and storage space is usually at a premium in their homes.

Go back over the sales you've circled and stake out a route. Time is of the essence in finding bargains in antiques at garage sales, because many other people have the same idea that you have. You can beat them to the punch by getting to the goodies first.

Plot a route with a colored felt pen. Mark

the sale closest to your house *1* and continue numbering those farther away *2, 3,* etc. Drive to *1* first, then on to *2,* and so on down the list. That way you won't waste time backtracking all over town.

Surprisingly, the best buys are *not* usually at the home where the ad lists *antiques* in bold letters as the main attraction. Often you'll find beautiful furniture at these sales, but it will be expertly restored, and the prices asked will be retail. The owners of much of this furniture bought it at *other* garage sales and refinished it with the express purpose of reselling it for a profit.

Garage sales yielding the best treasures are those where the ads list *antiques* buried in small type right along with a laundry list of old records, Avon bottles, ski boots, and kitchen sinks. Almost without exception you'll find these to be your best hunting grounds.

That's the way I acquired a handsome china cabinet that now holds many of my smaller treasures. As is usual in the suburbs, the garage sale ad listed numerous items from kids' toys to kitchenware. But within the list was the item that caught my eye: antique china cabinet. Given that the location of the sale was just down the street from my house, I figured this had to be a piece from the 1940s or '50s, but to my surprise it turned out to be a bit older than that.

The cabinet stood in the dining room along with some mismatched chairs and a rather sad-looking table. Though the cabinet itself was in pretty bad shape, I realized that it was probably from about 1900. Standing about 6 feet tall, it had a wraparound glass cabinet supported by six legs. Structurally, it was sound enough, but it had been neglected over the years and needed some TLC.

I asked the owner how much she wanted for the cabinet. After thinking for a moment, she replied, "Oh, this old thing! You can have it for $25." I didn't even stop to think and immediately said yes. Before the owner had a chance to change her mind, I made out a check for the amount and said I'd be back later to pick up the cabinet. Today, it's the centerpiece of my living room and holds many smaller collectibles.

Once you have your route planned, you're ready to start out on your antiques hunt. Begin early! If the first sale is scheduled to begin at 8:00 A.M., you should *be there* by 7:50 at the latest. Look the merchandise over carefully and quickly and buy anything that looks promising, then drive on to the next sale on your list. Don't linger. This may not be quite as much fun as a neighborly chat with the other shoppers, but remember, in order to *find* the bargains in antiques first, you must *get* there first.

One important word on strategy: If you see something you're even remotely interested in—pick it up! You may still be trying to decide whether or not a wobbly frame, for instance, is worth buying, but as long as you have it in your hands, It's potentially yours. The Code of the Garage Sale is that possession is nine-tenths of the law. You may decide after a few moments' inspection that the frame is really circa 1965 and not the Art Deco treasure you thought at first. You can always put it back on the table for someone else to examine. But as long as it was in your hands, you had first dibs on it.

One enthusiastic shopper named Kate learned this lesson the hard way. She arrived at a garage sale early and immediately spotted a charming little table with spiraled pedestal legs. She bent closer to try to get her bifocals in focus to read the price tag. Before Kate got there, though, a cagier shopper picked up the table and walked off with it. She got it for $10! If Kate had picked it *up* to read the price tag, she would have had squatter's rights to the table and it would be in her home now.

Always go to garage sales with plenty of change and small bills. Many people who hold garage sales don't have enough change and dollar bills at the very beginning of the day. They're often confronted right at the start of the sale with people coming straight from the ATM machine with $20 bills. You can frequently get them to lower a price a bit by offering coins and dollar bills in payment for an article.

You may also discover that cash comes in handy when an owner first refuses to lower the price of an item. For instance, let's say you come across a high-backed chair in excellent condition at a garage sale. The price on it is $35. You ask the owner if he would take less. He says, "No, the price is firm." You reach into your wallet and pull out five $5 bills. You hold them out to him and ask, "Would you take $25 cash for the chair?" After a moment he says yes and sells you the chair!

Approached scientifically, going to garage sales is not the time-consuming activity that going to auctions certainly can be. The best buys in inexpensive antiques go very quickly. Remember, start early and get there first. You should be finished and back home by 10:00 A.M. on Saturday with at least one or two treasures.

FLEA MARKETS

Flea markets are the next step up in the buying resource chain. They're held by many dealers instead of by individual homeowners. The same rules that apply at garage sales can be used profitably when searching for antiques at flea markets.

Arrive early, while the different dealers are still setting up their tables and arranging their merchandise—in other words, *before* the scheduled opening time. If you should see a really desirable item, you just might be able to buy it then, before the crowds arrive.

Move quickly through the selling area to assess which dealers might have any stock you'd be interested in buying. Make a note of their locations so you can easily find them later when you're ready to buy.

Carry cash and come prepared to dicker. Good-natured bargaining is the name of the game at most flea markets, and you should at least try to get a dealer to lower his or her price. But don't bargain for an item and then not buy it.

The real difference between garage sales and flea markets is that dealers at the latter will often trade merchandise, both among themselves and with their customers. It's entirely possible to buy a picture frame from one dealer, for instance, walk a few tables down the aisle, and trade the frame to another dealer for something of greater value to you.

Many towns have regularly scheduled flea markets that have operated every weekend for years. They draw dealers and customers from miles around. While they are not the best sources for antiques, they're certainly worth looking into.

Flea markets present some good opportunities to purchase old chairs, small tables, boxes, etc. for restoration and renovation.

SECONDHAND STORES

Secondhand stores are a minor source of antiques for restoration. But lightning does strike once in a while, so don't discount them. The big advantage you'll find here is that most secondhand-furniture dealers aren't too knowledgeable about or interested in antiques. They simply want to move the merchandise out of their shops as quickly as possible. On the rare occasion that they acquire a good old buffet or chest of drawers, they'll probably sell it to you for the same price they would a ten-year-old one that really *is* just used furniture.

Your best hunting grounds are secondhand stores in rural areas or very small towns. They're off the regular routes of the dealers, who are always on the lookout for bargains in antiques. And few serious collectors will take the time to scour the countryside on the outside chance that they'll find a gem for their collections.

Considering the price of gasoline today and the value of your time, you shouldn't invest too much of either in checking out secondhand stores. Anytime you're driving through a small town on vacation or business, however, by all means look for the local secondhand stores. A few minutes' detour off the highway and down a back street on such a mission can prove profitable.

You may find antiques in need of restoration

in the most unlikely of places. I found a large old steamer trunk that I bought for $20 in the basement of an antiques shop. Part of the trunk's bottom had rotted out. The owner of the shop had intended on repairing it but never got around to it, so she sold it to me. After repairing the bottom and restoring the rest of the trunk, inside and out, I ended up with a fine antique.

But the most bizarre find I ever had was an elegant Edwardian silver cabinet. As I was driving down a side street in a nearby town on a snowy day, I noticed a panel with a carved crest sticking out of a snowbank. I stopped my car to go take a look. As I was lifting the panel out of the snow, a tiny old woman yelled, "If you want that, then you'll have to take these." And with that, she opened the door of the antiques shop behind me and brought out two magnificently carved legs in the shape of dolphins. And there was more. By the time I had finished, I had a whole carload of pieces, all for free.

It took more than eight hours to figure out how all the pieces of this puzzle fitted together, but once I had them assembled, I realized what a true find I had discovered. After careful restoration—the solid walnut piece needed some extensive preservation—I ended up with a piece of furniture that not only dominates my dining room but is worth several thousand dollars. This was one of my first large restoration projects and, to this day, is still one of my favorites.

So, whether at a city auction attended by hundreds of eager buyers or in a dusty barn on a lonely ranch in Wyoming, the bargains in antique furniture definitely are there. And you can find them, just as hundreds of others do.

To make this delightful hobby/business both fun and profitable, you must learn to recognize the antiques that have real potential. In the next chapter, you'll learn how to distinguish styles of furniture so that you can recognize them on your antiquing hunts.

CHAPTER 2

THE "REAL" ANTIQUES: THE COLONIAL PERIOD TO THE VICTORIAN PERIOD

What is an antique, anyway? After all, *antique* means "old," doesn't it? Yes, certainly, but "old" is an abstract and highly relative term. *Antique,* like *old,* means different things to different people.

Those who live on the East Coast of the United States, the oldest part of the country, generally consider a piece of furniture an antique if it predates 1825 or so. In the lower South, where a Camelot-like civilization flourished during the mid-nineteenth century, *antique* and *Victorian* are almost synonymous terms. In the West, however, any piece of furniture built around the *close* of the nineteenth century is considered an antique!

In 1930 the U.S. government declared an official antique to be any piece made before 1830, the approximate date of the start of the Industrial Revolution. Faced with the passage of time, though, the Congress ruled in 1966 that antiques had to be only one hundred years old to be authentic. So, now any antique made around the early part of the twentieth century is officially an antique.

As mentioned earlier, this book isn't intended to show you how to buy (and perhaps sell) those exquisitely lovely early pieces that bring four- and five-figure prices at the higher-end shows and auctions. It discusses the more easily located pieces that are less rare but just as beautiful. It certainly will be to your advantage, though, to be able to recognize all the major American furniture styles of the past few centuries. This knowledge will add immensely to your own enjoyment of good furniture. And who knows, you just might get lucky someday and discover a treasure trove of beauties that will make not only your fortune but your reputation as an antiques expert. This chapter and the next describe the several furniture styles that are a part of our American heritage. Some are unquestionably antiques. Some are borderline cases—all depending upon your point of view.

COLONIAL PERIOD: EARLY TO LATE SEVENTEENTH CENTURY

The earliest settlers to the American colonies made only the crudest sort of furniture. Rough and strictly utilitarian, it bore little resemblance to the Jacobean styles they had left behind in England and Europe. The term *Jacobean* comes from the Latin word *Jacobus,* meaning James, and refers to the period during which James I was on the throne of England (1603–85).

A few examples of this early period—pieces constructed around the middle of the seventeenth century—are on display in several New England museums. Old inventories and wills gives us a still better idea of the way the first Americans furnished their homes. Settlers in rural areas used plainer, simpler furniture than their city cousins. Well-to-do city folk, however, hired turners and joiners—which are early terms for the craftsmen who later were called cabinetmakers—who emulated their English peers of that period.

By the mid-seventeenth century, these men began producing furniture that closely resembled the heavy medieval styles favored in England during the reigns of Queen Elizabeth I and King James I. The furniture was elaborate, massive, and ornate, with bulbous table legs and deeply carved cabinet fronts.

Colonists favored simple stools and benches in their homes. They often placed a settee, a long bench with a high back that shielded a person from cold drafts, beside the fireplace.

Since houses were small, homeowners preferred any piece of furniture that could do double duty or could be folded away when not in use. So many homes had gateleg tables, which had a fixed top in the center attached to a frame of legs and sturdy stretchers, carved by cabinetmakers in the better pieces. Two large drop leaves hung on either side of the center section, ready to be lifted and supported on movable legs that swung out on either side of the table.

Virtually every home of any substance had, by the end of the seventeenth century, a press cupboard and/or a court cupboard, for storage. Colonial housewives used the press cupboard or linen press to hold linen or clothing that had been ironed or pressed. The court cupboard, on the other hand, was more elaborate, with open areas to display cherished silver plate and precious utensils. Most of these large pieces of furniture featured heavily carved and decorated Tudor-style motifs of medieval England. Some, however, had simpler and straighter lines, influenced by the furniture brought to the new country by immigrants from Sweden.

By the end of that century, beds featuring high posts dominated the small bedrooms.

This Jacobean-style chair looks similar to the seventeenth-century Jacobean pieces the colonists had in England.

Housewives hung these with curtains to keep out the chilled night air.

What little is known about the furniture of this period shows that it was stiff, formal, and probably miserably uncomfortable. Puritan philosophy, with its strict religious code and abhorrence of anything that smacked of "worldly" pleasure, still held sway in the colonies. Ease and comfort were definitely not the major criteria for the furniture of the time.

Cabinetmakers favored woods that grew most plentifully in the forests—oak and pine—although walnut, ash, hickory, maple, apple, and cherry were used when and where available.

WILLIAM AND MARY PERIOD: 1689–1702

William of Orange and his queen, Mary, followed the hated despot James II onto the throne of England in 1689. Their reign was like a breath of fresh air. More than ready for a change, England quickly adopted the new ideas William and Mary brought with them.

The new monarchs soon moved out much of the stolid English furniture from their apartments and installed their own more cheerful and elegant pieces. They contributed lighter, more graceful, interior decoration to English life. The royal court followed suit, and then the English people as a whole. At about the same time, Dutch colonists introduced the same styles into the American colonies. So it was inevitable that in America, the massive Tudor furniture of the later seventeenth century should be replaced by the more comfortable and attractive designs inspired by the Dutch monarchs on the British throne.

As life became a bit easier for the colonists, they began to use more discretionary furniture. The popularity of letter writing, for instance, increased, and the long table that served in most homes for food preparation, dining, children's lessons, family conferences, and everything else was often in use and not amenable to long sessions with a quill pen. Besides, the writer needed a place to store that pen, ink, and paper. To fill this need, cabinetmakers began offering small desks. The first, little more than boxes with slanted tops resting on frames with four legs, resembled simple desks on frames. The slanted top served as the writing surface and opened on hinges, usually at the upper edge, with writing materials being stored inside. In time cabinetmakers began putting the hinges on the lower edge of the writing surface instead of the upper edge. Thus, the top opened down instead of up, and the inside became the writing surface. They supported the top, when lowered, on sliding rails that pulled out of the desk itself. Soon, they added drawers to the lower frame, and finally installed a bank of small pigeonholes and drawers in the upper section.

Small- and medium-size tables found their way into these homes, too, for the first time. Colonists used them for playing cards, serving tea, and displaying treasured objects, all embellishments of a more leisurely way of life.

Rather ornate dressing tables also came into vogue around the beginning of the eighteenth century. Typically, a dressing table was a small table with a shallow center drawer and two deeper side drawers. The table often had an elaborately shaped apron and usually rested on four turned legs with X-shaped cross stretchers—the horizontal braces between legs used to strengthen a piece. They used similar tables for preparing food, adding slate, marble, or tile tops, which were impervious to heat and resistant to knife cuts. These tables became known as *slate* or *slab tables*.

A variation of the dressing or slate table was the high chest. Cabinetmakers attached an attractive chest with three or four tiers of drawers to the top of the small table. Eventually, they added more drawers to the bottom half of this piece of furniture, resulting in a chest-on-chest of drawers that became known as the *highboy*. This tall piece of furniture replaced the press and court cupboards for storage of linens and clothing, although many homes used both well into the nineteenth century.

This movement toward more vertical styles became a distinct hallmark of the William and Mary period. In addition to the new tall chests of drawers, beds had higher posts and chairs had higher backs. These taller, more graceful, designs indicated the delicacy in furniture that William and Mary favored and encouraged.

Caned seats, an Oriental innovation, appeared on side chairs about this time, and the immensely popular *wingback chair* developed. This chair, now a classic design, became the first easy chair. Well padded and fully upholstered, the wingback chair became the first real breakthrough in seating comfort. Originally designed as a sickroom chair, it provided a place for the sick person to sit upright in front of the fireplace in the bedroom. The wings helped gather the warm air to keep the person from getting chilled. Since many people suffered from respiratory ailments during this time, colonists believed that it was better for the sick to sleep in an upright position to prevent the onset of pneumonia. A small stool elevated the sick person's feet. Eventually, the wingback chair made its way into the latter-nineteenth-century living room, and it is still a popular style today.

Most of the furniture built during this period looked more comfortable and attractive than that of early colonial days. Cabinetmakers began using more walnut and maple than before, adding a delicacy to their work with fine veneers, inlay, arched panels, and generally less ponderous turnings.

Wealthier colonists even began ordering cabinetmakers to adorn their new tables and high chests with gilt stencils and fine lacquer work. The ponderousness of Tudor England gave way to a new elegance and individuality as men and women established their roots in America.

QUEEN ANNE PERIOD: 1702–50

This period of American furniture, named for Queen Anne of England, who held the throne from 1702 until 1714, actually flourished long after her reign ended. And from old prints and inventories, it's obvious that life became increasingly easier for the colonists as the century advanced. Cabinetmakers introduced few innovative furniture forms during these years, but instead modified several of the earlier William and Mary styles to accommodate a more leisurely way of life. Thus, more sophisticated folding card tables and delicate tea tables, for instance, could be found in wealthier homes than a few years before. Those tea tables, whether rectangular or round, almost invariably had a *dished,* or recessed, top. Some, known as *bird-cage* tables, rested on a square framed, open boxlike structure, and their

This Queen Anne chair features the distinctive double-curved cabriole leg and shell motif.

Japanning, or decorating furniture with black lacquer and Japanese illustrations, became popular at the end of the eighteenth century.

tops could be folded down to stand against the wall when not in use.

During the first quarter of the eighteenth century, cabinetmakers began using the *cyma curve,* a form that got its name from the Greek word for "wave form." A classic shape, the cyma curve is a double curve, simple and elegant. It eventually became the dominant motif of the period, seen in pediments, dressing-table aprons, and chair backs, but most notably in the distinctive *cabriole leg.*

The balance of two curves produced a stability that belied its delicate appearance and helped make the cabriole leg a hallmark of furniture design throughout much of the eighteenth century. It appeared on virtually every table, chest, and chair produced during the period. The lower portion usually ended in a thick pad or shaped foot. Some designers preferred the more ornate claw and ball foot. Later in eighteenth-century America, cabinetmakers used an eagle's talon gripping a ball, a symbol of the new country.

Architects and furniture designers during the Queen Anne period also became entranced with the shell as a decorative motif and used it as much as the cabriole leg. Many fine homes of the period still boast elaborate shell carvings and moldings over fireplaces and inside cupboards. Following suit, cabinetmakers embellished the front panels of chests, knees of tables and chair legs, pediments of all kinds, and chair backs with classic, open shell carvings.

Inlay and marquetry faded from style, but skilled cabinetmakers used a great deal of lacquer and veneer to decorate the plain surfaces of their furniture. Carving wasn't quite as heavy as a few years before, with far more restrained paneling and molding on the flat surfaces. *Japanning,* a method of applying a Japanese-inspired lacquer with a hard, glossy finish, came into vogue during the Queen Anne period. It usually featured brightly colored and fanciful birds and fruits decorating a black background. Sometimes animals, human figures, and stylized Oriental buildings literally covered the larger and more expensive tall chests. The effect was one of opulence and wealth.

As the period advanced, cabinetmakers began to replace the flat top on case or storage pieces with the more elaborate *broken pediment,* often punctuated with central finials. These vase-shaped carved decorations presented a final touch of elegance. The broken pediment topped almost all the surviving secretaries—or combination bookcase and desk pieces—of this period, and it has come to symbolize, as much as do the cabriole leg and shell motif, the graceful Queen Anne period.

Along the same line, chair makers began inserting flat sections of wood, called *splats,* into the backs of their chairs. Replacing the spindles of earlier days, these splats were often cut in the shape of fiddles or classical vases. Also, with an eye to the comfort that seemed to be ever more important to this generation, chair makers shaped these chair backs to conform more closely to the curve of the human spine.

Cabinetmakers favored walnut during this era, with maple and cherry close seconds. Although shipping merchants introduced mahogany to the colonies during the first few years of the eighteenth century, it didn't take hold as a major wood for fine furniture until the latter part of the century.

An important addition to the history of furniture in America occurred during the Queen Anne period. It didn't in any way reflect that style, but it did turn out to be totally endearing, enduring, and firmly wedged in the hearts of the American people. This was the Windsor chair.

Windsor Chairs

Around 1725 one of the most durable chair designs ever devised arrived in America from its native England. This was the Windsor, and inventive Yankee chair makers quickly took to its simple, sturdy form. Basically, the Windsor is an all-wood chair with a solid seat shaped for comfortable sitting, legs that spread out at about a 20-degree angle, and approximately twelve to twenty-four slender, straight spindles in the back. Originally designed as a garden chair and painted a dark green, it eventually served as general seating both indoors and outdoors. Homeowners often placed these chairs along the walls of entryways so that visitors could sit and wait to be presented to the master or mistress of the house. A comfortable chair, it seems to fit well in just about any setting, from country cottage to millionaire's mansion. Perhaps that is the secret of its success. No other individual chair style, except perhaps the wingback chair, has retained its consistent popularity through the years.

Thomas Jefferson loved the Windsor chair, and historians believe he sat in one when signing the Declaration of Independence. We do know he bought forty-eight of them in black and gold to seat his many illustrious guests at Monticello.

The Windsor, used both indoors and outdoors, was the everyday chair of the eighteenth century.

Benjamin Franklin ordered twenty-four Windsors at one time and specified that they be painted white. George Washington bought twenty-seven for Mount Vernon, but we don't know his preference in color.

Early Windsors were nearly always painted, often green, red, or yellow. They were humble chairs, usually made from a motley collection of woods, and the paint disguised the mismatched parts. Chair makers often used poplar or pine, both softwoods and easily shaped, for the saddle seats. The legs, spindles, and arms might have been beech, hickory, maple, ash, or any other hardwood, often a combination of two or more.

Chair makers assembled these early Windsor chairs without nails or screws. In fact, they owe their sturdiness to a unique construction method. Craftsmen turned the legs and spindles from seasoned wood. The chair maker then set these pieces into well-fitting holes in plank seats that he carved from green wood. In time the green wood dried and shrank, gripping the ends of the legs and spindles with all the tenacity of a bear trap. This made a first-rate bond that didn't let go with time. They produced later models, however, using conventional methods with glue and screws and usually one wood throughout.

Windsors come in all forms—fan-backed, straight-backed, and curved-back. The most valuable for the antiques collector are those with two to four braces behind the back spindles. Springing from an extension of the seat at the rear, they rise to meet the upper edge of the back, forming quite an effective brace.

The value and quality of a Windsor chair can be determined by the number of spindles in its back. The very earliest, and, therefore, rarest, Windsors often had eleven spindles. These are still quite valuable. Windsors made in the late nineteenth century have as few as five spindles, are fairly common, and don't command high prices.

CHIPPENDALE PERIOD: 1754–85

Thomas Chippendale was an English cabinetmaker and designer whose styles had a tremendous influence on American furniture during the mid- to late eighteenth century and for years

Thomas Chippendale prepared a book of furniture designs that other cabinetmakers used to develop the Chippendale style, featuring claw and ball feet, cabriole legs, and pierced back slats on chairs.

afterward. Most people associate Chippendale with Chippendale furniture of Philadelphia, but he actually lived and worked in England. Besides being a cabinetmaker himself, Chippendale published a book of furniture designs, *The Gentleman and Cabinet Maker's Director,* in 1754, the most important that had ever been issued in England. American cabinetmakers purchased his book of designs and, in 1755, began making them, albeit quite a bit simpler than the English originals, using almost totally Georgian and Queen Anne derivations.

Many of Chippendale's designs borrowed from the rococo appearance of French Louis XV furniture, and most showed an embellishment of the simpler Queen Anne style by means of elaborate lines and touches. Some of his designs reflected the Chinoiserie or Chinese style, with pagoda motifs, bamboo turnings, the claw and ball foot, carved latticework, and considerable lacquering, while yet others showed a Gothic influence, featuring pointed arches and fretworked legs.

Though Chippendale brought new and fresh ideas to furniture design, he always carefully fitted and joined his pieces, enabling them to last a long time. Mahogany, which appeared about 1750, became his favorite wood. He employed lots of deep and sharp carving as his chief decorative technique. Besides shells, he fancied elaborate scrolls, foliage, and gadroons. Chippendale also used gilding, some veneer, and fretwork galleries around small tables and the tops of cabinet pieces as other forms of decoration.

Side chairs and armchairs became Chippendale's masterpieces. No one ever did so many things to make them look different. Unbelievable versatility distinguished the backs, which always had a distinctive pattern. He gave both the vertical-splat back and the ladder back with horizontal splats new treatment.

The *highboy,* a chest of four drawers on top of a matching aproned dressing table, continued its popularity in America throughout the Chippendale period, even though it had become passé in England. Invariably, cabinetmakers topped these Chippendale highboys with a broken pediment and finials carved in the shape of vases. Many had fan- or shell-shaped inserts below the pediment or at the joining of the top and lower sections.

Also during this period, cabinetmakers introduced the *kneehole dressing table* or chest of drawers. A refinement of the earlier dressing table, it had a bank of drawers on either side of the open kneehole, with the two joined by a small center drawer.

For the first time, too, cabinetmakers produced elaborate *breakfront bookcases.* Most of these large pieces of furniture had upper sections with glass paneled doors, some with arched panels, and many topped with a broken pediment. The lower section might be a bank of drawers with a central writing section, similar to those found in secretaries. Or it could have wooden doors, often veneered with fine woods cut into fanciful patterns to display the elaborate grains.

The *Pembroke table* was another newcomer to the growing list of small tables being produced for early Americans. Often used as a breakfast table for two, the Pembroke was a simple rectangular table with short drop leaves and usually a small drawer for storing cutlery. Most often the legs were square, with cross stretchers, sometimes decorated with elaborate openwork carving and sometimes quite plain.

During the former Queen Anne period, tea tables often had a *dished,* or slightly recessed, top. Chippendale cabinetmakers refined this feature a bit by turning that low ridge into a fancy fluted piecrustlike rim. This embellishment can be found almost exclusively on round, often three-legged, tables, the legs of which were usually deeply carved with some of the most elaborate patterns of the period.

The eighteenth-century highboy: A chest of drawers placed on a matching bottom piece that has some drawers and legs.

Nearly all side chairs and armchairs of this period had splats instead of rails, but during the Chippendale era, they became far more ornate than before. Frequently pierced in graceful designs, they echoed the cyma curve, which continued to be a favorite motif of American cabinetmakers. Most Chippendale-inspired furniture, in fact, made free use of graceful curves, including the cabriole leg. Most often that leg terminated in an elaborate claw and ball foot. Some furniture makers, though, continued to use the simpler pad, club, web, or drake foot of previous years. Acanthus leaves, swags, shells, and scrolls decorated chests, desks, highboys, and breakfronts.

By this time merchants imported mahogany into the young colonies in great quantities from Santo Domingo and Honduras, and it soon became the favored wood of sophisticated cabinetmakers of the period. The native woods—walnut, maple, cherry, pine, and poplar—still appeared, though they were mostly used by craftsmen in small towns and rural areas.

The Rocking Chair

Like the steadfast Windsor chair, which developed during the Queen Anne period but wasn't a part of it, a furniture maverick appeared during the Chippendale period—the ubiquitous rocking chair.

The rocking chair is one piece of furniture that actually has its roots in the United States. The idea has been credited to Benjamin Franklin, our master inventor. No one knows for sure, though, who first came up with the idea of putting runners on chairs, or when the rocking chair was first made. All evidence, however, points to a date of

The rocking chair originated in the United States during the second half of the eighteenth century. This Shaker rocker with arms became common during the mid-nineteenth century.

around 1760. Regardless of the exact date, more than two centuries of Americans have rocked their babies to sleep in this delightful chair.

Chair makers didn't build the earliest rocking chairs as rocking chairs but instead converted regular side chairs by adding runners to the legs. At first chair makers and homeowners simply cut a notch into the inner or outer side of the lower 2 or 3 inches of the chair legs and fit the runners into these notches. These early runners were quite thin and deep—some were little wider than ¼ inch but were 3 inches from one edge to the other. Understandably, they became known as carpet cutters.

Other than the obvious addition of a runner to an existing chair leg, the shape of the leg can indicate a conversion. Most chairs have a slightly tapered leg, wider at the upper edge than at the lower. Side chairs converted to rocking chairs will still have this tapered leg, but chairs made as rockers have legs with essentially the same circumference from top to bottom. To attach the rockers to the chair, chair makers cut a notch into the center of the lower edge of the leg and slipped the runner into that notch. They then drove a pair of pins or dowels through the legs and the runners to secure them to the chair.

Appalled at the destruction of carpeting, chair makers began making runners with the approximate dimensions we see today—about 1 inch wide and 1½ to 2 inches deep. At the same time they discarded the notch system and began applying the runners directly to the base of the chair leg.

Regardless of the way chair makers applied the runners, they made rocking chairs in every conceivable style and size. Some were pure Windsor. While others show Sheraton and Duncan Phyfe influences, there were also distinctive Boston and Hitchcock rockers. Victorian rocking chairs abound, as do the charming little low-seated sewing or nursing rocking chairs. All found a place in the homes and hearts of Americans.

FEDERAL OR CLASSICAL PERIOD: 1790–1815

Many designers whose names are household words may be grouped under the general heading of the Federal or classical period in American furniture. Among others, these include Hepplewhite, Sheraton, and Duncan Phyfe. Also a part of this era are the styles known as Empire and Directoire. No one motif can be said to typify this era of great change in the United States. It was a blend of many styles, covering some fifty vastly disparate years, from shortly after the American Revolution until the ascent of Victoria to the throne of England.

The style known as Duncan Phyfe was the only one that originated in the United States. The others had crossed the Atlantic from England and Europe. After winning their independence, Americans were ready and willing to throw off the old and take on the new. In reacting against the rococo curves, the Gothic ostentatiousness, and the pseudo-Chinese influences of the previous half century, they joyfully embraced the straighter, more classical, lines of "the new look."

The curving lines of the cabriole leg with its pad and/or claw foot all but disappeared as chair and table legs became slender and tapered. Cabinetmakers replaced ornate shell and leaf carvings with *reeding,* decorative molding characterized by several slender, rounded reedlike shapes as on a column, and simple turnings. A relatively plain oval, shield, or heart-shaped back appeared on side chairs, creating a more delicate and airy design than the formal pierced and carved Chippendale splats. The elegant and elaborate highboys and lowboys became unfashionable, and

Chair Backs

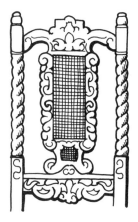

Caning, carving, and spiral twist
(Stuart, second half seventeenth century)

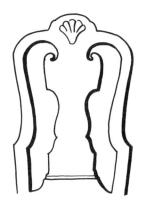

Solid splat
(Queen Anne and early Georgian)

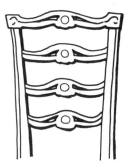

Ladder back
(Chippendale, mid-eighteenth century)

Wheel back
(Hepplewhite, late eighteenth century)

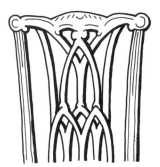

Gothic
(Chippendale, mid-eighteenth century)

Ribband back
(Chippendale, mid-eighteenth century)

Chinese
(Chippendale, mid-eighteenth century)

Shield back
(Hepplewhite, late eighteenth century)

Stuffed oval
(Adam, late eighteenth century)

Prince of Wales plumes
(Hepplewhite, late eighteenth century)

Sheraton
(late eighteenth century)

Balloon back
(Victorian, mid-nineteenth century)

The American Empire period—a transitional period between the Federal and Victorian periods—featured rounded shapes and veneered surfaces.

homeowners went back to storing their clothing and linens in plainer chests of drawers.

Gentle and restrained curves could also be seen in slightly bowed-front chests and desks. Instead of ornate carvings, cabinetmakers employed simpler lyres, urns, and inlaid ovals as motifs on furniture of this period.

The two most important innovations of this period were the *commode* and the *sideboard*. The commode was a small chest, usually about 3 feet high. The most beautiful examples, often semicircular and intended for use in the parlor, had

drawers and shelves to store the niceties of upper-middle-class living of the time. More commonly, cabinetmakers built the commode for the bedroom, where it served as a washstand. It had a marble or wood top with drawers and shelves below for linens and toiletries.

The sideboard, a trademark of this period in furniture, featured three sections and four to six legs. Each section contained drawers for cutlery and shelves behind paneled doors for china, linens, and silverware. Many had a serpentine front, the new undulating style achieved with a series of gentle convex and concave curves.

The American people developed a great deal of empathy for France during this time, since the French people had recently fought for their liberty from a tyrannical monarchy. Therefore, when France embraced the rather austere style known as Directoire (1790–1804), Americans happily took the new ideas to their hearts. This style had an almost military ambience, with sofa legs that resembled sabers and table legs shaped like flaming torches. Cabinetmakers began using other common motifs, such as wreaths, laurel branches, stars, rosettes, battle axes, shields, and palm leaves. Wherever possible, designers worked a patriotic red, white, and blue color scheme into a painted cabinet, desk, or chest. In America, an eagle, the symbol of the new nation, topped thousands upon thousands of mirror frames and pediments and often served as an ornamental support for occasional tables.

Within a few years the spartan designs of the Directoire period gave way to a heavier style that became known as American Empire (1810–30). Less graceful than its parent, the Empire style of France, this massive and stolid furniture lacked much of the beauty and elegance of Directoire designs. Beds, often fashioned with huge sleigh-like headboards and footboards, had brass hardware frequently molded into the shape of lions' heads, with rings for pulls. In addition, many pieces of mid-nineteenth-century furniture featured carved pineapples, animal feet, and elaborate cornices.

About the same time, both Europe and America rediscovered the classics. No longer did fashionable men and women look for freshness and innovation in their furniture. Creativity went out the door as antiquity came in. The public demanded furniture, silverware, clothing, houses, even outhouses, that duplicated the possessions of those who lived in Greece, Rome, and Egypt thousands of years before. Suddenly *Doric, Ionic,* and *Corinthian* became household words. The simpler taper disappeared from table and chair legs, and ornate columns appeared, emulating the columns that supported the roofs of ancient temples. The motifs on friezelike borders along table aprons and around mirrors could have enhanced the Roman Senate or an Egyptian altar.

Since this vogue for the classics ran parallel to that of other, more developmental, styles, designers frequently superimposed one element on another. *Pier tables,* for instance, those low pieces built to stand between two long windows, could have a top and lower shelf that was pure Directoire, yet boast lovely Grecian figures as supports for the upper sections. A pair of winged sphinxes might serve as arm supports for a chair whose back was pure Duncan Phyfe.

The entire Federal period, in fact, was one of transition. One style melded into and overlay another as many talented designers worked at satisfying the demands of the time.

NINETEENTH-CENTURY FURNITURE

Some of the furniture produced during the nineteenth century was undeniably in the worst possible taste, replete with as many scrolls, carved motifs, rococo curves, and general embellishments as a hardworking cabinetmaker could tack on or gouge out of the wood. Some of the furniture produced during this period still showed the restraint of earlier periods, though, with simple lines and near-classical ambience. Plus, furniture of this period is certainly the most available of all in today's antiques market. The trick for the collector or investor is to weed out the good from the awful.

Shaker Furniture (1820–60)

Shaker furniture also flourished during the nineteenth century, but it can in no way be described as fitting into the mode of most Victorian styles. The religious sect that developed this sturdy and simple furniture came to the United States from England about the time of the American Revolution. Hardworking and thrifty, they prospered, and by the mid-nineteenth century some eighteen Shaker communities existed throughout the Northeast.

The Shakers were an industrious and businesslike people who sold their products far outside the realm of their own communities. Their furniture clearly defined their own belief in the virtue of the simple life. It was attractive, functional, sturdy, and quite devoid of ornament. In many ways, Shaker styles resemble those of the American colonial period.

In time Shaker chairs became popular. Some Shaker communities began making chairs, and only chairs, for sale to the public as a way of producing income. One of the most popular and comfortable is the rocking chair, with its high ladder back, rush seat, and simple tapered finials. Though the basic design remained the same, each community added a particular style of finial to distinguish their chairs from those of

The Shakers originally made chairs to use in their communities and then decided to make them to market to outsiders. They only sold the chairs. The case pieces they made were only for community use. Each community identified its chairs by using particular finials and seat weaving patterns.

other communities. Shaker craftsmen made other pieces, such as candle stands, tables, and cupboards, strictly for use within their communities. Shaker candle stands have round tops, and generally have three legs, which are often shaped into a restrained cyma curve.

Many of the small worktables had tops that extended several inches past the supporting apron, and most had a drawer for cutlery set into one end. The *trestle tables* used in Shaker living and dining rooms were rectangular, with pedestals at either end. The trestle table had a flat stretcher between the pedestals, often placed quite high, sometimes just inches below the top of the table itself.

Shaker cabinetmakers preferred the simpler native woods of their adopted country—maple, cherry, butternut, birch, and pine.

Spool Furniture (1815–65)

Another simpler style, known as *spool furniture,* appeared in the the Victorian age. These casual designs, first introduced in *Godey's Lady's Book* around 1815, remained popular for some fifty years. Turned out en masse by both large Eastern factories and local cabinetmakers, spool furniture resembled a series of spools, buttons, or balls strung together like beads on a necklace. The improved lathes of the time could turn the symmetrical spools quickly and efficiently. They can be found used on every conceivable piece of furniture, but most prominently as bedposts and side table legs. Though produced during the Victorian age, spool furniture is really not Victorian in feeling. It's more a by-product of the more formal styles popular during the late seventeenth century.

Cabinetmakers produced spool furniture in every wood from walnut to cherry. The less desirable woods, such as pine and poplar, were usually stained to emulate walnut, rosewood, or mahogany, the most fashionable cabinet woods of the time.

THE VICTORIAN PERIOD: 1830–1901

Victoria came to the throne of England in 1837. Though she was a romantic but stuffy young woman, her values quickly became the values of her time. Victoria's reign began just as the classical period was declining, so many of the excesses of the first years of the nineteenth century are evident in the early Victorian period.

During this transition time many furniture makers were trying to combine different styles into one piece of furniture. It wasn't at all unusual for a wardrobe to boast a French Renaissance top with elegant gold stenciling supported by classically styled Doric columns on the two sides. Central doors might have a graceful border with rococo curves surrounding Gothic panels. The whole thing could well be supported by massive claw feet. The inevitable result was a coarse medley that could claim paternity in no particular style. The difference between these hodgepodges of the early Victorian era and those of the late classical period was an abiding romanticism. Overall, the lines were a little more rounded, the carving a little more fanciful, the designs simply more *feminine* than in previous years.

The dominant theme of artists and writers of the period was nature in all its glory, everywhere tinged with the soft-focus lens of romanticism. Where art and literature led, architecture and furniture followed. The result was Victoriana, and many purists consider the 1830s and 1840s to be

Chair Legs and Feet

Legs

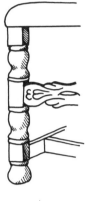

Turned

Cabriole

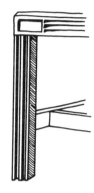

Moulded

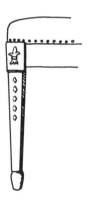

Tapered

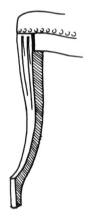

Sabre

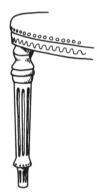

Turned and fluted

Feet

Pad

Hoof

Scroll

Claw and ball

Spade or peg

Furniture Mounts and Supports

Axe drop
(mid-seventeenth century)

Swan neck with shaped pierced plate
(early eighteenth century)

Pear drop
(late seventeenth century)

Swan neck
(Queen Anne)

Lion mask
(Regency)

Pierced back plate with Chinese influence
(mid-eighteenth century)

Neo-classical
(Adam)

Prince of Wales plumes
(late eighteenth century)

French Rococo
(mid-eighteenth century)

Ball

Bun

Ogee

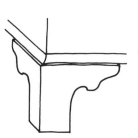

Bracket

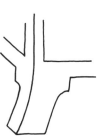

Splayed bracket

the beginning of the end of good furniture design in this country.

Gothic Revival (1840–65)

The first Victorian furniture definable as such became known as Gothic Revival, which flourished mainly from the 1830s through the 1850s. These vertical pieces of furniture, patterned after the soaring architecture of European cathedrals, featured as their dominant motif the pointed Gothic arch. Designers worked this into chair backs, secretary doors, whatnot fretwork, the pediments of frames and mirrors, headboards and footboards for beds, and the elaborate canopies that overhung many dressing tables. Furniture makers often combined an elongated arch with a *roundel,* a round, ornamental panel, to imitate the stained-glass windows of medieval European cathedrals.

The development and sophistication of furniture-making machinery about this time lowered the price of fashionable furniture to within the reach of most families. Until this time fine veneers had been expensive and available only in small sheets. By 1840, however, improved circular saws were capable of making exceptionally thin cuts on top-grade wood and in ever-larger pieces. As a result, furniture makers could cover entire tabletops with lovely quality wood veneers at a fraction of the price charged only a few years before.

Around 1850 an Ohio inventor perfected a bandsaw that could cut the most intricate designs in wood with, for that time, mind-boggling speed. The result was a nationwide flood of incredibly fanciful whatnots, sideboards, music stands,

The Gothic Revival style, featuring ornate motifs taken from Gothic cathedrals, was the first designated style of the Victorian period.

organs, mirror frames, and so forth, all overloaded with complex scrolls and intricate fretwork. Machines that carved wood almost as well as the human hand appeared shortly afterward. A torrent of inexpensive machine-made furniture soon adorned virtually every parlor, bedroom, and dining room in the land.

Rococo Revival (1845–60)

By the middle of the nineteenth century, romanticism had blossomed. Americans joyfully embraced the rococo period of Victoriana. This was the era best exemplified by the pretentious, proud, and unquestionably ebullient years just before the Civil War. Designers employed fluid lines, lavish carving, and lots of curves in furniture design.

The Victorians developed an intense love of naturalism and showed it by the profusion of floral and leaf motifs they attached to their furniture. Furniture makers built hundreds of thousands of dressers, commodes, and chests of drawers with wooden drawer pulls carved in the shape of leaves and fruit.

Renaissance Revival (1855–75)

Commonly known as "High Victorian," the Renaissance Revival style brought back the classical ideals of the Italian Renaissance during the fourteenth to the sixteenth centuries. Designers looked to classical proportions, shapes, and ornamentation, epitomized by a symmetry of form and the use of classical figures on bedsteads, arms of chairs, and table supports. Characteristically grandiose and luxurious, this style became the epitome of Victorian design. Rich drapery fabrics of velvet, brocade, and silk hung in rooms laid with fine Oriental carpets and decorated with bronze and marble statues in the homes of the nouveau riche. Homes had high ceilings during this time of

The Victorian Rococo Revival style, influenced by the Rococo period in France, featured lots of curves.

growing affluence, and furniture makers took full advantage of this fact. They built massive wardrobes, sideboards, and bedsteads 8, 9, even 10 feet tall. Many of their beds had four turned posts and either a full or half *tester,* a fabric-covered framework supported by the posts. In the North, canopies served a decorative purpose, while in the South, they served a practical one—supporting the framework for a mosquito net.

Iron and brass beds came into vogue about this time, as did fancy wicker furniture and the dainty little twisted-iron ice cream chairs with their tiny round tables for two. Every fashionable home had a fainting couch in the parlor to cushion the frequent falls of those tightly corseted women, and a hall tree near the front door to receive umbrellas, coats, and the hats of the men of the house.

The small whatnot evolved into the more elaborate *etagère,* often embellished with a marble-topped lower shelf and a mirrored back panel. For the first time dressing bureaus with attached mirrors and small shelves to hold kerosene lamps or candlesticks came into vogue.

Cabinetmakers heavily padded the backs of chairs and sofas for elegance and comfort. They then lavished the wooden framework of the chair or sofa with deeply carved roses, lilies, grapes, leaves, and open scrollwork. The typical fine sofa of the period had three humps to its back. Sometimes the back would also be divided to match the upper rail. A favorite first cousin of the sofa and a Victorian innovation was the *meridienne,* which had the base and seat of a regular sofa but only one arm and a sweeping high back. Dining chairs were usually built without upholstery on the backs, perhaps to discourage slouching at the table.

Victorian designers revived the cabriole leg with enthusiasm. It became so exaggerated on some small tables that the upper curve bowed out a full 6 or 7 inches before doubling back. Furniture makers often adorned these elaborate table legs with garlands of carved fruit and vegetables, wooden ribbons and swags, and delicately molded feminine heads.

Neoclassic Revival (1865–75)

During the same time that the Renaissance Revival style was popular, some designers turned even more to the forms and decorative motifs of ancient Greece and Rome. Straight lines replaced the curves of the Rococo Revival style as designers adorned their furniture with cherubs, dolphins, fluting, lyres, ram and lion heads, and urns. Pieces reflected a lighter, more delicate style during this short-lived period.

Eastlake Victorian (1870–85)

It was predictable that public taste would soon rebel against the excesses of the previous decades and begin looking for fresh ideas in furniture design. Charles Locke Eastlake, an English architect, stepped in to fill the need. In 1868 he published a book titled *Hints on Household Taste in Furniture, Upholstery and Other Details,* calling for a return to simpler, more geometric designs. He stressed high-quality construction and strong materials, an almost architectural approach to building furniture. Eastlake, like his contemporary, William Morris, was thoroughly revulsed by the excess of bad taste that filled homes on both sides of the Atlantic. Fashionable English men and women ignored him and his book, but

Americans, always ready for something new, soon adapted Eastlake's philosophy. After its publication in this country in 1872, the book had an immediate, if short-lived, influence on American furniture design.

Eastlake's furniture was far more formal and restrained than that coming from his exuberant contemporaries. His designs had a distinctly rural, almost utilitarian, ambience, quite in contrast to the elaborate romanticism that engulfed others. He advocated squared-off corners and flat surfaces. Undulating curves disappeared in favor of angles and geometric forms. Legs and supports became straight again, though often interrupted with bulbous details. He advised using many ceramic tile inserts on hall trees and washstands. Mirror and picture frames carried through with the geometric motifs, but like many of the sideboards of the period, they had well-proportioned finials on the pediments. Cabinetmakers frequently worked a simple spoon-shaped carving into the overall design.

Though furniture makers chose oak to construct Eastlake furniture, they also used walnut. This isn't surprising. Oak is one of the sturdiest, if not the most elegant, of cabinet woods, and thus quite in keeping with Eastlake's thesis.

However, the vogue for Eastlake furniture lasted little more than a decade, but it foreshadowed a change to come in American tastes.

Following on the heels of the romantic early Victorians and the austere Eastlake school, the furniture of the 1880s and 1890s is difficult to place into any category. A conglomeration of styles suddenly became fashionable again—Directoire, early Empire, Chinese—and designers added to these a

Charles Eastlake, through his book Hints on Household Taste, *influenced American cabinetmakers in the latter part of the nineteenth century. This Eastlake–style sideboard features incised, rather than carved, decoration, making the furniture less expensive to produce using mass-production techniques.*

few new crazes. Individually, some of this late Victorian furniture wasn't too bad, but some was terrible. As a whole, it showed the poorest taste in all of America's furniture history.

For all of its problems and excesses, the Industrial Revolution did have some positive qualities, one being that many more people had a great deal more discretionary income. Some Americans, however, were becoming wealthy with astonishing speed, and it seems they couldn't spend their money fast enough. They built massive mansions along the Hudson River in New York, on Chicago's Lake Shore Drive, and on the millionaire's playground, Jekyll Island in Georgia. And every burgeoning millionaire wanted his or her home to be more opulent than the one next door. They hired architects and interior designers and turned them loose with virtually unlimited expense accounts. The results, which all of America tried to follow, could only be described as gaudy.

Following the lead of English architect Norman Shaw, the architects abandoned interior doors on the ground floors of their clients' homes. In their place they put sweeping arches between rooms, then embellished these arches with every device at their command. They draped some of these openings between parlor and library or dining room and parlor with swags of heavy brocade and velvet, silken tassels and ropes. Some employed elaborate carved cornices and pediments that soared to reach the 12- and 14-foot-high ceilings. They subdivided other arches into smaller, usually Moorish-style, arches and pillars. A few managed to combine all this into one.

The craze for things Moorish permeated much of America during the latter part of the nineteenth century. Most of it was confined to architectural decor. About the only innovation as far as furniture was concerned was the *ottoman*. This was a round, deeply tufted, armless seat, usually placed in the center of a room.

Otherwise, homeowners tended to fill their homes with ornate antiques from other periods in a quite eclectic fashion. In keeping with the vogue of the time for collecting and displaying art and bric-a-brac, Victorians favored many fancy wall shelves, small tables, whatnots, and bookcases. Wicker furniture, originally used as summer furniture on open porches, gained much popularity in response to a growing trend toward lightness and openness in new homes. Following the same movement, and echoing the Victorians' love of things oriental, they began to buy furniture with a delicate bamboo motif. Both the wicker and the bamboo fit well with the new idea of bringing more light into a home. It was also about this time that people began to toy with the concept of bringing nature itself indoors. So, every fashionable home had at least one large potted Boston fern and a snakelike sansevieria or two. Homeowners usually tucked these plants into corners in hallways or parlors on *fern stands,* rather spindly tables some 3 feet high with a top seldom larger than 18 inches square. Furniture makers produced these stands in round, square, and octagonal shapes, sometimes with marble tops, and usually with a shelf some 12 inches off the floor.

The *rolltop desk* was a feature of every professional's office, along with at least one bank of glass-fronted stacked bookcases. Metal furniture, including tons of brass and iron beds, abounded. An English firm introduced the enormously popular *Morris chair* to America just before the 1890s. A forerunner to our modern reclining lounger, it offered an adjustable back, the ultimate in comfort for that time.

Victorians used wicker chairs on their wide porches during the summer, a practice that has remained to this day.

As the century drew to a close, furniture makers began using more and more oak. It was almost universal for the ubiquitous round dining table and the pattern-backed, armless chairs that served in every kitchen and dining room. They upholstered almost none of these chairs, most having solid, shaped seats or small caned sections.

The Victorian era ended as Edward VII ascended the throne of England in 1901. The entire English-speaking world figuratively threw open the windows, took a deep breath, and heralded the dawn not only of a new century, but of a new way of life. Out went the stuffy proprieties of Queen Victoria and in came a freshness and freedom of thought unlike any the world had ever known.

CHAPTER 3

THE NEW ANTIQUES

The term *new antique* may seem to be an oxymoron. It is, though, a phrase you'll hear frequently as you become more knowledgeable about antiques. It denotes high-quality furniture built from shortly before 1905 to approximately 1925. Though much of it isn't yet one hundred years old and thus cannot be legally classified as antique, it's nevertheless quite charming and a joy to collect and own.

A great deal happened in this country between 1895 and the years following the end of World War I. A few holdovers from the Victorian era existed, of course, but changes came, and they came fast. On both sides of the Atlantic, men and women threw off the somberness of the previous century and began to hunger for all things new.

The stereoscope that graced every Victorian parlor gave way to moving pictures at the local vaudeville house. Americans happily replaced gas lighting with Thomas Edison's new invention. The telephone soon made hand-carried messages a thing of the past. Millions of people abandoned privies as indoor plumbing became a practical reality for American homes.

Old mores broke down, and some entrepreneurs amassed great fortunes almost overnight. The new century spawned a generation of young men and women who were bright, restless, and grasping for the new and untried in their lives. Designers, most of whom were thoroughly sick of the gaudy, ornate, overworked, and overstuffed furniture of the late Victorian era, seemed only too happy to cater to their customers' desire for simplicity.

The Arts and Crafts movement that flourished in England during the 1890s greatly accelerated this movement toward simplicity. This movement protested the social, moral, and cultural turbulence that resulted from the Industrial Revolution. It opposed the imitative and often shoddy workmanship of the morass of factory-made furniture that flooded the market. The leaders of the Arts and Crafts movement called for a return to handcraftsmanship and high-quality construction. Unfortunately, this movement was short-lived, partially because most people simply couldn't afford to buy handcrafted furniture and accessories in the age of machinery. The movement left its mark, though, by finally putting an end to the fussiness and pretentiousness of late Victorian stylings. Such straightforward materials as bamboo, wicker, and bentwood became popular as designers smoothed out lines and eliminated the fanciful, frilly "gingerbread" motifs so loved by carpenters and architects during the last decade of the nineteenth century.

Most of the furniture built during these thirty-five years or so can be classed as one of three styles: Art Nouveau, Mission Oak, or Art Deco. Technically "collectibles," these are the antiques of the future. Many shops carry a large stock of these new antiques, and dealers buy and sell them daily for a tidy profit. In the last few years Mission Oak has experienced a rapid upsurge in price. Prices have skyrocketed on most Art Deco and Art Nouveau furniture as young urban professionals with an eye for quality, and good design, as well as a good supply of cash, have begun buying pieces to decorate their inner-city apartments and condominiums.

Another large and growing segment of the new-antiques buying public consists of those just learning about the field. Such people either don't have the money to invest large sums in antiques, or they wisely want to test the market with small investments before moving on to substantial purchases of more expensive pieces.

Regardless, absolutely no reason exists for *not* starting out with a few good pieces of furniture from one of the periods described in this chapter. You can always sell them or trade up later on to make room for more valuable furniture. What is more, with each passing year, these new antiques come closer to becoming legal antiques and thus more valuable as an investment. The law of supply and demand inevitably will come into effect as more and more people become collectors. The prices of all antiques, traditional and new, are thus bound to escalate in the near future.

Don't dismiss this period in American furniture just because the styles don't rate very high with collectors of more expensive antiques. Many a novice antiques buff has furnished a house or apartment with a delightful and lighthearted eclectic mix of new antiques. The effect can be charming. These really are the *fun* antiques!

ART NOUVEAU: APPROXIMATELY 1890–1914

Though the Art Nouveau movement was innovative, it didn't last long. It was important in American furniture history, however, because it heralded the end of the dismal darkness that came at the close of the Victorian era. Rebelling against the overembellished furniture that flooded the furniture marketplace of the late 1890s, some European designers developed new ideas that found immediate approval throughout the civilized world. They took a 180-degree turn from gingerbread and started designing furniture and accessories with simple, flowing, fluid lines. They took their cues from nature with its motion, curves, and endless cycling. Fairylike tendrils wove in, out, and around the leaves and stems of flowers, fruit, and nuts. Foaming ocean waves broke over nude women, and graceful tree branches swept the earth. The entire effect was one of delicate sensuality and naturalness, with faint overtones of sentimental decadence.

The Art Nouveau years found their greatest expression in accessories, not furniture. This was the era that fostered the whirlwind careers of Louis Comfort Tiffany and others who worked in glass, china, pottery, and metal. Those substances could be more easily shaped into the Art Nouveau forms than wood could. Most wooden furniture during this period was custom-made and therefore usually of high quality and fine woods. It's a real find to uncover a piece or two. Look for asymmetrical lines, stylized animal forms, and those slender nude or seminude women with their inviting upstretch- ed arms and long flowing hair.

Far more available than wooden pieces are the popular floor lamps made of cast iron and brass. Refinished, they're a useful addition to any home and are always in demand in antiques shops.

MISSION OAK: 1900–1920

This sturdy, completely utilitarian, almost peasant style of furniture, a direct outgrowth of the Arts and Crafts movement, was an attempt to emulate the simple and functional furniture used by Spanish priests in mission churches.

The designers who worked in Mission Oak used only thick planks of solid oak, a common, exceptionally durable cabinet wood. They worked

The Arts and Crafts movement in England spawned a style of furniture known as Mission Oak, featuring simple pieces, devoid of ornamentation, of dark-stained oak.

with the simplest construction methods, anchoring joints together, squared end against squared end, and fastened with substantial screws, pegs, and glue. Craftsmen seldom used more sophisticated joining methods such as mitering and dovetailing on Mission Oak furniture.

All Mission Oak has a squared-off, geometric feel. It also lacks curved lines or fancy carvings, but often craftsmen cut square or rectangular designs into the end panels of desks and library tables. Occasionally there's a simple geometric design glued to the front of a case piece. Almost never painted, Mission Oak furniture was, instead, stained a medium to dark natural wood tone.

Furniture makers upholstered their Mission Oak pieces in sturdy leather, usually cowhide. If not leather, they often used an open-weave homespun fabric reminiscent of the rough cloth worn by monks in early California missions.

While Mission Oak was usually plain to the point of being quite ordinary, an occasional piece did show the hand of an exceptional designer, such as Gustav Stickley, whose pieces now sell for several thousand dollars at auction and at high-end antiques shows.

Mission Oak had its virtues, but beauty was not often one of them. What it lacked in graceful-ness, it made up for in durability. It's extremely difficult to wear out or break furniture made of thick oak planks! As tastes changed, many people became bored with their solid and stolid Mission Oak but could hardly discard furniture with gen-erations of use left in it. So they relegated millions of out-of-style pieces of Mission Oak furniture to recreation rooms and summer cottages.

The resurgence of interest in Mission Oak today has caused people to see it with renewed appreciation. And those three-cushion couches, deep lounge chairs, library tables, and revolving four-sided bookcases are now finding their way into the antiques market.

ART DECO: 1920–35

Like Art Nouveau and Mission Oak, Art Deco was a minor and relatively undistinguished period in American furniture history. The Roar-ing Twenties followed right on the heels of World War I, causing a rapid and disturbing social tur-bulence in the United States. The depression brought a temporary hiatus to most creative thought among our artists and designers. As a

During the 1920s and 1930s, designers not only used sophisticated Art Deco designs on furniture, but also useful accessories such as table radios.

result, Art Deco in the United States never devel-oped the character and personality of most peri-ods. Lighthearted, useful, and quite practical, it opened the door to modern furniture design by popularizing simple, geometric designs. Pieces featured many oval and octagonal parts, as well as many angles and straight lines. Functionality, inspired by the revolutionary ideas of Frank Lloyd Wright, was the name of the game, so most furniture of this period had little ornamentation.

Unlike other furniture periods, Art Deco brightened up the home through the use of vivid primary colors. Many a breakfast table and matching set of chairs appeared painted in bril-liant yellow, blue, red, green, or white. Often the chairs would boast one of the new fanciful trims of the period—painted stylized floral decorations.

Furniture makers produced little high-quality furniture during this time. Ordinary woods and ordinary lines became the rule rather than the exception.

CHAPTER 4

HOW DO YOU KNOW IT'S OLD?

Rarely will anyone offer you a fake piece of antique furniture or accessory. A fake is quite different from a reproduction. The fake antique is a deliberate attempt to deceive you by artificially aging and distressing wood to simulate the effects of wear, and then passing the item off as genuine.

Only a great deal of skill and effort by an experienced and devious cabinetmaker can pull off this chicanery when faced with close scrutiny of the object by a knowledgeable person. Because of the costs involved in antiques forgeries, this faking is practiced only on pieces that command exceptionally high prices. No reputable cabinetmaker would be involved in such deception.

Every once in a while today, you'll read of a con concerning a dressing table reputedly from Marie Antoinette's bedroom or an inlaid desk supposedly used by Napoleon on Elba. When the whole truth comes out, you learn that someone actually constructed the "antique" three weeks before being offered for sale with a five-figure price tab. Such goings-on are rare, and most people will never encounter such a problem. Reproductions, however, are another story.

Some dealers sell reproductions, in contrast to fakes, as new furniture built in the style of another era. People have admired antiques for many years, both for their beauty and as an investment. The coming of age of machinery made it practical to duplicate earlier furniture styles at reasonable prices. The vogue gained momentum in the United States in the late nineteenth century and continues today. Reproductions abound, with virtually every furniture style available to today's consumers. Any large furniture store will have Duncan Phyfe dining room sets, Early American living room sets, and Queen Anne bedroom furniture. While the best of these reproductions are excellent, they do *not* have the monetary value of genuine antiques.

As a collector you must learn to tell these reproductions from the genuine pieces. Many times a piece of furniture is made in the style of another day and sold quite honestly as a reproduction. It then passes from one owner to another and garners a few nicks and a full coat of grime along the way. Within a few years all knowledge of its origins is lost. The last person to own it may quite honestly believe it to be an antique and offer to sell it as such. Yet, as a reproduction, it's still just used furniture.

How do you separate used furniture from the genuine article?

Your first step is to recognize furniture styles of the past. You must learn to spot the one or two "hopefuls" in a roomful of junk. Just being able to recognize the type of leg and foot that Chippendale used isn't enough. The lovely old chair you unearth in the dusty back room of a secondhand store may indeed have those legs and feet, and it just might be a genuine Chippendale. It is far more likely, however, that it will be a reproduction of the original Chippendale, a piece of furniture built within the past few years.

You can tell a reproduction from the genuine

piece by a series of tests and observations you'll learn here. They'll help you avoid the costly mistake of buying secondhand furniture when you think you're buying antiques.

Almost every serious collector and dealer is fooled sometime in his or her career. A collector of antique chairs thought he could tell. He found a beautiful rocking chair at an estate auction in his hometown. Out of a pile of used pieces, the chair was the only "antique" at the sale. It was in fine condition and was quite typical of the romantic style of around 1870 or so. His preauction examination showed that previous owners had worn out at least two seats. The chair had been made to hold a round leather seat. Nail holes within the seat channel showed him that one had indeed been there at some time. A series of nail holes on the upper surface of the wooden part of the seat indicated that the original leather seat had worn out and that another larger one had been tacked in place. This was a common practice, and he knew that many antique chairs are in this condition. That replacement seat, too, had obviously worn out. It was gone, and someone had nailed a piece of plywood on the underside of the wooden seat, then covered the hole with a foam-filled cushion. Those worn-out seats and the authentic design convinced him the chair was, indeed, an antique.

Someone had painted the chair a bright red, and foolishly, he didn't check beneath that paint. Once the chair had been stripped, he discovered two corrugated fasteners had been used for reinforcement on the underside of the seat, and they certainly appeared to have been put in during the original construction. That was his first indication that something was wrong, since corrugated fasteners are a fairly recent innovation.

Some of the glue holding the stretchers in the legs had dissolved during stripping, and that gave him a second clue. He saw that the previously hidden wood at the ends of the stretchers was far too light to be a hundred years old. As described in this chapter, all wood darkens with age, even that which hasn't been subjected to wear, grime, furniture polish, and air pollutants.

His conclusion was that he had actually bought a reproduction, probably one made during the 1920s or 1930s. This episode taught him an important lesson. Be wary if you go to an auction or estate sale and find only one "antique" in the lot. Most people who love beautiful antique furniture will own more than one piece. So, if their households are put up for auction, the offering will contain several pieces of antique furniture.

On the other hand, don't take it for granted that every piece of furniture at an antiques sale is really old. Sometimes a reproduction or two will be slipped in among the genuine antiques. Detection can be difficult if all the furniture at the sale is dusty and many pieces need repair, as often happens at estate sales and country auctions.

Your best defense against the costly mistake of buying reproductions is to become knowledgeable about the ways craftsmen made furniture. Be aware of the ways wood ages and furniture wears. Learn to recognize the ways they cut wood years ago and the old ways of joining different parts of furniture. Learn what old screws and nails look like. All this, plus the ability to recognize authentic styles, will help you know whether that Vic-

torian table you discover in a secondhand store in Atlanta is from 1865 or 1965.

You should also develop a healthy skepticism when buying from people you don't know. Just don't believe every story you hear that starts off, "This belonged to my great-grandmother. . . ."

In contrast to many other substances, wood undergoes marked changes as it ages. It shrinks. It darkens. It shows the effects of daily use. It acquires a soft patina that can't be duplicated by any modern finishing method. These are some of the reasons antique furniture has so much character and is so beautiful. They also can be some of your primary aids in determining the age of a piece of furniture.

SHRINKAGE

All live, growing wood contains natural moisture. Once a tree is cut, though, the moisture begins to dry up. Properly cured wood will retain most of its finished size and shape, but some shrinkage will inevitably occur through the years as natural moisture continues to evaporate. The hardwoods (cherry, rosewood, teak, mahogany, maple, ash, oak, walnut) will shrink less than the softwoods (pine, poplar, spruce). So any of the distortions or problems mentioned in this section will usually be more acute with softwoods than with the hard varieties, assuming the woods are the same age.

Most of the shrinkage in wood takes place across the grain. Very little occurs with the grain—lengthwise of the tree. This peculiarity of nature causes many little problems in old furniture.

You'll frequently find framed panels of wood that have split, resulting in a crack ¼ inch or more wide. You'll find these cracked panels in

The enclosed panel in the door of this Mission Oak cabinet has a split from natural shrinkage, a common occurrence in antique furniture.

desks, commodes, dressers—any case piece in which the cabinetmaker set a fairly thin panel of wood into grooves of a thicker wooden frame. The really astute fellows knew what would likely happen with time and just inserted the panels loose. That way, the thin wood was able to shrink and pull in without splitting. As a rule, any panel that shrank without splitting will be a little lighter at one or both of its side edges. This is because those edges have been exposed to the air for less time than the main part of the panel.

Some cabinetmakers insisted on gluing or nailing the panels in place, perhaps thinking they were doing a better job. In time that wood began to dry out. Something had to give as the wood shrank, and inevitably, the thin panels could not compete with glue and hardware. They split from the tension.

Drawer bottoms and the backboards of some case pieces were nearly always made of thin, soft pine boards, so they shrank more than the hardwood from which the body of the piece was made. Many of the dressers, chests of drawers, and desks you'll find suffer from this problem. The drawer bottoms become split or pulled out of the shallow grooves of the side or back of the drawer, depending upon which way the grain of the wood in the drawer bottom lies. Backboards

The maker of this tabletop assembled it from straight-cut wood.

were nearly always nailed to the body of the piece, so they split even though the dresser, chest, or desk itself remained quite sturdy and solid.

Some furniture will even shrink out of shape in time. This is most noticeable on round tabletops that become slightly oval as the boards contract from side to side. You can be pretty sure, then, that a pine table is old if the top is an inch or so out of round.

Every once in a while you'll find an antique that was put together with wooden pegs. If the piece is very old, those pegs may be protruding a fraction of an inch beyond the surface of the table apron, chair, or whatever. This is because furniture makers whittled the pegs lengthwise of the grain of very hard wood, so they shrank little. Yet the body of the piece of furniture shrank noticeably across the grain, allowing the pegs to project in time.

TOOL MARKS

Rub your fingers along the underside of an antique tabletop and along the backboard of an old case piece. You'll find that those old craftsmen, who had to do all the finishing work by hand, seldom wasted much energy planing unexposed surfaces of wood. Only the very finest and most expensive pieces got the royal treatment of having back and undersides as smooth and well finished as the tops and fronts.

Usually this rough, unexposed wood will still bear saw marks, which can give you a good indication of the approximate age of the piece. Any piece of furniture constructed before 1830 will have been made of wood cut and sawed by hand. The resulting saw marks on those rough surfaces are straight and usually quite irregular. By 1830 the age of machinery made possible power-driven sawmills that still used straight blades and that made relatively smooth but still straight cutting marks on the wood. Around 1850 sawmills began using buzz saws, which left clearly definable circular cutting marks on wood. So if you're debating about the age of an antique, just hold the rough, unplaned surfaces up to a strong light and let it shine across the item at an angle. You should be able to see quite easily whether or not the piece was sawed by hand, by straight saw, or by circular saw.

Even the planed exposed surfaces of wood in old furniture will not usually be as even as that in new furniture. For one thing, antique furniture predates electric belt sanders, which can remove surface irregularities in wood in minutes. Run your fingers lightly over the surface of an old table, for instance, and you'll be able to feel those slight valleys and hills typical of antique furniture.

CUT OF THE WOOD

Be aware, too, of the width of the boards when inspecting an antique. Some old tabletops have boards 18 to 20 inches wide, much wider than any cabinet wood used today. Also, furniture makers a few generations ago frequently used random widths of lumber in constructing a tabletop or desk. Modern furniture makers usually use boards of identical width, unless they're trying to emulate an old style. The lumber used in antique furniture was also heavier than that used today. A few generations ago furniture makers were concerned not only with turning out a beautiful product but also with making one that would stand up to hard use. These are two of the main reasons antique furniture is still good looking and usable after so many years of wear.

During the nineteenth century, many furniture makers constructed pieces of quarter-sawn oak. Quarter-sawing is a method of cutting wood in which a sawmill sectioned a log into quarters before cutting it into boards, resulting in a distinctive wavy grain. The pattern looks much like the ripples on a pond. This fashionable style wasted a lot of wood and soon went out of vogue.

PATINA

Patina is that much-prized glow wood acquires after many years of handling, polishing, and just plain aging. The best way to learn to recognize this natural patina is to place an old, well-cared-for piece of furniture, which has never been stripped, next to a new piece of a comparable color and wood. The difference will be obvious.

Assuming an antique is constructed of one type of wood and isn't a mixture of several, it should exhibit the same patina on all exposed finished surfaces. Be suspicious if you find an antique where one section of wood is markedly different from the rest. That section could be a recent repair or replacement. Such an alteration would substantially reduce the value of the piece.

Notice the difference in the grain of this quarter-sawn oak tabletop. You can easily spot the characteristic wavy grain.

The above caution goes double for applied trims. Some unscrupulous people will try to upgrade a fairly common and plain antique by gluing on fancy trims to simulate a more expensive one. These additions can include entire borders of pressed or carved trim on a table or china cabinet. Other alterations could be fancy wooden motifs on the back of a plain rocking chair or the fronts of dresser drawers.

The people who vandalize a good antique this way aren't only dishonest but usually foolish as well. Quite often a simple primitive antique—that is, one of plain design, made long ago with local materials and hand tools—is far more valuable than a later style complete with factory-made decorations.

These additions aren't hard to spot. The wood will lack the patina of the piece of furniture to which they're applied. Often they'll be lighter in color or will look new in comparison to the rest of the piece. Check the edges of the trim—where it joins the drawer front or whatever. If the trim is firmly affixed on an antique, you'll see a slight buildup of old varnish and wax or even dirt at the joining. If the trim is loose, pry it out a bit and peer at the wood underneath. The trim's design should be clearly evident there. If the color and patina of the wood extends unbroken around and under the trim, however, you can be quite sure that someone applied the decoration recently. Old wood that has been exposed to the air acquires a different patina from that which has been protected, such as the wood under a trim that a craftsman applied at the time he made the piece.

Unfinished but exposed wood, such as that on the backs of chests of drawers, usually becomes much darker than the finished wood on the front of the piece. You'll learn to recognize the characteristic tone of old, unvarnished wood in time. Coupled with a deep patina on the finished wood, it's a good indication of an authentic antique.

If you're at all suspicious about the age of a piece of furniture, try to check the condition of any completely unexposed and unfinished wood in the piece. For instance, check the ends of chair stretchers, the parts that are inserted a half inch or so into the chair legs. Although unexposed, this wood will have darkened on a genuine antique. On relatively new furniture, this unexposed wood will still look fresh and new. The stain or finish applied to the exposed surfaces of the wood of new furniture usually does not penetrate into those joints.

Another way to test for authenticity is to scratch the finish of a piece of furniture in some concealed spot. On new furniture the color will extend just under the surface, with light-colored wood under the stain. On old furniture the wood will be dark all the way through from natural aging.

NORMAL WEAR

Only furniture that's never used survives without nicks and scratches. Look for worn edges, cuts, stains in the wood, and any other evidence of everyday wear and tear. Hardwoods will show less wear and tear than softwoods. You can do a little test to demonstrate the relative "wearability" of one wood over another. Place a scrap of a hardwood such as walnut or oak next to a scrap of a softwood such as pine or poplar. Hit each with a hammer, using about the same force. The blow will have little effect on the hardwood but will make a major dent in the softwood. This should prove to you quite graphically that a softwood table should show a great deal of wear if it's a genuine antique, while a hardwood table would show proportionately less wear.

When examining a piece of furniture, ask yourself, "How would I use this?" Pick it up or sit on it or open the drawers or place an object on it. Multiply any action you took by a lifetime of use, and you'll know where that piece of furniture would show normal wear.

The front stretchers of chairs will sometimes be worn down on top from generations of people resting their feet there. The back edge of the two rear legs may be worn from those same people leaning back in the chair. On very old chairs the finials that decorate the top of the back posts may be slightly worn. They may even be dark and greasy-looking from years of use. A series of concentric nail holes in a wooden seat shows that several wood, fiber, or leather seats postdated the original leather or cane when it wore out.

Often you'll find ink stains on office furniture, a lasting memento of the days before ballpoint pens came into being. The underside of the front edge of kneehole desks will sometimes be worn. You'll find scars on the front inside corners of those kneehole desks from people pushing chairs in and out.

Knobs and handles and the areas around them often show undeniable signs of age and use. Many case pieces such as pie safes and secretaries, especially if made of softwood, will have distinct gouges around the knobs—usually on the right side—where generations of fingernails collided with the wood. These knobs, if made of wood, will almost always have a characteristic dark, greasy look.

Even metal hardware can leave signs of age on old wood. Brass will tarnish, of course, but this usually leaves no lasting marks on the wood. This isn't the case with some of the cheaper hardware previously manufactured. A dealer once spent a couple of frustrating hours trying to get rid of the deep black marks on a dresser left by some miserable copperplated hardware. The drawer pulls were at least a hundred years old, and for ninety-nine of those years they had been corroding away, leaving a deeper and deeper imprint of their pattern in the wood. He finally got most of the marks out with sandpaper and bleach and replaced the old pulls with some antique brass ones of almost the same shape.

Many times you'll find antiques whose hardware has been replaced at least once. Sometimes the evidence is not black marks but plugged-up holes that indicate where the original bolts went through the wood. You'll usually see these holes most easily from the inside of drawers because the replacement hardware wasn't the same width as the original, and someone drilled new holes to accommodate it.

These holes are no problem. They indicate

The front stretchers on this ladder-back chair show signs of normal wear.

only that the hardware is not original. While that may detract a bit from the value of the antique, it's so common that no one worries about it. In fact, if replacement hardware itself is very old, it just shows that the antique is far older.

Drawers are another good indication of age in an antique. Furniture makers constructed sides and bottoms of most old drawers of a softwood, usually pine, which wears quickly. You can look for three signs of age on softwood drawers: First, the bottoms should be worn quite smooth. Second, the tops of the sides may be worn down a little at the very back of the drawer. Third, the bottoms of the sides may be worn concave at the very front of the drawer as a result of the drawer being lifted forward as someone opened it. This common type of wear is the reason so many old dresser drawers drop down a little when pulled out.

JOININGS

Your most obvious clue to the approximate date of antiques may be the way furniture makers assembled them. Always check the edges of drawers. On most furniture styles the hardwood front will be joined to the softwood sides with some

sort of dovetail joint, except for some primitives and Mission Oak, which used butt joints. Most dovetail joints look very much alike—a series of alternating and interlocking wedge-shaped joints. Early cabinetmakers cut them by hand and often made the "tails" an inch or more wide. These handmade dovetails are often crude and uneven. By the mid-nineteenth century, furniture makers used machine-cut dovetails. The first machine-cut dovetails were smaller and more uniform that the old hand-cut ones and were often round rather than wedge shaped. Around 1880 most dovetail joints were similar to the wedge-shaped joints used today.

Early cabinetmakers frequently used pinned mortise-and-tenon joints for tables and chairs. The basic part of this joint was identical to that of modern mortise-and-tenon joints. Then, as now,

These three drawers represent, from left to right, dovetailing from the eighteenth, nineteenth, and early twentieth centuries. Notice the hand-cut dovetails of the left-hand drawer as compared with the machine-made dovetails of the right-hand drawer.

In the eighteenth and nineteenth centuries wooden pegs were often used in the construction of pieces because they made for stronger joints.

they cut a thin slot into one half of the joint (the outside edge of a bed footboard, for instance) and cut a projection to fit the slot in the other half of the joint (the upper edge of the leg). These craftsmen went one step further, though, by drilling a small hole through the finished joint and inserting a wooden pin for added reinforcement.

They often used wooden pegs in furniture construction, not always because nails weren't available, but because hardwood dowels made stronger joints. Before the advent of power-driven machinery, cabinetmakers whittled these pegs by hand. Therefore, any piece of furniture with irregular wooden pegs can be dated before about 1840. After that date furniture makers used machine-made dowels, which were about as cylindrical as the ones in use today.

HARDWARE

You can't always judge an antique's age by the type of nail or screw used in its construction, simply because it is too easy to replace hardware. A very old piece could have modern screws because someone recently reinforced a weak joint, for instance. On the other hand, a forger could use very old salvaged hardware on a cleverly made fake.

Assuming the hardware on an antique is the original, though, you have some guidelines to help you. Until about the end of the eighteenth century, cabinetmakers used hand-forged nails. Around 1790, though, nails stamped out of sheet iron with blunt ends but hand-forged heads became available. Some twenty years later blacksmiths began producing the entire nail by stamping. And by 1850 cabinetmakers were using wire nails with round heads and sharp points, quite similar to those in use today.

The very earliest screws were wide and crude and had irregular threads cut by hand with a file. Makers likely cut slots in the heads with a hand-held hacksaw, making them off center. Around 1800 machinists developed efficient screw-making machinery, and from that point on screws were fairly similar to those in use today.

Handmade hinges on very old primitive antiques will usually be made of crude, uneven sheets of iron with irregularly placed screw holes.

LABELS AND OTHER IDENTIFYING FACTORS

An authentic pasted-on manufacturer's label always adds to the value of an antique. If the label is dated, you also have incontrovertible proof of

This attractive walnut piece was once a shoeshine stool as indicated by the "shadow" of the shoe form that was left after that part disappeared. Often it's what remains today that can give you an indication of how a piece may have been used originally.

the piece's age. On dressers you'll most often find the labels pasted to the upper side of one of the drawer bottoms. On an old desk look for the label on the back of the small door that separates the bank of pigeonholes. On tables the label will be on the underside of the tabletop, and on chairs it will be on the underside of the chair seat.

A young woman once bought an old mahogany dental cabinet at an estate auction. It turned out to have a complete finishing record on a label pasted to the bottom of one of the drawers. The label listed eleven finishing steps, including staining, filling, two coats of varnish with sanding in between each, rubbing, and the final inspection. Beside each step was the finisher's code number and the date he worked on

Early cabinetmakers often carved their names or initials onto their pieces. As mechanization took over at the end of the nineteenth century, however, they began to stamp labels into their furniture or use paper ones applied to the backs of case pieces or undersides of chairs.

the cabinet. The record covers five weeks from November 6, 1917, until December 12 of the same year. This unusual cabinet, with its twenty-two shallow drawers, glass-fronted sterilizer compartments, beveled mirror, and beautifully paneled back, is not a "legal" antique yet. It will be within a few years, however, and that label will add a great deal to its value then.

An old label may be quite brittle and its glue completely dried out. One in this condition is easily lost, but you certainly want to preserve it to verify the age of your antique. I suggest one simple but effective method: Gently push some all-purpose glue under the label with a cotton swab or small brush. Press the label down and allow it to dry. Brush on a coat or two of satin-finish polyurethane varnish to protect the paper from further deterioration. If the label is in good condition, just cover it with a sturdy piece of clear plastic film. Then securely tape the edges of the film.

Late-eighteenth- and early-nineteenth-century furniture makers used another form of labeling. It seems that some manufacturers of Windsor chairs branded the undersides of chair seats with their names. Such a chair would be quite unusual and therefore even more valuable than an unbranded chair. Early chair makers took pride in their work and branded it to be sure everyone knew who made it. Chair makers sometimes branded a Windsor chair with the name of the buyer, too. This "label" probably served to identify ownership in case of theft.

You may also find other types of "labels." Old newspapers can be just about as good as a manufacturer's label in setting the approximate date of an antique. Before the advent of commercial shelf paper and relatively inexpensive wallpapers, people frequently used old copies of the local newspaper to line shelves and trunks. Be extremely careful to preserve any such treasures you find pasted into an antique. Not only can they date the item, but the papers themselves are quite interesting, with their old steel engravings, quaint type, and fascinating copy.

A collector of old trunks found a British seaman's trunk that had been lined with a copy of the *London Illustrated Times.* The newspaper was in pretty bad condition but still intact enough that he could read some of the articles. In one he found a reference to that week's date—in October 1867. The trunk of heavy planks and crude handmade iron hardware had obviously been used for many years before someone lined it with a British newspaper. So he had authenticated information for the approximate age of the trunk. He preserved the paper as described above and ended up with a one-of-a-kind gem of an antique. And guess where he found this beauty— at a garage sale, no less. The family had been using it as a toy box for its little son. They only decided to sell it because he kept dropping the heavy lid on his fingers!

CHAPTER 5

GENERAL REPAIR TECHNIQUES

All right. You've brought that rickety antique home from the garage sale, and now you're ready to restore it from early Secondhand to late Victorian. Before you grab your rubber-tipped hammer, though, you need to make a checklist of possible damage and problems. That way you'll be prepared with all the necessary materials, equipment, and parts at the time you need them. You'll also know exactly what you face in the way of repairs so you can take the proper steps in logical order.

1. Clean the piece thoroughly with paint thinner and/or a weak ammonia-and-water solution.

2. Remove all past Band-aid–like repairs, including nails, scrap-wood braces, and baling-wire tourniquets.

3. Test for loose joints.

4. Check the condition of the hardware.

5. Look for broken or missing parts.

6. Test the stability of the drawers and doors.

7. Look for warpage.

8. Test the level of the piece, determining if any problem stems from uneven legs or loose joints.

9. Check for any "glorification" with modern trim or decorations.

10. Look for loose, blistered, or cracked veneer.

With this information you'll know how much effort and time you'll have to expend to repair the monster. Take one word of advice, though: Certainly, you'll take care of any problem that threatens the stability of the piece or detracts from its inherent beauty. *Do not,* however—and this caveat applies to the finishing process, too—go too far. Remember, you want the final result of your work to look like a genuine antique that has seen years of loving use and care. You don't want a piece of furniture that could pass for a reproduction straight out of the showroom window of your local furniture store. Leave a few imperfections. Let your antiques retain the dignity of their years, of their own personalities. After all, isn't that why you love them?

Since bookstores and libraries carry many books on woodworking techniques, you won't

Nineteenth-century chairs received a lot of heavy use and often became loose as the wood shrank. Often people used heavy wire to reinforce these chairs from the bottom. The wire extended up the rear of the chair to keep the back tight.

find that information here. Instead, you'll find information about dealing with the special problems you'll encounter in renovating antique furniture.

With that in mind, let's start at the beginning.

GLUING

You'll want your finished work to look as authentic as possible. Always use glue in preference to screws when securing a joint. A well-glued joint is far stronger than one joined only with screws since metal tends to wear out, especially at stress points. In time the joint will loosen, simply because the screw works loose. Old wood is often dry and brittle. You can easily split a delicate piece by trying to join it to another with a screw. This doesn't mean that you'll *never* use metal fasteners in renovating your antiques. Many times you'll combine glue and screws on hidden joints, just as the craftsmen did when they first constructed the piece.

Early furniture makers used glue made from animal hide or fish products, which they heated to a liquid before each use. While a few purists today still contend this is the only way to get a good strong joint, you can get excellent results with the yellow wood glue available in most hardware stores. It requires no mixing, stays liquid in the bottle, dries fairly quickly, cleans up with water, and forms a strong, water-resistant bond when dry.

Should You Take It Apart?

One school of thought regarding antiques renovation says a piece of furniture must be completely disassembled and every joint reglued. This isn't necessary unless the piece is falling apart. If an antique is still sturdy after generations of use, the chances are it will continue that way for a long time to come. You're only asking for a lot of extra work if you take apart joints that do *not* need repair or regluing. Work on the wobbly or damaged parts and leave the solid ones alone.

When you *do* have to dismantle an antique, you should use either a rubber-tipped mallet or a regular hammer with the head covered with a thick pad of rags. Tap gently at first, then with more force as the old glue begins to give way.

Removing Hidden Hardware

Occasionally, while you're dismantling an antique, you'll find that the parts refuse to separate, even though you know the glue bond is broken. The answer usually is a hidden nail or two buried inside the wood, its head right at or below the surface. Years before, the old glue lost its grip on life, and some home-repair buff probably tried to shore up the wobbly legs or stabilize a top rail by *nailing* it together.

Often you aren't able to see the head of the nail, so you won't know where to dig. One solution is to try to force the two parts apart a bit until you can actually see a portion of the nail's shank. Use a hacksaw to saw through the nail. If you can't get the entire hacksaw in, around, or under the nail, just take the blade out of the tool and use it alone. After you separate the parts, you can use pliers to pull the nails out of the wood.

Another method of getting a buried nail out of wood is to drive it through. This works if the nail is very slender and has essentially no head, and if the point lies close to the outside edge of

Sometimes digging is the only way to remove nails that have been used to repair antique furniture.

the wood. Rest the antique on a horizontal surface to brace it, then force the nail through with a *nail set*—a small tool used to pound nails below the surface of wood.

The last alternative is one that *always* works but does cause considerable damage. Take a tool such as an awl and dig some wood away from, around, and under the nail's head. This gives you enough room to get a pair of needle-nosed pliers or a diagonal cutter in to pull the nail out. You'll have to repair that hole with wood filler later on.

Occasionally you'll have a similar problem with an old screw whose head breaks off when you try to remove it. If the remaining shank is loose in the wood, you can sometimes dislodge and remove it with a magnet. More often than not, the shank remains firmly embedded in the wood. You can nearly always get such a shank out, however, by drilling around it with a small drill bit until you've created enough space to remove the shank with tweezers. If this problem

occurs on a hinge, remove the other screws, which should allow you to lift the hinge off the wood. Then remove the shank, using the method described previously.

Coding Identical Parts

Be sure to mark any seemingly identical parts you remove from an antique, coding them so you'll know just where each should go upon reassembling. That way you won't be confused about which stretcher went on the top left and which on the bottom right. Surprisingly, even the matched spindles from the back of a chair are often of different lengths, and the ends may have different diameters.

Removing Old Glue

Once the necessary parts are disassembled, you need to sand away all the old dried glue. Fresh glue will not adhere over the old stuff. Old glue can be especially difficult to remove, too. Sometimes boiling vinegar will dissolve old glue. Or you can use coarse sandpaper on those sections that will be hidden once the antique is reassembled.

Often the hardest glue-removal job is trying to get the old glue out of sockets. You'll find the easiest way is simply to drill it out with a drill bit of the same diameter as the hole.

Getting Started

Remember, don't try to glue fifteen different pieces back together in one operation. This is about as efficient as trying to paper the ceiling and four walls of a room at one time. Something will always be falling out or down while you're pushing something else in. Glue a few pieces at a time,

Often the easiest way to clean old glue from a socket is to drill it out with an electric drill. Use a bit the same diameter as the socket and take care not to enlarge the hole.

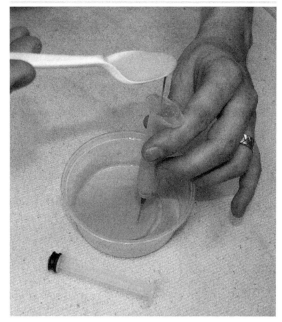

Mix one part water with three parts yellow woodworking glue and pour the mixture into a hypodermic syringe. The thinned glue will flow easily through the needle.

clamp them, and allow the section to dry overnight before you tackle another section. Be sure to wipe off with a damp cloth any glue that oozes out of the joints. Once it's dry, wood glue is difficult to remove and will quite effectively block your stain or oil from penetrating the wood.

Periodically, throughout the regluing of several parts of an antique, you should set the piece of furniture on a flat surface and check its level. Check both horizontal and vertical planes.

At times you may not need to take an antique apart for regluing. Perhaps one leg of a chair, for instance, is just a little loose. The answer in that case is to force glue into the joint while the two

parts are still in place. This method also works when you're faced with a narrow crack on a tabletop or solid wood seat, a crack too small to accept a glue-laden spatula. The most satisfactory tool for this operation is a hypodermic syringes filled with a diluted solution of glue and water. Yellow glue as it comes from the bottle is usually too thick to flow through the needle, so mix about one part water to three parts glue. You can buy inexpensive hypodermic syringes in drugstores in some areas or ready-made gluing kits in home-improvement and hardware stores.

Insert the needle of the filled syringe deeply into the joint or crack and press the plunger.

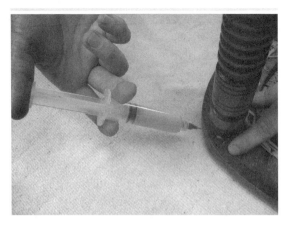

Use the syringe to force the thinned glue into joints that need tightening.

Use a cloth furniture clamp to tightly hold the glued joint until it's dry.

Don't skimp. Remember, this glue is diluted, and besides, much of it will probably run out of the joint while you're working. Wipe off any glue that drips onto the finished surface of the antique, tap the joint with a wooden mallet, and then clamp overnight.

Clamping the Glued Antique

You can't do a good job of gluing wood without using clamps. Natural tension between parts, the weight of the antique, or just plain gravity can cause freshly glued joints to pull apart slightly, thereby substantially reducing the quality of the repair. To be effective, joined parts must be firmly butted together, and the glue must penetrate the pores of the wood. The only practical solution is to clamp every glued joint firmly immediately after joining the parts.

C clamps and pipe clamps are the old standbys in most workshops, and they're indispensable in repairing antiques. C clamps in two or three sizes will take care of the small jobs. Pipe clamps of 4 to 6 feet can help stabilize even large dressers, chests, or buffets. Pipe clamps come in two pieces. Attach one piece to the end of a section of lead pipe. This part of the clamp has a screw handle that moves the clamp along the pipe with each revolution. The other piece of the clamp has a locking mechanism. Place it along the pipe and slide it back and forth as needed. To clamp a 40-inch-wide cabinet, for instance, you would place the locking section about 41 inches down the pipe. After gluing the cabinet, place the assembled pipe clamp along its length. Tighten the screw handle until the clamps firmly grab the cabinet. One or two more revolutions, and the clamps form an excellent vise to hold the cabinet while the glue dries.

A good selection of clamps can be quite expensive, and while you're building up a collection, you can certainly use less-expensive surrogate types. Plain cotton clothesline can be quite effective. Pass a length of clothesline around the glued antique twice and tie the ends securely. Tighten it by placing a screwdriver or a short length of dowel between the two lines and twisting them until you reach the desired tension. Secure the screwdriver or dowel behind some part of the furniture to hold the tension. Bungee cords are another inexpensive alternative to hardware clamps. Their end hooks and strong elastic cords make them ideal for irregularly shaped pieces. Bungee cords are especially useful when clamping chair legs and spindles.

Even more unconventional "clamps" can be improvised for those hard-to-secure gluing jobs. Old inner tubes can be cut into gargantuan rubber bands that have endless possibilities. Spring-type clothespins are good for clamping edges and very small work. And you can use tape to hold sections of delicate trim in place while glue hardens.

Regardless of the type of clamp you use, though, be sure to place thin wood or rags between it and the wood to prevent damage at the point of contract. A thin strip of wood is known as a *caul* and is especially useful when gluing long edges such as tabletops or when clamping softwoods. Just be sure to place waxed paper between the caul and wood to prevent excess glue from wedding the two together.

A caul helps to distribute pressure from clamps when you're working with a piece such as this tabletop.

Inexpensive bungee cords can be used to hold glued joints together.

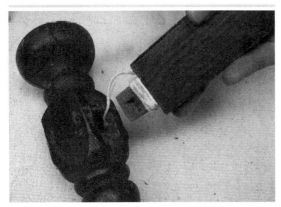

1. One way to make sure an old mortise-and-tenon joint stays together is to wrap cotton string around the tenon.

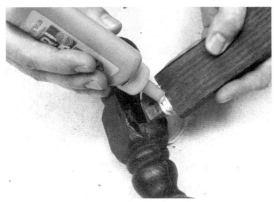

2. Apply wood glue to the string and tenon.

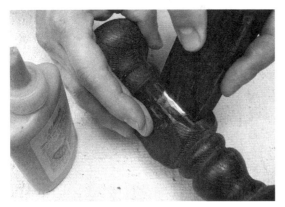

3. Glue the joint together, tapping it with a wood mallet.

TIGHTENING SOCKETS

Some sockets in antiques are too large to grip the companion piece, even when fresh glue is used. Don't ever bank on a thick layer of glue filling in gaps of ⅛ inch or so. It just won't happen. One way to increase the size of a spindle end so it *will* fit a socket that's too large is to brush on a coat of glue, then wrap the end with thread or a few thicknesses of nylon stocking. This artificially enlarged end should fit the socket once it is given another coat of glue. Or coat the end of the spindle with glue, insert it into the socket, and fill any remaining space with short pieces of glue-dipped wooden toothpicks.

A more professional, although more troublesome, way does exist to tighten sockets. Use a piece of hardwood dowel as long as the depth of the socket but a bit larger in diameter. Drill out the old socket with a drill bit the same diameter as the piece of new dowel. Glue the dowel into this new, enlarged socket and allow it to dry overnight. Then bore a new socket in the center of that dowel, using a bit the diameter of the old spindle's end. Insert the spindle, along with plenty of glue, into this new socket. Once the glue hardens, this type of joint has an exceptionally tight bond. You'll find this an excellent method to reinforce worn sockets.

SPLIT AND CRACKED WOOD

As mentioned before, old wood dries out as its natural moisture gradually lessens. Add to that the drying effects of centrally heated homes, and you have the catalyst for one of the most common problems in antique furniture—split wood. A split will often begin as just a hairline crack. At

The thick boards that formed the seat of this captain's chair have separated. The arrows point to the resulting cracks.

first it's barely noticeable. Bit by bit, though, it creeps along and gets deeper, until finally the desk side panel, tabletop, or whatever splits into two pieces. Sometimes a piece of wood, usually one under pressure, such as a chair seat, will develop a crack along the length of the wood, apparently spontaneously. Almost any split, though, regardless of its nature, can be repaired with glue and clamps. The sooner you catch it the better.

Cracks on large-surface pieces such as table-tops and chair seats are easy to repair. Just spread glue generously along both sides of the crack and clamp the two parts together. Place a level across the surface to make sure the pressure of the clamps hasn't bowed the parts out of line.

As described in chapter 4, framed panels in old furniture often split because they were glued firmly into place when made. After years of natu-ral shrinkage, the panels cannot slide out of their channels, and since wood won't stretch, they did the only thing possible: They split down the grain.

When faced with such a split panel, first try to loosen the panel's pieces from the side channels. Slide a flexible spatula into the groove and try to work the glue loose. If you can manage this, the panel will slide freely. If you're successful, work some glue along both edges of the split and push

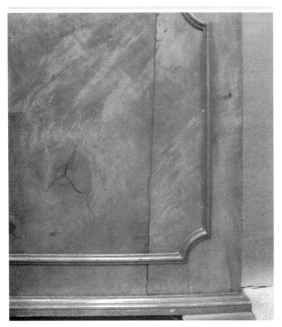

This detail of the base of a tall-case clock shows the damage that can occur on an antique when panels of wood shrink because of the dryness caused by fireplaces and woodstoves in eighteenth- and nineteenth-century homes.

This desk spent the first one-hundred-plus years of its life in misty England, where the damp air prevented the wood from excessive drying. A returning serviceman shipped it to the United States after the end of World War II. It eventually found its way to Arizona. When a woman bought it a couple of years ago, the exceptionally dry air there had taken its toll. A side panel had split, leaving a gaping ⅛-inch-wide crack. There was no way to get the panel out of the desk, and the glue would not release its hold.

The only solution was to cut a long wafer-thin sliver of mahogany and, after spreading glue along all edges, force it into that crack. While the repair is still visible, even after touch-up refinishing, most people aren't aware of it.

When the split in a case piece is too thin to insert a wood strip, the only thing to do is fill the crack with wood dough or filler of a matching color.

Fortunately, the natural graining and variations in color of wood help disguise these repairs very nicely.

Sometimes the boards in a chair seat will dry out and shrink along just one section of their joining, nearly always at the back, between the hip rests. The result is a thin space about 3 or 4 inches long between two of the boards. The rest of the joining between those boards will be quite firm and solid.

Wood dries and shrinks because of a lack of moisture. You can *sometimes* make those boards swell and meet again by dripping warm water into the crack. This technique can take many days, with several applications each day. Unfortunately, it doesn't always work.

the two pieces together. Wipe off all of the excess glue with a rag and hold the wood together with masking tape until the glue dries thoroughly.

Many panels won't come loose that easily. Assuming the split panel is on a framed door, take the door off its hinges and disassemble the framework. This will free the panel. Glue the split panel together, then reassemble it with the framework, allowing the panel to slide freely in the channel.

You're faced with a bigger problem if the damaged panel is part of the permanent structure of a case piece. A typical example of this situation would be a marble-topped early Victorian mahogany desk.

HARDWARE—USING IT, REUSING IT, REPLACING IT

Count yourself fortunate when you come upon an antique with all its original hardware. Few desks, chests, dressers, or cabinets survive the years with all their pulls, escutcheons, locks, and keys intact.

Excellent reproduction hardware is available at fairly reasonable prices, however. (Check the catalogs of the suppliers listed at the back of the book.) You can buy just about any piece of hardware you need cast in quite authentic period styles. Your only real problem may be in trying to decide just *which* of the pulls, knobs, handles, or whatever you want to use.

Make certain, though, that the new hardware you buy for an antique matches the style and period of that piece. A sure mark of a neophyte restorer is delicate Queen Anne pulls on a late Victorian chest or Hepplewhite escutcheons on a Mission Oak bookcase. Study style books in a library and the antiques in museums to absorb this knowledge.

Antiquing New Hardware

Most of the reproduction hardware you buy will be too new to look authentic on an antique. And only an amateur or someone who really doesn't care about antiques would put some of this flashy hardware on a lovely old piece of furniture. Several ways exist, though, to "age" new brass hardware. The following are two of the simplest. In the first method, use a pair of pliers to hold the piece of hardware carefully over a burning candle until the brass is smoked and black. Take a rag and gently wipe some of the black off, leaving enough to

A dealer "fancied up" this early Victorian chest with chunky brass knobs. Most likely it originally had round wooden knobs.

You can "antique" new reproduction hardware with a commercial product especially made for this purpose. It will eliminate the objectionable brassy finish within minutes.

give an old and slightly tarnished look to the brass. Spray on a couple of coats of waterproof lacquer to seal the black onto the brass.

The second method calls for a commercial fluid especially made to mottle brass. You wipe the fluid on with a rag or cottonball, allow it to cure a few minutes, then rinse it off. No protective spray is necessary.

Duplicating Old Hardware

Quite often you'll find a lovely antique that has all but one or two of the original pulls or knobs. This may be the case with a charming mid-Victorian commode that you might find at an auction. It may be missing one pull out of its four originals when you find it. It would be a crime to discard three original pieces of hardware in favor of replacing the set with four matching reproductions. The solution is to have the missing one copied.

Only the workers at a brass foundry can do this copying successfully. Look in your yellow pages for a foundry in your area. You'll have to take one of the old pieces of hardware to them to use for a mold, but the duplicate will be exactly like the original, even down to the natural oxidation of the metal. The cost of having hardware copied doesn't fit into the bargain-basement category. In fact, the bill for that one pull can be as much as you'd spend to buy four new matching reproductions. But the money will be well spent to retain the authenticity of the commode. Obviously, any antique with its original hardware is more valuable than one with reproduction hardware.

Reactivating Old Locks

Furniture makers put locks on the doors and drawers of desks, dressers, and cabinets. Often these locks seem to be jammed, but you can nearly always free them. Get a can of any silicone lubricant and spray the liquid generously into the lock. Take the original key, if you have it, or a reproduction and gently "work" the lock until it opens smoothly. This method almost always works. Most old keys have long since disappeared, however, by the time you come upon an antique in need of restoration. You can buy new ones from one of the suppliers listed at the back of the book. They offer several styles, each listed in their catalog with the type of furniture it will fit—kitchen cabinet, desk, dresser, etc. Most of these old locks are quite generic, so you shouldn't have any trouble getting a key to fit any lock.

Before you order a key, check with your local locksmith. Many locksmiths carry a supply of old keys, and they might find just what you want.

Replacing Casters

Late-nineteenth- and early-twentieth-century furniture manufacturers also built their office chairs, tables, and case pieces to accept casters. Time and hard wear, though, have often dealt a hard blow to these quite practical rollers. Replacing them is a cinch, however, unless the wood that surrounded the original metal socket is badly deteriorated.

Let's take the easy cases first. Very often you'll find a chair or table with the casters missing but the metal socket still intact and in good condition. All you have to do then is just insert new casters into the old sockets.

You may, however, find both sockets and casters missing. In that case you'll find a hole drilled into the base of the leg. Measure that hole for depth and diameter to make sure it will accommodate a new socket. Most new sockets require a hole 1½ inches deep and ⅜ inch in diameter. If the socket you're working with is smaller than that, drill it out to that measurement. If it's considerably larger, plug it with a dowel and redrill, as described on page 68. Then insert the new socket and caster. If the original hole is just a trifle more than ⅜ inch in diameter, you can fill out the extra space with wood dough. Assemble the caster's stem into the socket *before* you insert it into the leg. Push the caster firmly into the dough, making sure the teeth engage either the wood or the wood dough. Flip the roller around several times to make sure it will move freely once the dough hardens.

How do you handle the situation if the sockets are missing and the wood at the base of the legs is partially rotted away? This is quite common with furniture that stood in damp basements too long. You can't drill satisfactorily into wood that is loose and crumbling. You can, though, rebuild that wood until it's solid enough to support the socket and caster.

One way is to scrape away the soft wood and fill the resulting cavity with wood dough. Then cut a piece of thin wood to the same dimensions as the leg. Glue or screw this piece of wood onto the bottom of the leg to act as a cap. Once the wood dough is dry and firm, sand the cap and any visible wood dough to conform to the original design of the leg. Now, drill a ⅜-inch hole through this cap and the hardened dough. Insert the new metal socket into the hole, then add the caster. You can even level a piece of furniture that tilts a bit by making the cap for the short leg a bit thicker than for the others.

You may someday come upon a fine old office chair or cabinet with one or more legs deteriorated to the point that the above repair method isn't feasible. In that case, the only practical solution is to trim the legs down to the solid wood. You can then add enough new wood to bring the leg or legs to the former dimensions. Or, simply attach the casters to the newly cut bottom of the legs. You can do this if the comfort or design of the piece of furniture does not depend upon the wood you cut away. In most cases an inch or two missing from the height of a cabinet makes no difference at all in its usefulness or design. That isn't the case with some chairs, but you'll never miss that bit of length from the legs if you're working with an office chair that has a mechanism to adjust the height. You can compensate for the wood you cut away by raising the seat an inch or so.

Tightening Hinges

Tiny hinges with even tinier screws attach the doors to the bodies of commodes and other case pieces. These little screws nearly *always* work loose in time, resulting in a dragging door. All you have to do to shore up the door is to remove the screws, insert a piece of wooden matchstick into the screw hole, add a squirt of glue, and then reinsert the screws. It's the easiest repair you'll ever make.

Lengthening Bed Rails

Most beds made a century or more ago were several inches shorter than our modern beds. Therefore, the old rails, even if in good condition, won't allow the use of a ready-made commercial box spring and mattress. You can, of course, have a mattress company construct a custom-made mattress and box spring to fit the bed, but that will be an expensive proposition.

It's far more practical, and easier than you think, to make new rails. Buy two solid 1-inch X 6-inch X 6⅓-foot planks, in the same hardwood as the bed. Attach new hardware to the end of the new rails and to the head- and footboards. This hardware is available from one of the suppliers listed at the back of the book.

You can buy metal mattress supports that hook over the top of the rail to hold the box spring in place. Or you can attach wooden supports of 2-inch X 2-inch X 4-foot stock to the insides of the rails. The latter method adds an hour or so to the repair time, but it results in a more authentic-looking antique.

Reusing Old Screws

It's always a good idea to reuse old screws whenever possible in repairing antique furniture. The shine on new screws screams "repair!" and really detracts from the overall appearance of the piece. So save all the screws you remove from old furniture, and watch for coffee cans full of old screws at garage sales.

These old screws will go into wood just as easily as new ones if you lubricate them first. All you have to do is twirl the screw once or twice across a cake of soft soap or dip it in lubricating oil or dishwashing detergent. Lubricate all screws, even

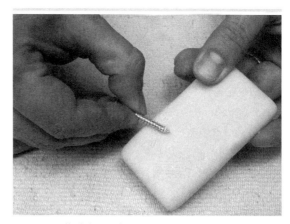

Screws will slide easily even into the hardest wood if you lubricate them first by drawing the screw across a cake of soap.

new ones. It's amazing how easily they'll glide into even the hardest wood after this treatment.

Overlarge Screw Holes

One common problem with trying to reuse old screws is holes that have become too large. To solve this problem, stick the ends of a couple of wooden matchsticks into the hole, squirt in a bit of glue, and then reinsert the screw. This trick is just about foolproof.

Embedded Screws

On the other hand, if a screw seems to have taken up permanent residence in a piece of antique furniture, here are some suggestions to get it to *release* its grip.

First, try to lubricate the screw and its hole with a few drops of kerosene or the commercial liquid especially made to loosen stubborn screws. Allow the lubricant to soak into the wood for an hour or so, reapplying it several times.

Then use a sturdy screwdriver whose blade tip fits the screw's slot exactly. A screwdriver that's too small may damage the slot, sometimes terminally. Put all your weight behind the screwdriver, pressing down on the screw as you try to turn the screwdriver counterclockwise.

No luck? Don't despair. Put the screwdriver tip back in the screw's slot and strike the end of the handle with a hammer as hard as you can without dislodging the screwdriver and mashing your hand. Then take a nail set in your left hand and place its tip at the far right-hand side of the slot, holding the tool almost parallel to the flat head of the screw. Again, use your hammer, this time striking the blunt end of the nail set, trying to force the screw counterclockwise. If anything will break the hold of a stubborn screw, it's the combination of lubricant, a sharp blow, and the leverage action of the nail set.

Sometimes you'll come upon an old screw whose slot has been obliterated by years of rust, grime, or paint. You can cut a new slot by literally sawing through the gunk with a hacksaw blade. Be careful, though. Old metal can be pretty soft, and it's easy to cut too deeply into the screw.

Disguising Screw Holes

Most of the furniture makers who built the antiques of today were perfectionists. They took a great deal of pride in turning out *finished*-looking work. You'll seldom find, for instance, the raw heads of screws exposed anywhere, except perhaps on hip rests and the backs of chair side posts. As you try to emulate the old-time quality of an antique, make an effort to conceal all screws, too.

All screws on exposed surfaces should be countersunk, and then the holes should be plugged.

Ready-made plugs come in a variety of woods and two styles, button and flat. Use the button style when you would like to add a little decorative detail to the antique. Use the flat type when you want to hide the fact that you put a screw into the wood at that spot. Both types can be finished to match the body of the piece, but remember, they are of new wood and lack the patina of old wood. You'll probably have to blend two different batches of oil, as described in chapter 6, to get a good match.

1. Countersink the hole for any screw that is inserted on an exposed surface.

2. Once the screw is in place, squirt a little wood glue in the depression and insert a wooden plug or make one from a dowel.

3. Trim off the dowel at the surface and sand lightly, then finish to match the surrounding wood.

4. Once refinished, the dowel blends into the original finish of the piece, as it does on the arm of this chair.

REPLACING MISSING PARTS

Earlier in this book you read that you could diminish an antique's value if you replaced any original part or section with a new one. This admonition applies most especially, though, to those rare pieces that, for some reason, are exceptional examples of their periods. These are the antiques destined to become museum-quality exhibits.

Common antiques, however, generally need some TLC. They've been hauled from Pennsylvania to California in jolting wooden-wheeled wagons. They've made the journey from New Hampshire to New Orleans by steamer, paddle boat, and open barge. They've been romped on by lively children and sat on by visiting aunts who were a bit too fond of ice cream. They've been used as stepladders to reach top shelves.

Most need a broken or missing part replaced. No purist will perform a "marriage" on them. This travesty is literally *building* an antique from scratch with several major parts taken from as many unrelated old pieces. But in reality you must sometimes add a bit of wood or a small replacement part. By doing so, you can take a neglected and essentially worthless piece of old furniture and restore it to beauty and usefulness.

Replacing Stretchers and Spindles

Chairs receive the heaviest use of any furniture in your home, and so it's logical that antique chairs frequently have missing parts. And, next to seats, those delicate members known as *stretchers* and *spindles* seem to be most in need of help.

The back and side stretchers that brace the legs of antique chairs often are just simple straight dowels. Replacing them is a cinch. All you have to do is measure the diameter of the ones still on the chair and buy dowel stock of the same size at your lumber company. Once home with the dowel, your first task will be to remove the old, dried glue from the holes that held the old stretchers. The easiest way to do this is to drill the glue out with a drill bit the same size as the hole. You may find the splintered remains of an old stretcher still in the socket. Drill that out, too.

Cut the dowel length, allowing for the distance it must extend into the chair legs. If it's too large to fit into the socket, trim the ends with a utility knife, a rough file, or sandpaper. Rub glue around the ends of the dowel, squirt a little more into the socket, and set the new stretcher in place.

Sometimes you can spring a chair's legs apart enough to insert this new stretcher. More often, though, you'll have to take your rubber mallet and knock the legs apart. This will mean you'll loosen the other stretchers. You'll have to remove them all, sand their ends, drill out the old glue from the sockets, and reset them with glue, too.

Most old chairs have elaborately turned *front* stretchers. If one or more of them is missing, you'll have to duplicate it to restore the chair. The only practical way to duplicate a turned stretcher is on a modern lathe. Most of us don't have workshops equipped with the sophisticated and expensive machinery necessary to do this work. That's no real problem, though, since any custom woodworking shop can make duplicate replacement parts for a nominal fee. Take the stretcher you wish copied into the shop, and the craftsperson there can turn out a duplicate in a matter of minutes. Just be sure to specify that he or she use the same type of wood from which the original part was made to construct the new one. You should insert a replacement turned stretcher into the sockets in the same way as a plain dowel, of course.

Inserting a replacement spindle into the back of a chair is usually more of a problem than replacing a stretcher. You'll have to knock the upright outer posts of the chair outward to release the top rail and free the spindles. Unfortunately, many old chairs have had those top rails

File the ends of a replacement chair stretcher or spindle so that it will fit the existing socket. Here the stretcher has come from another old chair.

"tightened up" somewhere along the line—with nails. This so-called repair will effectively stop the removal of the rail. You'll have to dig those nails out as described on pages 63–64.

Once any nails are out and the old glue is broken, that top rail should be easy to remove. Tap it off the top of the existing spindles. From this point on, replacing a spindle is similar to replacing a stretcher.

Replacing Hip Rests

Most old side chairs came equipped with *hip rests,* those curved pieces of wood that join the back of the seat at each side. Hip rests do *not* serve as a place to rest your hips but as a brace between the back and seat of the chair. Without them the chair would be unsteady, and the back side posts would be in danger of breaking about 2 inches above the level of the seat.

One or more of these hip rests are often missing from antique side chairs, but replacements are plentiful and not too expensive. You can order them from one of the suppliers listed at the back of the book.

Just attach the new hip rests to the chair's back and seat with screws. You'll even find the old screw holes still there to guide you in the proper placement. These screws will be quite visible, so don't use shiny new steel ones. Use old screws or "age" new brass ones with one of the methods mentioned on page 71–72.

Integrating New Wood Sections with Old

Every once in a while, you'll find an antique that's missing some minor panel or piece of trim. A young refinisher found a marble-topped walnut Eastlake commode at a moving sale. A panel at the bottom of the piece was missing. Who knows why this had been removed. Even though he had to replace the panel with new wood, he was able to match the finish to make it look like the rest of the piece.

The important thing to remember in constructing a new part for an antique is to keep the design compatible with the body of the piece. For instance, when the refinisher was working on the commode, a friend asked him why the refinisher didn't cut some attractive curves into the new panel. His friend couldn't understand why he was planning to glue on a perfectly straight board when he had a saber saw in his basement workshop that could be used to make it more ornate. His answer was that nowhere on the lovely little antique had the original craftsman cut any curves, an austere philosophy typical of the Eastlake style of the 1870s. You can easily ruin a piece's appearance by attempting to make it fancier than its maker intended.

The only problem the finisher had in replacing that missing board was in trying to get the new wood to blend with the wood that was more than a hundred years old. His lumber dealer stocked only one type of walnut, but the maker used a different type on the commode. The old wood had a richer, deeper brown tone than the new board, which had definite gray undertones. Add to that the issue of age and patina. Plus, he had to strip the commode to remove all the old paint and varnish, which altered the old wood's color to a certain extent.

At first glance it appeared he was working with two entirely different types of wood. But he put the replacement board in the hot summer sun and poured bleach and water on it for several days. Then he carefully mixed two blends of the colored finishing oils, putting one mixture on the new board and another on the old wood. The result was worth all the trouble, because no one who has seen the commode has ever realized that piece of panel is not original.

Recycling Old Parts and Wood

You previously read about buying new wood replacement parts and using new wood stock to construct replacement parts for an antique. The only real problem you'll encounter in doing so is in trying to blend the colors of the old and new woods. Chapter 6 gives some hints on ways to do that.

This American Empire mahogany card table, an auction find, was missing one curved section of the lower right leg. The replacement part will be undetectable once it's finished to blend with the older wood.

You can sometimes bypass that little problem, though. One way is to reuse old parts. This is an especially practical alternative when restoring a chair. You'll often come upon broken-down chairs as you search for antiques to refinish. Useless as they are in their present condition, you can nearly always salvage a stretcher or two or a pair of hip rests from these chairs. There's no way these wrecks can be restored, but, considering the few dollars or so you'll pay at garage sales, they're real bargains. The parts from these disasters are of

oak or other hardwood and have acquired that treasured patina of age. With just a little care, you can usually finish them to blend very nicely with your antique chair. Besides, you save yourself the trouble and expense of buying new parts.

Save all *scraps* of old wood, too. Keep a box in your workshop, garage, or utility room and throw in it every scrap of mellow wood you come by. And watch for such treasures as old table leaves, odd drawers, and other orphan pieces of furniture at garage sales. They're all invaluable when you need old wood to patch an antique or construct a replacement part.

Replacing Wooden Escutcheons

Nineteenth-century furniture makers often used wooden escutcheons instead of brass ones over the keyholes on their pieces. Placed as they were, these thin pieces of wood took a lot of abuse, so you'll often find them missing or broken. To replace them, merely pry off any wood remaining from the original escutcheon, sand the area beneath well, and glue on the replacement. You can order replacements in several woods from the suppliers listed at the back of the book.

If it's properly finished to match the body of the antique, you won't be able to tell the difference between this new escutcheon and any originals on the piece.

Shaping Curved Chair Slats

You'll find many old office chairs constructed with shaped back and side slats. Reproducing and installing a duplicate to take the place of a broken or damaged one certainly isn't the easiest of repairs. It can be done, though, and a few hours' effort will salvage a valuable chair for another century of use.

Your first step is to pry or drill out the remains of the damaged slat. Then make a pattern for the new slat, using one of the intact slats as a template. Press a piece of paper against the narrow dimension of the slat and reproduce its curve by drawing along it with a pencil. Transfer this pencil line, which duplicates the curving side of the slat, to a block of scrap wood at least as long as the slat. Cut along this pencil line with

a saber saw. The result will be two pieces of wood that fit together like the pieces of a jigsaw puzzle, whose inside edges exactly duplicate the curve of the slat. Place a straight replacement slat in this curved jig you've made and shape it under pressure. You'll have better results if you laminate two thin slats rather than try to bend one of the finished thickness. Cut, or have your lumber company cut, two thin slats, each half the thickness, the same width, and 3 or 4 inches longer than the original slat. For instance, consider a hypothetical chair as an example. If the exposed measurements of the slats in this chair are $\frac{1}{2}$ inch X $\frac{3}{4}$ inch X 12 inches, cut two thin slats, each $\frac{1}{4}$ inch X $\frac{3}{4}$ inch X 16 inches. The extra 4 inches will give you plenty of wood to fit into the sockets, as well as some for trimming and an allowance for error.

To laminate and shape these slats, spread glue on one side of each slat, then press them together. Place a strip of waxed paper on either side of this wooden "sandwich," and put the whole thing between the curved edges of the jig. Clamp the jig together, forcing the slats to conform its shape. Allow the laminated slat to harden overnight. The next day sand the edges and trim the ends to the desired length.

How you insert this replacement slat into the original sockets is largely determined by your chair. You may want to take the top rail off, as described on page 77. Or you may try this: Cut a shallow channel in the wood of the seat behind the bottom socket. This will give you enough space to slide the new slat into the sockets with the top rail still in place. You'll have to add some more new wood to fill in that channel, but it eliminates taking a very solid chair apart.

WORN AND STICKING DRAWERS

Someday you'll undoubtedly acquire a chest or dresser whose drawers will become the bane of your existence. You'll be able to close them fairly well until about the last inch, when you'll have to lift them to complete the movement. While irritating, that little problem is at least an indication the antique is genuine. The trouble comes from the drawer sides and the runners inside the dresser itself usually being made of softwood while the body of the dresser and the front of the drawer were hardwood. Through the years that softwood wore down, sometimes ¼ inch or more, while the hardwood front panels remained essentially unchanged. When you close the drawer, it slides along until it jams against the front panel. The only way to close the drawer completely is to lift it, allowing the front panel to clear the framework and slide in.

If the sides of the drawers are noticeably worn, you can build them up to their original dimensions. Use a utility knife to shave thin slivers of wood to fit the worn area. Wooden paint stirrers, tongue depressors, and ice cream sticks also make good replacement parts. Once the *shims,* the new pieces of thin wood, are glued onto the bottom of the drawers, sand all surfaces smooth and finish off with a coat or two of varnish. Then run the new edges with a cake of soap or spray them with some lubricant to ensure smooth gliding in the future.

Runners wear down almost as often as drawers. These little strips of wood stretch from front to back inside the body of the antique, supporting the drawers. If the runners are stationary, simply add slivers of wood to them with glue as described above. If they're removable, try turning them over. You may find an adequately smooth surface there. If not, make new runners by cutting new wood to the measurements of the runners. That will be far simpler than trying to build up the old ones.

After you get the drawers closing efficiently, you may find they go too *far* into the piece of furniture. If so, chances are the *stops* have fallen out. These are small pieces of wood (usually a 1-inch-long piece of 1 x 1-inch wood) glued inside the back of the drawer cavity. To replace them you need to locate the marks left by the original stops. As a rule you can find these areas without trouble because there will be a difference in the patination of the wood at those spots. Or there may be bits of old dried glue still clinging to the wood there. If you can't find the old stop marks, just measure the depth of the drawer front to back. Then measure the drawer cavity front to back the same distance and place a pencil mark at that point. Glue your stops behind the pencil mark. This will keep the drawer from sliding in too far.

CORRECTING WARPAGE IN FURNITURE

Furniture warps when one surface of the piece, the convex side, absorbs more moisture than does the opposite surface, the concave side. You can usually correct this common problem in antique furniture if the warped piece is removable.

This is one repair job where stripping is absolutely necessary. Remove every bit of paint, varnish, oil, wax, or other finish so the wood fibers will be free to absorb moisture, then dry uniformly. Your goal is to add moisture to the dry side and gradually allow the piece to dry under pressure. This helps the wood stabilize both its moisture content and form. You don't need professional equipment to correct a warp—either a below-ground concrete floor or a shady spot on the lawn will do nicely.

If working on the concrete floor of your basement, soak several towels in water, wring them out, and lay the warped board, separated from its base, on the wet towels. Place the board concave side down. Place heavy weights—concrete blocks or bricks—on the upper side of the warped board. Shut the door and let nature take over.

Depending on the amount of warp, you should see results in a couple of days. Once the board appears to be flat and level, lift it, remove the towels, turn the board over, and lay it down on the same spot. Some moisture should remain in the concrete—enough to continue the re-forming process. If not, dampen the concrete and replace the weights. Continue this daily turning of the top for three or four more days. At that point the board should be about as flat as it will ever be and ready for the final drying. Take it to a warm, dry room and continue turning and weighting it down for a few more days.

Reassemble the top and its base, using good-quality wood glue and hidden screws. Refinish the piece. Seal the underside of the board as well as its top side to help forestall any problems in the future.

You don't have a damp basement at your home? How about a flat spot on the lawn? Soak a section of your lawn with the garden hose. Lay a cotton sheet on the ground to protect the wood from dirt and grass stains and follow the procedure described above, weighting and turning the top for about a week. Then move it to a dry, but still shady, spot in the yard for the last few days of drying, again turning and weighting as described above.

REPAIRING MAJOR BREAKS IN WOOD

One of your primary objectives when restoring antique furniture is to make a repair without any external evidence of that repair. Professional restorers often use a repair technique called *blind doweling* to achieve this result. The repair is strong, invisible, and actually quite simple to master. You'll find it especially valuable when faced with a broken chair or table leg, or with a split chair seat.

This repair involves joining the broken pieces with one or more hardwood dowels. First, remove any broken sections still attached to the body of the furniture. Gather the sections and place them on a flat surface, aligning them at the break. Take a pencil and draw one line across the break of a narrow chair leg, drawing several distinct lines for a thicker table leg. Separate the broken pieces. Using a drill bit the diameter of the dowel you'll use for the repair, drill holes ½ inch to 1 inch deep (depending on the thickness of the leg) into only one side of the break.

No formula exists for the correct size dowel to use in any specific situation, but a good rule of thumb would be to use one about one-third the diameter of the broken piece.

Cut a dowel, one for each line you drew, into lengths twice as long as the depth of the drill hole. For instance, if you drilled a ½-inch hole, you would cut each dowel into 1-inch lengths. Brush glue onto half of the dowel and tap it into the hole you drilled—the remaining half of the dowel should protrude from the break.

Using the line you drew across the break as a guide, align the broken sections again. At the point where the protruding dowel touches the remaining section, trace the circumference of the dowel. Drill out this spot to the same depth you drilled the first hole.

Brush glue on the projecting end of the dowel and along both sides of the break. Tap the two sections together, using the lines as a guide, and you should have a perfect match and a virtually invisible repair. Wipe the excess glue off, clamp, and allow the repair to dry overnight.

TIGHTENING OLD WICKER

Wicker furniture sometimes becomes a bit loose, and the seats start to sag after many pleasant summers on the front porch. You can often firm it up without doing any major repair work. Just take the piece to the backyard and scrub it down with a mixture of one quart hot water, one cup vinegar, and one tablespoon laundry soap. Rinse well with the garden hose and allow the pieces to dry outdoors. The canes will shrink and tighten up as they dry, usually leaving you with a much more substantial piece of furniture. *Warning:* Use this technique only on wicker in good condition, with no broken or missing sections. The same technique works to firm up saggy cane seats on chairs. Refinish wicker by spraying it with exterior paint, and seal caned seats with polyurethane.

REPAIRING DAMAGED VENEER

Veneering is the process of gluing a thin layer of expensive cabinet wood to a base of ordinary wood.

As furniture ages, the glue between these layers loosens either from excess moisture or dryness. The edges of an old veneered piece often become chipped or warped. Many times small pieces of the veneer will be missing. While only an experienced professional can restore badly damaged veneer to its original state, you can repair some minor damage yourself.

Blisters

Veneer blisters, which look like bubbles, are small areas where the glue has loosened surrounded by large areas of firmly affixed veneer. These bubbles are easy to see. The veneer will be raised slightly above the base wood at that spot, and often you can press down the blisters with slight pressure from your finger.

Faced with such a blister on veneer, your first try at replacing it should be to simply *iron* it down. Dampen the blister first with hot water, then place waxed paper or a brown paper bag over the spot. Top with two or three thicknesses of a folded rag. Turn your dry household iron to a medium setting and place it on the folded cloth. Leave it there for thirty seconds or so. Remove the cloth and paper and immediately place a large cold item—a cast-iron skillet, for instance—on the blister. Weight it down and allow it to set overnight. What you've done is soften the old glue with heat and then harden it again with the sudden cooling and pressure.

If that doesn't work, you can try this: Take a razor blade and carefully slit through the center of the blister along the grain of the wood. Lay a hot, wet cloth on the blister for a few minutes. Once the wood feels damp and flexible, carefully slip a table knife under one side of the slit. Lift the knife to raise one side of the slit. Squirt some glue under the raised side. Remove the table knife and repeat the process on the other side of the slit. Wipe off any excess glue, cover with waxed paper, and firmly weight down the repair overnight or until the wood is thoroughly dry.

Missing Veneer

Pieces of veneer sometimes break off the edges of tables, often at corners. You can patch this damage, but often the results may not exactly match the original.

Cut a piece of veneer slightly larger than the part or missing part you need to replace. Place a piece of replacement veneer, available from suppliers listed at the back of this book, over the damaged area, allowing an inch or so of extra material all around. With a razor blade, X-Acto knife, or utility knife, carefully cut through both the new veneer and the old. Cut with the grain along one side of the repair and in a straight line when going across the grain. Remove the new veneer patch, any scrap veneer from the patch, and the old, damaged veneer. Sand away any dried glue that remains in the area to be patched. Your patch of new veneer should fit perfectly into the section cut out of the old veneer.

Now measure the thickness of the old veneer against the replacement patch. If the new veneer is thinner than the old, cut two or three more sections of veneer exactly the size of the first to bring the patch up to the level of the old veneer.

Spread a layer of yellow wood glue onto the core wood and place the patch onto it, taping it down with masking tape or clamping it if the patch is larger. If you need to clamp your patch, be sure to place another piece of scrap wood between the veneer and the clamp to prevent the clamp from denting it. Make sure the grain of the final piece of veneer patch follows the grain of the body of the furniture. If the veneer isn't thick enough, repeat with more yellow wood glue and another patch. Do this until you've built up to the thickness of the original veneer.

Clean off any excess glue, allow the glue to set for an hour or two, and then trim the edges with a razor blade if necessary. Using very fine sandpaper, lightly sand it smooth to blend in with the original veneer.

Apply several coats of finishing-oil stain until you get a shade that blends into the original finish of the surrounding wood. By applying successive coats of finishing-oil stain and rubbing gently with extra-fine (0000) steel wool between coats, your new patch should begin to blend with the old veneer on your piece.

1. Cut a piece of veneer slightly larger than the part you'll need to replace, and place it over the damaged area. Cut a patch with a utility blade, working through both the replacement veneer and the original veneer. By cutting through both the new and old veneer at the same time, you'll be able to make the patch exactly duplicate the area into which it would fit.

2. Glue the veneer with wood glue, and then use masking tape to hold it down until it's dry.

3. Trim the veneer with a razor blade.

4. After the veneer has been trimmed, sand it smooth to blend it with the surface.

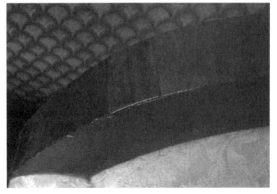

5. Apply several coats of finishing oil until you get a shade that blends into the original finish of the surrounding wood. Your patch should blend in perfectly with the piece.

Chipped Veneer

Sometimes tiny chips of veneer will be broken off raggedly along the edge of a tabletop or dresser. The only attractive solution to this problem is to sand the broken edge of veneer back, canting the sander down at about a forty-five-degree angle. Carefully done, this technique results in a smooth edge, even though the angle formed by the top and sides of the piece will be quite different from the original angle. You *could* trim the veneer back and insert a new strip along the edge, but this repair would be highly visible and unattractive.

Lifted Edges of Veneer

Frequently, veneer will lift from the core wood along the edges of an antique without any pieces breaking off. This problem is usually the easiest of all to repair.

First clean the space between the veneer and the core wood to remove any dirt lodged there. Insert yellow wood glue into this cavity and press down firmly.

Cut a strip of waxed paper long enough to cover the repair and lay it over the veneer. Place a long board on top to equalize pressure, and clamp. This last step ensures that the glue will adhere equally all along the edge of the veneer.

Replacing an Entire Veneer Top

You can put a completely new veneer top on an antique if you're willing to take the time and trouble. Veneer is available in many different woods, several sizes and thicknesses, and a wide range of prices.

Actually, putting the new veneer on is the easy part. Removing the old veneer is the hard part. Old-veneer glue can be very tenacious. You may, however, feel your antique justifies the effort if its top is too badly damaged to repair yet the piece is worth saving.

Using any thin-bladed tool such as a utility knife, putty knife, or spatula, begin prying the veneer off the core wood around the edges. Expect to hit a great deal of resistance once you get past the first few inches. At that point you can try dissolving the old glue. One of the best solutions for this job is full-strength, boiling vinegar. Plan on using at least a gallon of white vinegar for the average 24- X 24-inch table. Wearing rubber gloves to protect your hands, turn the table over on its side and carefully pour the boiling vinegar along the edges of the veneer, trying to pry it up at the same time. This process may take quite a while. If the glue doesn't release its hold after the first application of vinegar, wait fifteen minutes and try again. You might have to make several applications.

Let the table dry completely once you get all the old veneer off. Then sand away every scrap of glue that remains on the core wood. Fill any gouges with wood putty and sand again. The surface must be smooth and clean for the new veneer to adhere.

Measure and cut a piece of veneer at least ½ inch longer and wider than the surface you are covering.

Apply a coat of high-quality contact cement to the surface of the table. One manufacturer of cement especially made for veneer work recommends using a small roller for this job. Let the cement dry for approximately thirty minutes, then test it by pressing a piece of paper onto the adhesive. If the paper doesn't stick, you're ready to proceed. Apply a coat of contact cement to the back of the veneer. Allow it to set for about fifteen minutes. Test it as above, but now you want it to be slightly tacky.

Cut a sheet of heavy paper at least ½ inch larger than the surface of the table. Place this *slip sheet* over the surface of the table to separate the veneer from the base until it is in position. Put the veneer on top of the slip sheet.

Carefully, a few inches at a time, slip the paper from under the veneer. Enlist someone's help before attempting this, because once that veneer with its coat of cement touches the cement-covered base, it will stick—permanently! You will *not* be able to reposition it.

Smooth the veneer in the direction of the grain as you slowly slip the paper, inch by inch, from beneath it and the base. Take your time.

Once you're through, take a deep breath, sit down, and relax for half an hour. Then go back and trim the edges with a razor or X-Acto knife. Wait at least twenty-four hours before sanding and finishing.

INLAYS

The old glue under inlays sometimes dries out, causing a section to bulge slightly above the surrounding area. As long as the inlay is in relatively good condition, you can correct this problem in minutes.

Press the inlay down into its channel to make sure it will lie flat again at its original depth. If it won't, check to see if dirt or bits of glue lie in the channel. Clean out any obstruction, then squirt yellow woodworking glue into the channel, using the technique described on pages 65–66. Press the inlay back into the channel, then wipe the surface with a damp rag to remove excess glue.

Continue holding the inlay down with your fingers for a few minutes, and, with luck, it will lie flat almost immediately. If it doesn't, place a piece of waxed paper over the glued section, put a caul over the wax paper (described on page 67), and clamp the whole thing.

BROKEN MARBLE

Though you can *refinish* marble, as you'll learn in the next chapter, only a professional can successfully *repair* broken or badly damaged marble.

Check your yellow pages for the name of a company that specializes in repairing marble. You'll find them listed under "Marble" or "Monuments." Take the damaged piece to them, and chances are, they'll return it to you unblemished and beautifully polished.

They can join broken pieces with a mastic that closely resembles the marble's natural graining, making the repair virtually undetectable. They can even fill in small missing sections with a marblelike substance. They can rebuild chipped edges or trim the edges down, cutting a lovely new pattern in the process. Don't expect them to replace large missing pieces, though.

Only a skilled craftsperson can do this work, so these repairs aren't cheap. Expect to pay anywhere from $150 for a minor job to more than $500 for a major renovation.

CHAPTER 6

GENERAL REFINISHING TECHNIQUES

Perhaps the most useful knowledge you acquire in refinishing antique furniture will be an understanding of the various characteristics of the different cabinet woods. Stop in at a good lumber yard or home-improvement center and ask to see the sample display of raw and finished lumber. Seeing and touching actual samples can show you the diversity of these woods. You can compare the open grain of oak to the close grain of rosewood. You'll see which woods are almost white in their natural states and which have a distinct brown or reddish tint. You'll notice how these colors react to finishing oils and stains.

Every lumber yard has a scrap bin, so while you're there, ask for a few small pieces of these cabinet woods to take home with you. You can then make your own comparison tests. Put a little penetrating oil on a piece of ash and then the same amount on mahogany. You'll notice they don't absorb the oil at the same rate, and one will absorb quite a bit more than the other. Hit a piece of oak with a hammer, and then hit a piece of poplar with the same force. You'll see quite graphically that one would resist the ravages of time while the other would soon become worn and scarred in daily household use. Cut geometrically identical pieces of pine and walnut. Notice the difference in their weights.

The following chart lists some of the basic characteristics of the most popular cabinet woods that have been used in antique furniture:

Wood	Color	Density	Grain	Distinguishing Characteristics
Ash	light, creamy	medium	wavy, close	veined, streaks in direction of growth
Beech	light brown	medium	straight	easily worked, takes color well
Birch	cream or reddish brown	hard	plain or curly	similar to maple
Butternut	light brown	soft	close	similar to walnut
Cherry	reddish brown	medium to hard	straight or curly	similar to some mahogany
Chestnut	brownish yellow	medium	straight	similar to some oak
Hickory	cream	hard	fine, straight	tough, resilient
Holly	light brown	hard	close	mostly used for marquetry and inlay
Mahogany	light to dark reddish brown	hard	straight to wavy	attractive grain, durable, often in wide pieces, popular for veneer
Maple	rich, light brown	hard	close, straight, curly, bird's-eye	strong, heavy
Oak	light cream to light brown	hard	open, straight	heavy, tough
Pine	light, creamy	soft	straight	resinous, flexible, often used for core wood
Poplar	yellow to brownish	medium	straight, close	even texture, barely visible pores, takes color well
Rosewood	blackish brown	hard	wavy, close	pleasant fragrance
Satinwood	yellowish	medium	straight	lustrous surface
Tulipwood	light rose	medium	straight to wavy	pink stripes
Walnut	grayish brown to rich brown	hard	straight	strong, easily worked

These differences in wood determine, among other things, the way woods react to certain finishes. An understanding of these differences will help you know in advance, for instance, that a walnut table will become darker when treated with a certain color of oil than would a pine table. This would happen because walnut is naturally darker in tone than pine. You'd know that a chestnut cabinet would absorb more oil, and therefore probably be darker, than would an oak cabinet, since the chestnut is less dense than the oak.

Once you become really knowledgeable about these differences in wood, you'll be able to control final colors to your satisfaction. For instance, you could take an oak dining table, a set of ash chairs, a chestnut commode, and a pine buffet—all made at different times by different craftsmen—and refinish them so the colors would be almost identical. If you tried to use the same blend of oil on all, you'd end up with a dining room full of mismatched colors instead of a harmonious grouping that will be a pleasure to use and live with.

You'll also discover, if you haven't already, that some furniture makers of the past had a very cavalier attitude about mixing various woods in the *same* piece of furniture. You'll discover a couple of oak panels in an otherwise all-walnut cabinet, for example, or a mahogany occasional table whose bottom shelf turned out to be maple. Those old craftsmen knew how to mix their stains to make diverse woods blend as one. You can do the same in refinishing these pieces today.

You'll probably use this skill most frequently when trying to blend the color of a new replacement dowel with that of a century-old chair. Most home-improvement centers carry plain dowels in walnut, oak, and birch. Manufacturers made many press-back chairs of ash, so you'll have to blend oils that will make oak look like ash.

Old wood also takes color differently than does new wood, even if they are of the same variety. Any new piece of wood inserted into an antique, be it a spindle, patch, or whatever, will be several shades lighter than the old wood. Its sharp, clean tone must be blended in with the older, more mellow tone with two different shades of oil. You can learn to do this by experimenting with scraps of new and old wood of different varieties.

SHOULD YOU REPAIR OR REFINISH FIRST?

Ask any two antiques refinishers whether they refinish an antique before they repair it or vice versa, and you'll probably get two different answers. There's no right or wrong technique— just whatever works for the individual.

However, it's far easier and more practical to repair a piece *before* you refinish it. It's almost impossible to repair an antique without imposing a few scratches on its surface. If you refinish the antique first, you'll have to touch up those scratches afterward. By repairing first, you can be sure to glue any loose splinters. It's too easy to lose them during a stripping process.

Many of the antiques you'll bring home from yard sales will be coated with peeling paint. They *must* be stripped to the bare wood before you can restore their original tones. The strippers you use in your workshop won't penetrate a joint or repair that has been well glued. But they can easily leave a residue on dismantled or loose joints that leaches out later, softening the glue and weakening repairs.

For these reasons you should always repair your pieces before stripping or the final finishing.

TO STRIP OR NOT TO STRIP?

That is indeed the question, and you'll hear contrasting opinions about the subject as you get more into this hobby. One theory says you should never remove the original finish of an antique. And undoubtedly, an antique in good condition with its original finish is certainly one to be desired and cherished. On the other hand, many people agree with this theory but also argue that many antiques have finishes no one but a nurturing alligator could love. Actually, both theories are correct.

You should certainly try to save the finish of any antique you find if it hasn't been painted over. Some people assume that *any* antique with a darkened and rough finish has to be stripped before it can be renovated. After much useless work, you may discover that a great many of these unattractive finishes could have been restored to their original beauty *without* stripping.

Many antiques appear to be black because years of grime and furniture polish have created a thick opaque covering. Often it takes only a good cleaning to revitalize the finish. If, however, someone has painted the antique, or if the old finish is in really deplorable condition, you have no choice but to strip off all the finish and start over.

Begin by cleaning the antique with a mild soap-and-water solution, applied with a soft fiber brush. Murphy's Oil Soap is especially good for this since it contains essential oils needed to revive and moisturize old wood that harmful detergents would dry out. Don't soak the piece, as you could easily dissolve the old glue. Instead, using an old washcloth or a piece of terry-cloth towel, work on a small area at a time, washing gently but firmly, then immediately drying that area. *Never put water on any antique that you suspect might have inlays or marquetry, or one with a veneered surface*—instead apply the soap and water using a wrung-out washcloth, being careful to quickly dry the small area.

Allow the wood to dry for twenty-four hours. Working in a well-ventilated area, go over the wood thoroughly with a rag soaked well in paint thinner, turpentine, or carbon tetrachloride. You may notice a distinct lightening of the color. You can sometimes remove more dirty old finish by rubbing the wood with a mixture of linseed oil and powdered pumice. Put a few spoonsful of pumice in a container and add linseed oil until the mixture has the consistency of thick cream.

Caution! Never use flammable cleaners in any enclosed space unless you can open the doors or windows. *Never* allow anyone to light a match, smoke, or cause a spark near these solvents. It's safest to work outdoors and then leave the piece of furniture out there until all flammable solvent has evaporated from the wood.

The finish on old furniture sometimes acquires an unpleasant pebbled roughness with time. You can often remove this graininess by dissolving the old finish with its original solvent. This process is called *amalgamation*.

Many furniture makers, well into the 1920s, finished their pieces with shellac. Shellac dissolves

Thoroughly clean any antique before you decide to strip it. You may find that only dirt and furniture polish obscure its natural beauty. You can use a kitchen "scrubby" sponge, a synthetic scouring pad, or both.

in denatured alcohol. To discover if your antique has been finished with shellac, dip a pad of fine steel wool into some denatured alcohol and rub a concealed area. If the rough surface begins to smooth out under light pressure, the finish is, indeed, shellac.

You must work quickly when smoothing an old finish by amalgamation since alcohol evaporates fast. Dip the pad of fine steel wool into the alcohol and rub it briskly over the finish, working in the direction of the grain. Add more alcohol as necessary to keep the surface wet, continually moving the steel-wool pad with moderate pres-

sure over the surface. The defects and pebbling of the old finish will begin to dissolve. Turn the steel-wool pad as necessary to keep it clean and unclogged. As soon as you are satisfied with the smoothness of the finish, go back over it with clean alcohol and a fresh pad.

You can buy prepared commercial amalgamators that also do an excellent job of removing an old dark and wrinkled finish. They are quite expensive, though, considering the amount it takes to rejuvenate most antiques.

Amalgamation, whether with alcohol or a commercial product, results in a fine, lustrous finish that preserves the deep patina of the wood. Once it's cleaned, you need only polish the wood to restore its original beauty.

If you find that the finish does *not* dissolve readily with alcohol, you might try the same process with lacquer thinner. If that works, then the finish is lacquer. It's highly unlikely that you'll find lacquer on a genuine antique, however. It was almost never used until the 1920s.

Almost every town has at least one company that can strip paint from furniture. These companies can be a blessing when you're faced with a lovely old piece that's covered with multiple coats of pink, ivory, gold, and green enamel. Their powerful commercial solvents and equipment can cut through numerous layers and return a piece of furniture devoid of *any* paint, varnish, or finish.

You don't need a professional stripper for every antique in need of stripping, however. The solvents they use are powerful. They often dissolve old glue right along with the paint. And on occasion, if the worker has to dip the piece too many times, the solvent can eat into the pores of the wood itself.

You do have the option of doing your own stripping, using one of the commercial strippers available at any paint or hardware store. These thick liquids remove layers of old varnish in just a few minutes. However, they aren't always as effective or fast on multiple layers of paint.

You'll find two kinds of strippers on the market today—one can be washed off with water while the other must be removed with paint thinner. They are equally effective, but many people prefer the water-soluble type for two reasons. First, water is less expensive for the rinsing process than paint thinner. Second, many people try to avoid caustic and flammable substances as much as possible. Always follow the manufacturer's directions carefully when using a stripper.

Apply a thick coat of stripper to the wood, brushing in one direction only. You don't have to worry about going with the grain. Give the stripper time to work. Sometimes you'll see results in five minutes, and sometimes you may have to wait twenty minutes or more. The amount of time you wait depends not only on the thickness and condition of the finish but also on air temperature and humidity.

When the varnish or paint wrinkles up and appears to lift from the surface of the wood, you're ready to scrape the resulting goo off with a putty knife, paint scraper, or metal spatula. Use an old toothbrush to get into the deep crevices of carvings and elaborate turnings. Once you have most of the old finish and remover off, you're ready for the rinsing step. Depending on the type of stripper you used, go back over the piece of furniture with a stiff fiber brush and either hot, sudsy water or paint thinner. Rinse off quickly and allow the antique to dry in the open air but out of the sun.

Once in a while you'll find that stripping does not remove all the paint from the pores of an open-grained wood. In that case, you might try mixing equal amounts of shellac and denatured alcohol and brushing this mixture into the areas that still contain paint. Allow the shellac to remain on the wood for a few days, then repeat the stripping process on those areas. If this doesn't work, the only solution is to pick the tiny bits of paint from the pores with an X-Acto knife. But this can be tedious.

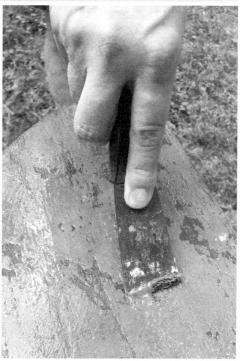

(above) *Scrape the softened finish with a putty knife, paint scraper, or old metal spatula, going with the grain.*

(left) *Apply stripper in even strokes with the grain of the wood. Let stand for a few minutes to soften the finish.*

Paint applied over varnish is usually easy to remove. Sometimes, however, paint has been applied directly onto bare wood. It soaked deeply into the pores of the wood, and, in most cases, even commercial stripping won't remove the color.

You may someday be lucky enough to find an antique chair, chest, or table that a maker finished with milk or casein paint. One popular nineteenth-century recipe for milk paint was to mix boiling skim milk with either brick dust or animal blood. It was then poured hot onto the bare wood, where it penetrated into the wood's pores. The result was an attractive deep-red stain that was distinctive and highly durable. This type of finish is valuable and should *not* be removed, even if it's in poor condition.

BLEACHING STAINS FROM WOOD

Someday you may need to lighten all or part of the wood on an antique. Tabletops acquire stains through the years. Sometimes natural dark streaks detract from the beauty of the wood. Often stripping doesn't remove enough residue from an old stain (as mentioned in the preceding section) to allow the use of a lighter color in refinishing. And old desks and office chairs frequently arrive in our workshops complete with deep-blue ink stains, reminders of the days before ballpoint pens. Some form of bleaching will usually take care of these problems.

Professional furniture refinishers use a two-step bleaching compound that's quite strong and effective. Unless you get into refinishing on a large scale, though, you'll be just as happy using regular household bleach.

All the old finish and accumulated grime must be removed from an antique before bleaching. Small sections of old varnish or greasy spots will keep the bleach from penetrating at those points, and you could end up with a polka-dot effect.

After the antique is stripped and cleaned, sand it well to open the pores. Outdoors or in a well-ventilated room, brush or pour a generous amount of bleach onto the wood. (However, do not overbleach—this will give the wood a gray cast, which is impossible to remedy.) Reapply more bleach approximately every half hour to keep the wood wet. Plan on using about a quart of bleach for the average 24- X 24-inch table. A softwood will probably respond quickly to the chemicals in the bleach, while a hardwood may be far more stubborn. You can speed up and intensify

the action of the bleach by working in the sun.

The only caution here is to wear rubber gloves and old clothes, as you're almost bound to splash some bleach on you.

Once you feel the bleach has lightened the wood as much as it is going to, rinse the area well with water. If you're not satisfied with the removal of the stain, you could try pouring on some household ammonia. Allow that to work a few minutes, then rinse well.

Don't be discouraged if some part of the stain remains after all that. Some stains of long standing won't give way completely, regardless of how long you work at them or what you put on them.

All that water you've used will have raised the grain of the wood and roughened it, so you're going to have to sand the piece again to get the satin-smooth finish you want.

SANDING TECHNIQUES

Many times the success or failure of a refinishing job is determined by the thoroughness of the sanding that preceded the final finish. Here are some tips for successful sanding.

- Avoid rotary-disc and belt sanders. They remove too much material too fast and can leave scars on the wood.

- Avoid the very coarse grades of sandpaper. Use the medium grades for rough jobs such as paint and varnish removal and work up to the very fine grades for the final smoothing.

- Use a very fine grade of steel wool (grade 0000 or 4/0) to rub down your final coat of oil or varnish.

- Sanding blocks, especially the flexible ones, are great for hand-sanding.

- Paper-backed sandpaper can be made more flexible by pulling it, paper side down, over the edge of a table.
- Clean clogged sandpaper by tapping it against the floor or by raking a stiff brush across its surface.
- A fine grade of emery cloth is economical to use since its backing lasts much longer than that of paper-backed sandpaper.
- Pumice blocks wear away quickly (and smell awful), but they're excellent to use on elaborate turnings.
- Cut emery cloth into 1-inch-wide strips and use them see-saw fashion to sand elaborate turnings.
- Steel wool twisted around a string makes an excellent sanding tool for deep slits in turnings.

Using a pumice stone is one of the fastest and most efficient ways to clean old finish off elaborate turnings. It molds itself to the design and will cut away paint and old varnish from the deepest crevices.

COLORING AND FINISHING WOOD

Years ago all furniture finishers applied stains and fillers to bare wood, usually trying to get the deepest tones possible. They then followed these stains and fillers with multiple coats of shellac. As a result, they obscured much of the natural graining and beauty of the wood. Today finishers try to color and preserve the wood while retaining as much of the natural graining as possible by using a colored penetrating oil.

Many refinishers of antique furniture use a type of oil manufactured by several firms and sold as tung oil finish. It's a clear, light oil that has several uses and is ideal for working with antiques.

The wood in much antique furniture is quite dry and brittle. It needs some deep lubrication, not only to bring back its natural beauty but also to forestall future cracking and splitting. Tung oil finish does just that, soaking into the pores of the wood and helping to stabilize the fibers against future swelling, warping, and shrinking. As it dries in those fibers, the oil actually makes the wood itself about 25 percent harder than it was previously. Any antique so finished is less susceptible to all types of environmental damage than one finished in the traditional manner.

This oil comes in several colors, ranging from clear to a dark walnut tone. The refinisher can, therefore, color the wood of an antique in virtually any tone desired, without obscuring the grain in any way. You can mix the oils, too, to get special colors or to help you blend the different sections of an antique, the replacement parts with the old wood, and different woods into one tone.

Read and follow the specific manufacturer's directions for the product you purchase, though the basics are the same for all of them. Use either a brush or a rag—an old white crew sock works great—to apply the oil to wood that has been sanded to finish smoothness. Wait about thirty minutes for the oil to penetrate the wood, but add more oil if the antique is so dry it absorbs the first coat immediately. Allow some moisture to remain on the surface of the wood. Wipe the wood dry with a clean soft rag and then allow the finish to "cure" for an hour or so. Apply a second coat of oil, allowing it to penetrate the wood thoroughly. Wipe the wood absolutely dry after this second application of oil. Between applications, put the oil-soaked sock in a plastic sandwich bag and place it in your freezer. When you're ready to apply successive coats of oil, remove it and let it stand at room temperature for about fifteen minutes. This prevents the sock from hardening or drying out.

Wait twelve hours for the oil to dry and harden. Use this time to decide what type of final finish you want for the antique. If the piece will not receive hard wear or be subject to frequent spills of liquid, try this medium-protection finish: Repeat the oiling procedure of the day before, wiping dry between each coat. Give the antique a final polish by rubbing it down with a little oil on that ultrafine sandpaper known as *wet-and-dry sandpaper*. Professional refinishers dampen a piece of ultrafine wet-and-dry sandpaper with oil and then give their pieces a final rubdown. These multiple coats of oil and the final rubdown result in a lovely, lustrous finish that looks like old-fashioned hand rubbing. You can use it with confidence on hall trees, lamp tables, beds, or any antique that receives only moderate hard use.

Do not use polyurethane varnish on your antiques. Though it will give them a tough finish, it will destroy any value the piece may have had.

CARING FOR REFINISHING MATERIALS

Quality refinishing materials aren't cheap, so it pays to use them wisely. The first and foremost rule: Put the lid back on tightly!

Air is the enemy of almost every liquid or malleable product you use in your workroom. Oxygen trapped inside previously opened cans may cause many of them to harden or form skins that make them virtually useless.

Wood dough is probably the worst offender. How often have you reopened one of these little cans to find the stuff inside as hard as a rock. You can avoid this problem by doing two things: First, don't leave the lid off the can while you're working. Take out a little dab and, using pressure, press the lid back on the can until you need more. This means a few extra motions, but it's worth it to salvage that fairly expensive product. Second, when you have finished with your project for the day, *hammer* the lid back on the can and turn it upside down for storage. By following these two steps, you'll be able to use just about every amount in the can.

The channels on the tops of oil and paint cans always fill as we wipe brushes across them. It's virtually impossible then to reseal the can airtight. Drill or hammer a series of small holes in the channel *before* starting to use the product. This way, the paint or oil drips back into the can, leaving the channel clean enough for a tight seal.

If you have only a small amount of oil or paint left over, however, don't save it in the original can. There'll be too much air trapped above the product. Pour such leftovers into glass jars of the right size to hold all of the oil or paint. Screw the lid on tightly and label the jar as to contents, and it should last for quite a while.

SIMULATING OLD MILK-PAINT FINISHES

Milk or casein paint is one of the oldest and most durable finishes known. Examples have been found in ancient Egyptian tombs, and it was frequently used on both furniture and interior walls of homes in this country from colonial days until the 1940s. The advent of easy-to-use commercial paints, especially latex, made milk paint virtually a forgotten relic of the past.

As mentioned previously, any antique still carrying vestiges of genuine milk paint should be treasured and maintained in its original condition.

With the country look so popular now, refinishers have wanted some product that would simulate the flat, coarse, translucent colors of old milk paint. Although such a finish is not carried by paint stores, it is available by mail order, and it is virtually an exact duplicate of that used for thousands of years. An added benefit is that this milk paint is environmentally safe—free of lead, chemical preservatives, and hydrocarbons or other petroleum derivatives.

This paint can be used on any piece of furniture that has been stripped down to bare wood. The paint is shipped as a powder, which is mixed with water prior to use. It can be applied with a brush, sponge, roller, or spray gun. The depth of tone is achieved by the amount of water mixed with the powder—more for thin, wiping stains, less for deep shades.

To increase the durability of milk paint and enhance its delicate color, experienced refinishers recommend a final protective coat of paste wax or water-based varnish.

The manufacturer of this milk paint is listed on page 195 in Resources. You can also try www.realmilkpaint.com and www.oldhouseweb .com.

TOUCH-UP TRICKS

Granted, many times you must completely refinish an antique, all the way from stripping through the final finish. You'd have no choice, for instance, if you found a lovely old cherrywood china cabinet that someone had painted with avocado enamel to go with their 1970s kitchen.

You don't need to ruin the patina of an antique, though, by stripping, sanding, and refinishing just to remove a little minor damage. Many nicks and marks can be quite satisfactorily dispatched or diminished with some easy touch-up techniques.

The following techniques are simple to master and will cover some of the most common minor problems with the finishes of your antiques. But don't go overboard and try to eliminate every dent and stain. An antique should have a *few* "beauty marks" to testify to its use.

Minor Scratches

You can often remove a hairline scratch from a highly polished surface with fine steel wool and any lightweight oil, such as 3-In-One or sewing-machine oil. Just dip the pad of steel wool into the oil and *gently* rub the wood in the direction of the grain. This very mild abrasion will remove only the thinnest film from the finish, but it might work. If the scratch is still visible, try disguising it. Break a pecan, walnut, or Brazil nut meat in half and rub the cut side along the scratch. The oil in these nut meats sometimes blends perfectly with antique finishes. Iodine often will do the same on mahogany. Apply it with a tiny brush—old lipstick or eyeliner brushes are perfect—or dip the end of a toothpick in the iodine and draw the tip along the scratch. Add a bit of alcohol to the iodine if it appears to be too dark for your mahogany. Regular wood stain or penetrating oils can be used, of course, as can paste shoe polish. Even a child's wax crayon can sometimes be used to match an offbeat color. Once you've filled the scratch with any of these materials, rewax the entire surface of the antique with paste wax and buff to a sheen. The scratch should be virtually invisible.

Small Dents

A dent happens when wood fibers are compressed through pressure. To get rid of the dent, you must decompress the fibers. Heat and steam will usually do the trick. Remove all wax and polish from the dented area with paint thinner or turpentine. Wipe away any excess solvent with a dry tissue. Fold a piece of cheesecloth or other soft, loosely woven fabric into a tiny pad, dampen it thoroughly with water, and place it over the dent. Allow the pad to remain on the dent for an hour or so, adding more water if the pad begins to dry out. Place a metal

bottle cap, flat side down, on the damp pad, directly over the dent. Set your household iron to "high" and rest it on the cap. The heat from the iron will be transferred through the bottle cap, will create steam from the wet pad and should swell the dented fibers. Try again if the first attempt is not successful. Then rewax and polish.

Gouges

A gouge is deeper than a dent and can't be ignored. You can fill gouges with any of several commercial products made specifically for filling spaces in wood. These fillers are called by different trade names, but most have the word *dough, filler,* or *putty* somewhere in the name. Buy a filler in a shade as close to the finished color of the antique as possible. You can alter the filler's color somewhat by dabbing on some opaque stain.

Assuming you don't plan to refinish the entire antique, your best bet is to *not* sand the area around the gouge. Sanding removes the old finish as well as some of the old wood. You could end up with a light-colored area that's quite difficult to blend with the rest of the finish. Just push the filler material into the gouge and smooth it with your finger. This repair may be quite visible, since the filler material won't have the surrounding wood's grain. To camouflage the repair a bit, don't fill the gouge completely with the filler material. Allow an ⅛-inch or so depression between the top of the filler and the surface of the wood. Once the filler becomes hard, begin filling in that depression with successive coats of polyurethane varnish. Use a cotton swab as an applicator. Brush a coat of the polyurethane in the depression, allow it to dry, and swab on another coat. *Warning:* This can take days. Once you've raised the level of the depression to that of the surrounding area, buff the patch lightly with fine steel wool and rewax the entire surface. All this is time-consuming, but the resulting finish seems to have some depth to it and is usually less noticeable than the flat opaqueness of filler alone.

Ink Spots

The problem of trying to bleach ink spots out of bare wood was covered earlier in this chapter. When the ink spots are on the *top* of a finish, you stand a pretty good chance of removing them *if* the old finish is quite hard and in good condition. Rub the spots out with powdered pumice mixed to the consistency of heavy cream with a light all-purpose household oil. Just dip a rag into the pumice-and-oil mixture and rub briskly with the grain. You may have to touch up the shellac or varnish because of this abrasion, but you shouldn't have to recolor the wood.

Cigarette Burns

Cigarettes left burning on the top of a piece of furniture leave deep indentations, ones impossible to sand away. About the only option you have when faced with such damage is to scrape away the soft blackened wood with a sharp knife. Next, sand the charred area to remove as much dark color as possible, even if the result is an area considerably lower than the surrounding surface. Then refinish that space to match the rest of the piece.

Preserving Stencils

Furniture makers of less-expensive, mass-market pieces often decorated them with stencils. It's always a good idea to preserve these if possible. A grandmother found a charming little high chair that had a faint stencil design on the seat still visible through the old dark shellac. By using the following method, she was able to save the design, renovate the high chair, and then surprise her youngest daughter with it as a gift for her first baby.

You must use a very light hand to get the old shellac off the design. Scrape the shellac off with either a commercial scraper or a small knife. You'll probably have more control with a knife. Work in a good light, removing only a small amount of material at a time until you've cut through the shellac and seem to be right at the stencil. At that point put the scraper or knife away and begin working with fine steel wool and alcohol. Dab at the stencil carefully until the alcohol begins to dissolve the remaining shellac. If any of the stencil disappears with the shellac, stop immediately—you've gone too far. Use the amalgamation technique described on pages 92–93 to clean and renovate the rest of the antique, working *around* the stenciled area.

Removing Decals

A couple of generations back, it seemed the whole world acquired a bad case of "decalcomania." Whenever the urge struck to decorate some existing piece of furniture, the answer often seemed to be, "Brighten it up with some decals!" As a result, you'll often find certain antiques, most frequently high chairs and kitchen chairs, embellished with those shiny renditions of yellow butterflies and blue Dutch windmills. About the only good thing about these decals is that they were durable. You can remove them without damaging the wood underneath simply by soaking them in vinegar. They'll peel off with just a bit of encouragement from you and a blunt table knife.

Foggy and Milky-Looking Finishes

Moisture is one of the chief enemies of antique finishes. Moisture penetrating the finish causes the "blushes" found on some pieces of old furniture. You may have to try several different remedies before finding the one that will work on a particular antique. Start by removing all old wax and polish with turpentine. Occasionally, this cleaning will remove the problem, but if it doesn't, try one or more of these remedies:

- Dip a pad of fine steel wool into linseed oil and rub it over the finish, always moving in the direction of the grain.
- Mix two parts paraffin oil and one part white shellac. Dip a pad of fine steel wool in this mixture and rub with the grain.
- Mix equal amounts of linseed oil and turpentine and rub the finish with this mixture, always with the grain.
- Sponge the finish with a mild vinegar-and-water mixture.

In every case, rub the piece of furniture completely dry with soft rags after the treatment, and rewax with a good paste wax.

White Rings

Moisture from a wet glass or a potted plant produces white or dark gray rings on furniture. These rings usually don't reach down beyond the surface of the finish, so they're easy to remove.

You don't need any special product, either. Any one of several home remedies is almost bound to work on any white ring you encounter. One word of caution, however: Try the remedy on an inconspicuous spot before you rub it on the white ring.

Below are several tried-and-true methods to eliminate white rings:

- Dip a soft rag into any light oil (cooking oil, sewing machine oil, petroleum jelly, furniture oil, etc.), then into cigarette ash or baking soda. Rub the ring gently.
- Rub the area gently with a mixture of equal parts baking soda and toothpaste on a damp cloth.
- Dip a piece of fine steel wool into denatured alcohol and rub the area gently.
- Saturate a soft cloth with any good furniture wax and rub the area vigorously.

It shouldn't take you more than five minutes to remove the ring with any of these methods.

Black Marks

Moisture can also cause ugly, permanent black marks if it's allowed to penetrate through the finish and into the wood itself.

Some black marks can be removed, or at least lessened, if you invest a little time and effort. Roughen the surface lightly. This will open the pores of the wood to accept your bleach. Try to sand as little of the undamaged wood as possible. This may mean sanding across the grain on a circular mark, a real no-no in most instances, but it often can't be helped in this case.

Once you're down to the bare wood, you can

try bleaching the mark away, according to the directions in the section on bleaching, then refinish to match the surrounding finish.

Take heart if you can't get all the black marks out of your antique. Many are impossible to remove. A small amount of damage, if not too disfiguring, can actually be part of the charm of an antique, attesting to its years of usefulness.

Moisture can produce either milky or dark gray rings on furniture.

STAINED MARBLE

Marble, which is limestone recrystallized under heat and pressure, has been treasured for statuary and fine architecture since classical Greece and Rome. Its slightly translucent surface, which reflects a degree of light, makes it a subtle and desirable complement to the opaqueness of wood. Add to that the fact that marble is hard,

durable, and not readily damaged by extremes in heat or cold, and it's easy to understand why it's still valued today.

Some of today's most cherished and valuable antiques—especially side tables, dressers, and washstands—have marble tops. Yet, for all its durability, marble will absorb dirt and can stain if neglected. Unfortunately, the marble top of any antique whose wooden surface needs refinishing will probably need refinishing, too.

The first step in restoring marble is to give it a thorough cleaning. Begin by flooding the surface with hot water. Then scrub it with a hot, sudsy, nonabrasive detergent, using a soft fiber brush or nylon scrubbing pad. Rinse well by flooding again with plenty of hot water. Wipe dry with a clean, soft rag. Repeat the cleaning step if you're not satisfied that the marble is free of surface dirt. This washing won't remove embedded stains, most of which have been caused by long-standing contact with household liquids or rusty metal objects. You'll have to continue working with the marble to eliminate those.

Organic stains—caused by tea, coffee, tobacco, ink, etc.—can usually be removed with a bleach solution. Buy a small package of whiting from the paint store and a bottle of hydrogen peroxide from the drugstore. Mix the whiting with enough peroxide to form a thick paste. Add a few drops of ammonia. Apply this paste to the stain and cover it with an inverted bowl to maintain the moisture. Allow to stand for several hours, then wash off the paste with clear water. Some stains of long duration may not give up easily, so you may have to repeat the operation several times.

After cleaning, the marble top of this American Empire washstand is ready for use as a coffee and tea server in a dining room.

Rust stains usually are brown or dark orange, and they take their shape from the object that caused the stain. Use one of the commercial rust-removing compounds sold in hardware stores to remove rust stains from marble.

When the marble is free of stains, wash it again with hot, sudsy detergent to remove all traces of the cleaning compounds. Although clear, the surface of the marble may be quite rough. Surprisingly, you can actually *sand* most of that roughness away. Flood the marble with water

again and go over its surface with fine wet-and-dry sandpaper and lots of elbow grease.

You can use a chemical called *tin oxide powder* to help you achieve the gleaming polished surface that's part of the beauty of fine marble. Buy a package of it at your local chemistry supply house or university chemistry stockroom. Lacking one of these in your town, you might ask your pharmacist to order it for you. Wet the marble again and polish it briskly with the tin oxide powder on a pad of soft cloth. Keep the marble wet and the pad moving. Soon a distinct shine will appear on the marble. When you're satisfied with the polish, rinse the marble thoroughly and dry it with a soft cloth. Now, wax the marble with some clear paste wax to maintain that lovely sheen and protect it from future damage.

METAL FLOOR LAMPS

Manufacturers of antique floor lamps made them of solid brass, plated brass, and/or iron. The lovely solid brass ones need only polishing with a good commercial brass polish to restore them to their original luster. And unless the plating has worn extremely thin, you can usually polish even a brass-plated lamp back to its former glowing beauty. Count yourself lucky if you find one of these lamps in good condition. Rewire any old lamp you find, *regardless* of its condition. New replacement wires, sockets, and plugs are cheap, and old frayed wiring can start fires. Don't take the chance.

Many years of polishing can take a toll on brass-plated lamps, leaving the brass thin. If the base metal showing through thin brass is unattractive, buff on a thin coat of the gold-leaf metallic wax described in chapter 8. This wax gives a deep glow and is the only practical method to refurbish a badly worn plated lamp.

Iron lamps are a different proposition. Most of them have been painted over and over, and the surfaces are chipped, layered, and in generally poor condition. Therefore, I suggest you strip all the old paint off any iron lamp you find.

Spray on a good-quality black satin paint. Spray black satin paint on any iron sections of brass lamps, too.

You'll have no problem finding and attaching shades for those lamps that have four upright candelabra-type sockets surrounding a central socket. Just get a large glass reflector from the hardware store and a silk lamp shade of a corresponding size from a department or discount store. Drop the reflector into the cup that surrounds that socket, then rest the silk shade on the reflector's upper rim.

You may find that the central socket is quite large—far too big for the base of any standard light bulb. Manufacturers made these oversized sockets for light bulbs popular some fifty years ago that are unavailable today. No problem. Just ask the clerk at the hardware store for a *mogul converter socket*. This is a porcelain socket that screws into the larger socket, reducing it to the size of modern light-bulb bases.

You won't have that problem with the popular iron bridge lamps, but they will present

Use metallic wax to restore the sheen to badly worn sections of plated brass on metal lamps. This wax is easy to apply and forms a deep, attractive luster.

A bracket cap socket has been installed on this Art Nouveau iron bridge lamp. The shade adapter will be attached to the socket. The original reverse-painted glass shade will be attached to the adapter with three small set screws around its rim.

A bracket cap socket has the round, dome-shaped cap that comes on all standard lamp sockets. It also has a double bracket and a butterfly thumbscrew attached to the smaller end of the socket, the end the wires go in. Align the bracket's two sides around the hole at the upper end of the lamp. Place the thumbscrew through the bracket and the hole, and then tighten securely to the lamp column. Using about 12 feet of lamp wire, wire a standard socket, discarding its cap, using instead the cap you've just attached to the iron lamp.

After you've wired the socket, thread 5 feet or so of wire either through the lamp column or along its side, depending on the design of the lamp. This will give you about 6 feet of lamp wire extending from the base of the lamp to the outlet. If your outlets are spaced far apart, measure a longer piece of wire before wiring the socket.

The second problem you'll encounter with bridge lamps is in trying to fit a shade to that bare socket. Ask a lamp shop for a *shade holder*, an adjustable brass ring that fits around the body of the socket. Tighten the ring with a set screw and then attach the lamp shade to the ring with three other set screws. The whole arrangement is quite secure.

Authentic antique glass shades are rare, but you can buy reproductions at lamp stores. They come in all sizes, shapes, colors, and prices.

other difficulties. First, makers didn't build many bridge lamps with the sockets as an integral part of the design. All you'll find is a hole at the upper end of the upright iron column. To wire this lamp you'll need to go to a store that specializes in lamp parts or electrical supplies. Ask for *a bracket cap socket*. This isn't usually a stock item and may have to be ordered unless you live in a very large city and have access to a large lamp store.

CHAPTER 7

REPLACING CHAIR SEATS

For every antique table, washstand, or dresser you discover, you'll find at least two chairs. They may be simple ones with charmingly restrained lines, graceful ones with deep hand carving, or the enormously popular fanciful press-back style. Since chairs traditionally take the most abuse in any household, your finds will often be in pretty bad condition. Stretchers are frequently broken. A hip rest and spindle may be missing. The chair may rock and roll like a kid trying out his first pair of stilts. And the finishes are sometimes unbelievable. All of these sad conditions can be remedied with just a little TLC and the information in the various chapters on repairing and refinishing.

Often unsalvageable, though, are the seats. Almost any upholstered, caned, leather, or pressed-fiber chair seat used for a few generations will be worn out. Only solid wood seats usually survive intact. This chapter will show you how to replace those frayed and ugly beasts with new seats to highlight the beauty of your refinished chairs.

This book cannot go into the intricacies of a complicated reupholstering project. That's for professionals or for those who've had some personal instruction in the craft. Unless you're in one of these categories, you should take all chairs that have springs and webbing to an upholstery shop. The results will be worth the cost.

The vast majority of chairs you'll come upon, however, don't require this expense, since they're of much simpler construction. With a little practice you can do these reseating jobs, including recaning, yourself.

CANING

Few final touches enhance the beauty and value of a refinished antique chair more than a new woven cane seat. This sturdy and economical seat became popular in Europe around the middle of the seventeenth century and was in common use until the early nineteenth century. The earliest examples show a mesh much wider than that used today. As workers refined their techniques, later pieces were considerably finer and more closely woven. Furniture makers of the early 1800s had little use for this homely craft, however, preferring more elegant upholstered seats of brocade and velvet.

Toward the end of the nineteenth century, a revival of interest in caning occurred. Consequently, many late Victorian and turn-of-the-twentieth-century chairs you find today still bear remnants of their original cane seats. And remnants are usually all that *do* remain. Almost all of the chairs you'll find that were once caned had later been "refurbished" with a padded seat or one of pressed fiber, leather, or plywood. The evidence of having once been caned is always clear, though, and comes in two forms.

One type of chair has a deep groove cut into the surface of the seat framework. The groove is sometimes filled with old spline left from previous caning. *Spline* refers to long, thin strips of soft, wedge-shaped reed placed in the groove over cane to secure the cane and form a neat finish. This type of chair formerly held a seat of precaned webbing, which you can replace easily and quickly.

The holes on the seat of this chair indicate that it once had been caned. A former owner decided to replace the more expensive caning with a less expensive leather or fiber seat, as you can see by the remaining nail holes.

The other type of chair has a series of holes drilled through the seat framework, indicating that it held a hand-caned seat at one time. With some work you can restore this seat to its original condition.

Precaned webbing is just as attractive as hand-caned, although the latter will take you longer to install. You'll find both methods included here in case you come upon a gem of an old chair that cries for a new hand-caned seat.

The cane you'll use comes from halfway around the world. Cut from the outside bark of rattan, this honey-colored fiber comes from a tropical vine found primarily in China, India, and Sri Lanka. It's peeled off the green vine and cut into different widths, ranging from a minuscule 2-millimeter strand to a sturdy 6-millimeter band. Each has a specific use in some form of caning or rattan work.

You can buy caning materials at larger craft shops in metropolitan areas and on the Internet. Also, almost every handicraft magazine and many women's magazines carry ads offering kits. Each kit contains enough material to cane one chair, the necessary tools, and complete instructions. Almost anyone who's adept with his or her hands can do a credible job with one of these kits. Then, with the confidence of experience behind you, consider buying your material in bulk. See the Resources section for a list of these mail-order suppliers. Expect the price you pay for this bulk cane to be about one-third to one-half of the price of the kits. At this writing, for instance, a cane-webbing kit containing common (9⁄64-inch) cane costs about $36. The same material bought from an online supplier costs about $18.

Hand Caning

Before you begin recaning, remove any old cane that remains on the chair. Use shears to cut away as much as you can. Then use an ice pick or awl for cleaning out the holes. Make sure each hole is completely free of old cane, splinters, globs of varnish, and other debris. In an extreme case you might want to drill out this debris, using a bit the diameter of the holes. Sand the area around the holes and refinish the chair as needed.

You must determine which size cane to buy. Cane comes in a variety of widths, each identified by name. Determine your needs by measuring both the distance between the holes, measured from center to center, and the diameter of the holes. The measurements in the table below are pretty standard and will help you make the right choice.

It may turn out that someone spaced the holes in your chair to suit his or her idea of craftsmanship. If so, just order cane by the hole *size,* choosing a slightly smaller width cane if you have to decide between two sizes. In addition to cane for the seat, you must order binder cane, the wide strand that's woven around the edges of the finished seat to give it a neat, finished appearance.

IF DIAMETER OF HOLE IS:	AND DISTANCE BETWEEN HOLES IS:	ORDER THIS TYPE OF CANE:	WIDTH WILL BE:
1⁄8 in.	1⁄4 in.	Carriage	1.5 mm
1⁄8 in.	3⁄8 in.	Super fine	1.75 mm
3⁄16 in.	1⁄2 in.	Fine fine	2 mm
3⁄16 in.	9⁄16 in.	Fine	2.5 mm
1⁄4 in.	5⁄8 in.	Narrow medium	2.75 mm
1⁄4 in.	3⁄4 in.	Medium	3 mm
5⁄16 in.	7⁄8 in.	Common	3.5 mm

The traditional pattern of chair caning.

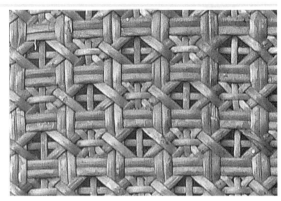
A variation on the traditional chair-caning pattern.

Binder cane is wider than seat cane and slightly smaller than the diameter of the holes.

If you elect to order your cane in bulk, you'll find that it comes in either 500- or 1,000-foot hanks. The 500-foot hank is sufficient to weave two average 14- X 14-inch seats. If you have an option as to the length of the strands in the hank, order the longest length available. This means less tying off of the strands, and therefore, less work overall.

Cane is quite stiff when you buy it. To make it pliable, soak it in warm water for about two hours prior to caning. One way to do this is to fill a sink or large basin with water, dunk the cane in, and put some sort of a weight on top to keep the cane from floating. A heavy skillet works fine.

Some professional caners put a spoonful of glycerine in the soaking water. They say it keeps the cane damp longer once it is removed from the water.

It takes six to eight hours to cane the average chair, once you get the hang of it. Soak

one-fourth of the cane needed at a time. Take the first batch out after two hours and put another in. Working at average speed, this should just about come out right. If you soaked all the strands you needed at one time and took them all out at the end of two hours, you would find that the last ones had dried out before you got around to using them. And leaving them in for eight hours would make them soggy.

If you find your bundle of cane contains strands of different lengths, separate them according to length and use the longest ones first. The first steps in caning are easier if you use longer strands, simply because you'll have fewer knots to tie.

Keep a bowl of water handy and dip your hands in it from time to time. This helps keep the cane soft and pliable as you work.

Step 1

Locate the center holes, front and rear, and insert a peg in each. Use either special caning pegs, available from the cane supply house, or golf tees.

Step 2

Remove the rear peg and pull a strand of cane up through this hole from underneath. Allow 4 to 6 inches of cane to hang below the framework of the seat, then peg the hole again. Remove the front peg and draw this piece of cane down through the front center hole. Don't pull too tight. Allow a little slack as the cane will tighten as it dries. Reinsert the front center peg.

Working toward the left, pull the cane up through the hole to the left of the front center peg and down through the hole to the left of the rear center peg. Keep the strands smooth, untwisted, and with the shiny side of the cane on top. Peg each hole as you work, removing the pegs (except the rear center one) when you proceed to the next hole. When you near the end of a strand, put it down through the last hole that will allow you 4 to 6 inches hanging down. Place a peg in that hole until you tie off the strand later.

Since most chair seats are wider at the front than at the rear, there usually are more holes at the front than at the rear. To compensate, use one or two side holes near the rear corners to keep the last strands of cane parallel. Peg the last strand of cane on the left, leaving 4 to 6 inches of cane hanging down.

You may notice that your chair has corner holes slightly larger than the other holes. Do not use these until you get to step 8.

After the left-hand side is finished, begin the right-hand side. Pull a strand of cane up through the hole just to the right of the rear center peg, peg it, pull the cane down through the hole just to the right of the front center hole, and continue as you did on the left side.

Step 3

Working from side to side, cane horizontally, just as you did from rear to front. Start at either the top or the bottom of the chair. It makes no real difference.

Step 4

Repeat step 2, pulling strands of cane from rear to front on top of the ones woven in steps 2 and 3. Keep these strands slightly to one side of the first row of back-and-forth strands worked in step 2.

Step 5

Begin weaving the strands from side to side again, this time weaving over and under the back-and-forth strands. Start from the last hole on the right at the rear. Weave the first from right to left *over* the strands of step 4 and *under* the strands of step 2. When you return the cane from left to right, weave *under* the strands of step 2 and *over* the strands of step 4. Peg each hole as you work until you return the cane on the next row.

Step 6

Go over the entire seat, aligning the strands, making sure they're in neat pairs from side to side and back and forth. The space between the holes in the cane formed by the weaving pattern should be open and even.

Step 7

By now you have quite a few pegs sticking in the holes, so it's time to begin tying off a few. To tie off, work from the underside, rewetting the cane if necessary. Grasp one of the loose ends of cane and weave it over and under one of the woven

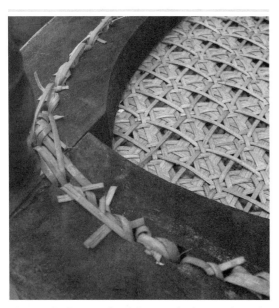

Weave the loose ends of the cane back onto themselves under the chair to produce a neat, finished look.

strands that pass from hole to hole. Make a simple knot and pull as tight as you can. As the cane dries it will shrink slightly, and the knots will become quite rigid.

Step 8

You now begin the diagonal weaving. Start in the rear right-hand corner, using that reserved hole mentioned in step 2. Peg the strand of cane and weave toward the opposite front left-hand corner, weaving over the vertical strands and under the horizontal strands. Remember you're weaving over and under *pairs* of strands at this point. Complete half the seat, then go back, peg another strand of cane, and weave the other half.

Step 9

Repeat step 8, this time beginning in the rear left-hand corner. This time you'll weave under the vertical strands and over the horizontal strands.

Step 10

Tie off all remaining tag ends now as you did in step 7.

Step 11

Cut your binder cane 8 to 10 inches longer than the perimeter of the caned seat. Bring the binder up through the rear center hole, leaving 4 inches hanging below the framework, and peg it. Lay the binder around the perimeter of the seat, over the holes. Take a long strand of the seat cane and bring it up the hole to the right of the rear center hole, over the binder cane, and down the same hole. Keep the binder cane snug and continue around the seat, up a hole, over the binder, and down the same hole. Stop at the last hole to the left of the rear center hole. Push the remaining binder cane down the rear center hole. Tie off all ends—and the seat is finished.

Allow the cane to dry overnight at room temperature and you'll find that it firms up beautifully, giving your work a most professional look.

You may occasionally come upon an old chair that has only a few canes missing or broken but is in good condition otherwise. You can repair this chair yourself using the method described above. Just remove the broken canes and fill in with new cane, weaving into the old design and tying off on the underside with the existing cane.

Traditionally, you should use a single piece of wider cane as an edging around your chair seat, tacking it down at every other hole with another piece of cane.

If you're *really* lucky, you may even find a chair once in a while with the old cane intact but just a bit saggy and dirty. All you need to revive it is a bowl of warm, sudsy water and a brush. Scrub the cane gently until you're satisfied you've removed as much of the grime as possible. Let it dry at room temperature overnight and you'll find that it will firm up very nicely for you.

Obviously, hand-caning is a labor of love, and you just may not have that much time to devote to one chair. There is a way around all this effort, though. You can cut a groove about ¼ inch deep on the chair seat just outside the drilled holes and then use press caning to reseat the chair. The results are satisfying. It's impossible to tell, once it has been press caned, that the chair was actually intended for hand caning.

You must either have a router in your own home workshop or go to a custom woodworking shop to have this groove cut. Decide where you want the groove to be placed, and then make a template to guide the router around the chair seat in that pattern. *Caution:* Don't place the groove so close to the holes that you weaken the seat framework and take the chance of its breaking through. Place the groove about an inch away from the holes.

After you cut the groove, make any necessary repairs to the chair, and then cane it as described below.

Cane Webbing or Press Cane

Cane webbing or press cane is a cane "fabric" woven by machine in a design identical to that achieved by hand caning. It's pressed into a groove in the chair framework and secured with glue and a length of spline.

Often old chairs have remnants of the spline from previous caning stuck in the groove. This old material must be completely removed before you refinish the chair and install new webbing.

With a chisel, go all around the outside edge of the old spline, tapping the chisel with a hammer to break loose the old glue and varnish. Do the same on the inside edge of the spline. Pry up one end of the spline with a narrow screwdriver or a *spline remover,* a tool especially made for this purpose, and pull it out of the groove. You may have to run the screwdriver or spline remover underneath the spline to force it out of the groove. Hot white vinegar will usually dissolve any stubborn dried glue that remains. The new spline won't fit properly unless the groove is

A cheaper alternative to a handwoven cane seat is to use press or machine-woven cane, which comes in sheets. You attach the sheet cane to your chair with a spline, a thick form of reed. Before you can redo your chair seat with new press cane, you'll have to remove any old spline that remains by digging it out with a narrow screwdriver or a spline-removing chisel.

completely clean of debris. Sand the edges of the groove to remove any gouges or rough spots.

Most cane webbing today comes with standard ½-inch holes. The only real decision you'll have to make is the amount to buy—assuming you don't use a kit—and the size of the spline.

Cane webbing is sold by the linear foot in widths of 12 inches, 14 inches, 16 inches, and so forth. You may buy as many linear feet as you want. To determine the amount you need for any specific chair, measure the deepest point of the chair seat from front to rear, groove to groove, and add 4 inches. Also measure the widest part of the seat from side to side, groove to groove, and add 4 inches. If a chair has a groove that is 10 inches deep at its deepest point and 12 inches wide at its widest point, it would require 14 inches of 16-inch-wide webbing.

The chair would also need 44 inches of spline, which is sold by the inch. Spline comes in different sizes to fit different-size grooves. Measure the width of your chair's groove and order accordingly. Every supplier has a chart in the catalog to help you choose the proper size spline. The important thing to remember is that the spline should fit easily in the groove, since two thicknesses of cane webbing must also go into that space. You should be able to drop it in and lift it out with your fingers.

Soak your webbing and spline in warm water for about two hours just before you install it on the chair. This will make the cane pliable enough to mold easily into the groove.

Step 1

Take the webbing from the water, dry it enough to keep it from dripping, and position it carefully on the chair, keeping the shiny side of the cane up. At least 2 inches of the webbing must extend past the groove on all sides. The holes should be lined up evenly from front to rear and side to side. Once in position, you can ensure the cane doesn't slip out of alignment by clamping it to the chair's framework with a couple of small C clamps. This is not essential, though.

Step 2

Once the webbing is in position, begin pushing it down into the groove with small wooden wedges. These wedges come with kits or may be ordered from bulk suppliers.

Start at the rear. Using one of the wedges, press the cane down into the groove. Tap the wedge firmly into place with a hammer, and leave the wedge in the groove to hold the cane as you work. Repeat this procedure, tapping a wedge into place on both sides and in the front. Remove any clamps if you used them.

With a fifth wedge, go back and begin tapping the cane into the groove on the sides of the first four wedges. Continue until you have pressed the webbing into the groove all the way around. Remove the four wedges. The cane will stay in place now.

The spaces between the webbing should be straight both horizontally and vertically. The webbing will be slightly slack, but don't worry. It will tighten as it dries.

Step 3

The grooves in some chairs have rounded corners; in others they are square. The two styles require slightly different treatments when cutting and applying the spline.

Since wet spline is pliable enough to mold around rounded corners, cut it in one continuous piece for a chair. Measure the distance around the groove, add about ¼-inch allowance, and cut the spline to this measurement. It can, however, be difficult to bend spline neatly to fit a very sharp corner. It's better to cut four separate pieces when working with a chair of this design. Measure all sides, add ¼-inch allowance to *each* measurement, and cut the spline to fit.

Step 4

Pour a bead of good-quality wood glue into the groove over the webbing. Beginning at the back, press the spline into the groove. Tap it into place with a wedge and hammer or a rubber mallet. Tap firmly but carefully so as not to crush the spline. If using one continuous piece of spline, join it at the rear center, trimming off any excess material. If working with separate pieces, press them into place and trim off excess material from each piece. Be sure the pieces butt securely against one another without any open space at the joints.

Step 5

Allow the cane to dry overnight at room temperature. It will be taut and beautiful in the morning.

Step 6

With a razor blade, utility knife, or X-Acto knife, trim off the fringe of cane that extends above the spline.

Step 7

At this point, varnish the spline and cane to keep it from absorbing too much of the finishing stain or oil.

Step 8

You may need to sand the seat again around the spline to remove any scratches left when you cut away the excess cane. Then apply whatever finish you desire.

PADDED SEATS

Many of the chairs you find will have neither holes for hand caning nor a groove for webbing. Yet there will be a large space in the seat indicating something was once there. That "something" might have been a padded seat. You can build these yourself using fabric to match your home's decor.

This type of seat is neat and professional looking and is quite easy to manage. Its big disadvantage is that the upholstery fabric isn't removable, for cleaning or replacing, without dismantling the entire seat. Use a fabric that can be cleaned on the chair as you would any piece of fine upholstered furniture. Use a piece of plywood or an old pressed-wood seat as a base. The beauty of this wooden seat is not important; your main concern is that it's still in one piece and not cracking down the middle.

Step 1

Place the seat on a sheet of newspaper and trace around it with a marking pen. Remove the seat and make two more outlines on the newspaper. The first should be 2 inches *outside* the original outline. The second should be ½ inch *inside* the original. The larger, outside line is your pattern to cut the upholstery fabric. The smaller, inside line becomes the pattern to cut a pad of foam rubber or polyester batting.

Step 2

If you want your finished chair to look tidy from all angles, you may want to disguise the underside of the seat. To do this, cut a cover-up from sturdy brown wrapping paper using the pattern you made for the upholstery fabric. Center the seat on the paper, bottom side down, and fold the 2-inch allowance over onto the top of the seat, the part you will soon cover with upholstery fabric. Tape the paper in place securely with masking or duct tape. The bottom of the seat is covered, neat, and quite presentable, even from a worm's-eye view.

Step 3

Place the seat right side up and dab a few spots of quick-setting glue, such as contact cement, onto it. The glue is not absolutely necessary but does help hold the padding in place while you position the upholstery fabric.

Step 4

Cut the padding the size of the smaller pattern, and then place the padding onto the top side of the seat. Press it down firmly so the glue can grab hold.

Step 5

Cut a piece of upholstery fabric the size of the larger pattern. Place the fabric, right side down, on a table and center the seat on it. The padding should touch the wrong side of the fabric. Fold one corner of fabric over the rear of the seat and secure it with a staple. You'll find that ¼-inch staples are perfect for this job. Pull the fabric taut and staple the opposite corner. In turn, staple the third and fourth corners, pulling the fabric taut each time. Then begin on the sides, left then right, top then bottom. It's important that you work from one corner to another as you staple, from one side to another, rather than circling the seat clockwise. This keeps the fabric centered and free of wrinkles. With all four corners and sides stapled, you can begin working in the spaces between the staples, making tiny pleats to take up the extra fabric in the corners.

Step 6

Turn the seat right side up and position it onto the chair. Tack it into place with the tiny nails called *wire brads*. You'll find that ⅞-inch ones work fine.

Step 7

Cut a piece of the upholsterers' trim known as *gimp* 1 inch longer than the circumference of your chair seat. Place it right side down on a table and spread the underside with a thin layer of good-quality fabric glue. Carefully, so as not to smear the glue on the upholstery fabric, press the gimp over the brads. Start at the rear center, work around the seat, and end at the rear again. Trim off any excess gimp and press the cut edges together. Wipe off with a damp cloth any glue that oozes onto the fabric or chair.

PRESSED LEATHER AND FIBER SEATS

Sturdy pressed seats were popular with turn-of-the-twentieth-century chair makers, and the originals often remain on chairs you'll find today. Many are beyond saving, but you can replace the tattered remains with handsome replicas in less than an hour.

Both pressed-fiber and pressed-leather seats come in sizes from 12 to 16 inches wide, and in round, rectangular, and bell shapes. A fanciful design is deeply embossed into the center of the seat, with the motifs ranging all the way from romantic valentine hearts to demonic fire-breathing monsters. You can order the seats by mail from several suppliers. See the list of mail-order houses at the back of this book.

The seat you receive will be larger than you ordered. It will have a border of plain material several inches wide on all sides of the pressed design. This extra material allows you to trim the seat to any finished size to suit your own particular chair. If your chair still has its old pressed seat, you can use that as a pattern to trim the new one to size. If the old seat is missing, make a pattern from paper, allowing *at least* 1 inch of overlap of the seat onto the chair's framework. You'll probably see holes in the wood where the original seat was nailed. This is also a guide to the finished size of your new seat.

Center the old seat or the paper pattern over the new pressed seat, and draw around it with a pencil. Trim the seat on this line with a utility knife or shears. After trimming, remove any pencil marks with an eraser, and sand the cut edges to smooth out any irregularities.

Leather seats are available in a natural tawny color or stained in one of several shades. Fiber seats come unstained and can be finished to match the stain on the chair. Fiber absorbs stain quickly, and it's easy to get a tone much deeper than you intended. So, when using a fiber seat, it's a good idea to test your wood stain on a scrap—a piece left over after trimming, for instance—to make sure you'll get the depth of color you want.

If the scrap is darker than desired, make additional tests with stain or oil of lighter shades on other pieces of scrap until you get the tone you want. After staining or oiling the fiber seat, brush a coat of sealer onto it before nailing it to the chair. Be sure to use a sealer that's compatible with your stain or oil—a water-based sealer with a water-based stain or an oil-based sealer with an oil-based stain or colored oil.

Position the trimmed seat on the chair and secure it with upholstery nails. Space the nails evenly around the edge of the seat. A rather flat-headed nail, instead of the hammered half-ball type sometimes used on old furniture, seems to look best.

2. Lay out a pattern that's approximately 1 inch larger than the embossed design.

1. This chair originally had an embossed leather seat. An embossed fiber seat is an ideal replacement.

3. Trim the fiber seat to fit the chair, based on the paper pattern, and then sand the edges to smooth them.

4. *Stain the seat to match the chair, and then install it with flat-headed or upholstery nails.*

5. *The finished chair is now restored to its original look and ready for years of use.*

If you're using a leather seat, you should have your chair completely refinished before the seat is installed. If using a fiber seat, hold off on the oiling and varnishing until after installation of the seat. Then do it all at once.

Both leather and fiber seats are tough. A little saddle soap once in a while on the leather ones and a quick wipe with a damp cloth on fiber is all that's necessary to keep them clean and in good condition.

REPLACEMENT OF VENEERED ROCKING CHAIR SEATS

One style of late Victorian rocking chair had an elongated, S-shaped, veneered seat that curved up in back and down in front. While you'll see a few of these original seats in good condition, most are warped or broken or have badly cracked veneer.

Replica seats are available, and installing one completely changes the appearance and usefulness of an otherwise unattractive chair. First remove the old seat by knocking the chair's seat framework apart. Lift it out, along with any slivers of wood that remain in the channels. Scrape out the old glue.

The replacement seat will purposely be a few inches too wide and too long, so trim it to the dimensions of the channel on your chair. Place a bead of glue inside both side channels. Insert the new seat into the channels, and then clamp the whole thing overnight. After finishing, you'll have a lovely old rocking chair whose seat is good for another hundred years.

CHAPTER 8

REPAIRING FRAMES AND MIRRORS

Many antique frames suffer from years of neglect. Often they're in fairly good structural condition but are covered with generations of dust and grease, so you should give any frame a thorough cleaning before deciding it if requires refinishing.

Begin by removing all loose dirt with a clean paintbrush or a soft old toothbrush. All old frames should be treated with great care, and when you wash one, use the gentlest possible cleaner. Two or three spoonsful of sudsy ammonia per pint of water should do it. Wring a cloth out in this mixture and rub gently over the frame.

Never get the frame dripping wet. Too much water can loosen old glue that holds moldings to the frame or dissolve exposed plaster trims. If the surface is still dull after treating it with ammonia and water, it may be covered with a heavy coat of thick, dirty wax. This will nearly always disappear if you clean it with a cloth dampened with turpentine or paint thinner.

Sometimes even the best cleaning job won't brighten a tarnished or dull old frame enough to make it attractive. Yet you may not want to remove or cover the original finish. Try highlighting the moldings with one of the metallic waxes on the market.

METALLIC WAXES

Metallic waxes are a mixture of metallic powders and pigment suspended in a fine wax base, usually carnauba wax. Sold in arts-and-crafts shops, they come in small 2-ounce tubes to one-gallon cans in a wide variety of tones, including gold leaf, silver, bronze, and a rainbow of colors. It's a thick water-based product that enables you to create any metallic effect.

You'll use the gold-leaf wax for highlighting. With your fingertip or a small cloth pad, rub a thin coat of wax evenly over the tops of all moldings on the frame. Use a gentle back-and-forth rubbing motion rather than long strokes, and be careful not to get the wax down into the base of the moldings. You will lose this highlight effect if you extend the gold beyond the very highest parts of the moldings. Then buff to a deep luster with a soft cloth.

To brighten an entire frame that has some color but is just dull, select a wax as close to the original color as possible. With a little practice you can even mix colors. Dampen a small soft cloth pad with turpentine and apply a bit of wax to the pad's surface. Use the wax sparingly. You don't want to obscure the original finish, just refresh it. One added benefit of this wax treatment is that it will often color and touch up small nicks in the finish, saving you the time and trouble of a complete refinishing job.

Buff the wax coating to a soft sheen, and you'll have a lovely, gleaming finish that belies the little work you put into reviving an old picture frame.

GOLD LEAF

Genuine gold leaf is valuable and often fragile, so you'll want to retain every bit that's left on an antique frame. Simply clean the frame as mentioned at the beginning of this chapter, then polish the gold leaf with a soft cloth. *Never* touch up bare or worn spots on old gold leaf with ordinary gold paint. An antique frame with worn gold leaf

Metallic waxes can be used to highlight and brighten the molding of antique frames. Touch just the tops of the molding design with the wax and buff to a gleaming finish.

is far more valuable and beautiful than the same frame amateurishly repaired with cheap paint. You can brighten an old gold-leaf-covered frame by rubbing a very thin layer of gold-leaf metallic wax over the entire surface.

Worn gold leaf can, of course, be repaired by the time-honored method of applying new sheets of gold leaf to the frame. Gold leaf is 22-karat gold beaten to a thickness of less than one-quarter of one-thousandth of an inch. It's sold in small squares that have a thin paper backing. The repairer peels the backing off, revealing a gummed surface on the underside of the gold leaf. Place the gummed side on the frame and press it into the molding with a small brush. The result is beautiful since the frame is, quite literally, covered with the finest gold. No one has ever invented a more elegant way to finish a frame.

These sheets are so thin and wispy, though, that they really are too difficult for most of us to manage. In addition, the price of gold today has sent the cost of gold leaf into the stratosphere. If you have a truly heirloom-quality gold-leaf-covered frame in need of repair, simply find a professional to do the job.

If you have or find an old gold-leaf frame that must have some small part of the molding reconstructed, as described on the following pages, buy the best-quality *gold-leaf paint* to gild the patch only. This paint contains karat gold and comes in miniature bottles. Apply it to the patch with a small artist's brush, and the repair will have much the same brilliance and durability of the original gilding. Depending on the extent of the patch and the condition of the old gold leaf, you may then want to layer on a thin coat of metallic wax over the entire frame. This will help brighten the old gold leaf and blend the patch in with the original gilding.

REPLACING MISSING MOLDING

Someday you may come across an antique picture frame decorated with a fanciful trim where some of the pattern is broken or missing. Many people pass these frames up, thinking nothing can be done to repair them. This isn't always the case, though. You can repair or replace many designs with just a bit of effort. And you don't have to know how to carve wood.

Almost all apparently carved decorations on wooden frames actually are molded from a substance called *gesso*. This is made from a mixture of plaster of paris and water. Workers molded the original designs from a similar blend at the time the frame was built, then glued them onto the finished frame. You can essentially repeat the process today to repair broken moldings.

Often you may have to replace only a small section of an elaborate design—a petal knocked off a rose or one edge chipped from a fluted shell, for instance. The easiest way to do this is to mold the gesso with your fingers and shape it to fill out the missing part.

Begin by thoroughly cleaning the frame according to the directions at the beginning of this chapter. Brush yellow glue onto the raw broken section of the molding. Make a small amount of gesso by mixing two or three spoonsful of plaster of paris with a few drops of yellow wood glue and enough water to make a soft, puttylike dough. The glue adds stability. Gesso dries quickly,

Many antique frames have decorative multiple borders. These borders are usually made of gesso, which sometimes cracks off with time, as illustrated by the damage on the inner edges of this frame.

Allow the patch to dry overnight and then sand with fine sandpaper to refine the design further. You'll discover that gesso sands easily, and the patch will soon be as smooth as the rest of the molding. Spray a thin coat of clear plastic or brush on a coat of orange shellac or polyurethane. This will waterproof the raw gesso and serve as a base for the final finish. Then finish the rest of the frame to match. If carefully done, the patch blends surprisingly well with the original molding.

With a little more work, you can actually duplicate a large and/or quite detailed design. This may be necessary if your frame has an elaborate design on three corners, but the fourth is badly damaged or completely missing. Sometimes an intricate design covers the entire frame and you need to replace a few inches of it. Many old frames, too, have one or more fancy borders separating large flat or curved panels. These very thin gesso borders often break off, especially at the corners and outer edges.

You'd have an extremely hard time trying to reproduce these detailed designs freehand, but you can make exact copies by creating a mold using portions of the intact design. To do this you need a package of children's modeling clay from a dollar or arts-and-crafts store. It comes in a package with four chunks, each a different color, and it stays soft even after exposure to the air, so you can reuse the same clay many times.

Tear off a piece of the clay and knead it in your hands until it's soft and pliable. Flatten it until the clay is about ½ inch thick and long enough to cover the damaged section and a narrow shoulder. Select a portion of the intact design that matches the missing section and dust

so you must work with small amounts. Make several successive batches if you have to repair more than one or two small sections of molding. It just doesn't remain pliable long enough to handle more than that.

Roll this mixture around in the palm of your hand until you have a smooth ball. Pinch off enough to make the repair, and press it onto the broken edge of the old molding. Quickly shape the gesso with your fingers to approximate the design of the missing part. Use a popsicle stick, the back of a spoon, a small screwdriver, a nail, or any other tool to help you mold the pattern. Don't worry about rough edges.

1. The first step in replacing a narrow molding is to remove all loose and badly damaged existing molding.

2. Brush a thin dusting of flour onto an intact portion of the molding. The flour keeps the modeling clay from sticking to the frame.

3. Press well-kneaded modeling clay over the floured section of the existing molding. Allow the modeling clay to set for a few minutes, then carefully peel it off the frame. It now has the exact design of the existing molding in reverse.

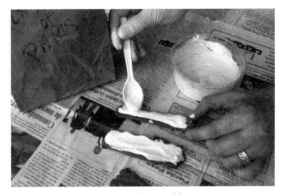

4. Spoon gesso onto the clay molds.

5. Allow the gesso to harden overnight, and then carefully peel the clay off the gesso. Trim the molds to fit the channel of your frame.

6. *Place a bead of glue in the frame's channel and press the replacement molding into place. Fill small cracks and holes with fresh gesso.*

7. *Once all the gesso and glue is dry, stain the replacement molding to blend with the existing molding. After staining, this frame was highlighted with metallic wax, and then the original glass and picture were put back. A few pleasant hours of work had increased the value of this auction buy many times over.*

it with flour. Place the modeling clay over the design and press down firmly. Wait a few minutes, then carefully peel the clay away from the frame, trying not to distort the shape.

Mix a batch of gesso to about the consistency of whipped cream and spoon it into the mold. If you're duplicating a thin edging, you'll just have to spread gesso along the mold. Don't worry if some runs off. Allow the gesso to dry overnight before carefully removing it from the mold. Trim away the excess dried gesso until the new part fits the broken or missing section of molding. You probably won't be able to make a perfect match, but small cavities can be filled later with thin gesso.

Brush a generous layer of glue onto the frame and press the replacement part in place. Tape or tie it to assure a good bond. Fill in any holes with that thin gesso and allow it to dry overnight. Sand rough spots and spray with clear plastic, shellac, or polyurethane. Finally, finish the rest of the frame to match or refinish the entire thing.

Large, dry, replacement molded sections are usually easy to work with since their bulk makes them quite solid. Thin, narrow borders are another matter. If they don't break coming off the mold, they probably will when you press them onto the frame. It happens to all of us. There's no way to avoid this problem. Just line up the broken sections as best you can. Again, small cracks and holes can be filled with thin gesso. Once the replacement sections of molding are finished to match the original design, the patches will blend almost imperceptibly into the old border.

REPAIRING SMALL CRACKS AND HOLES

Many frames constructed during the Victorian era were of a rough core wood with a complete overlay of thin, smooth gesso. Almost inevitably, the outside corners of square and rectangular frames will be worn and cracked, usually exposing the base wood. Most of the time, too, the glue that held the frames rigid has long since dried out and disappeared. The result is usually four pieces of frame with space at each point, the whole thing held together quite tenuously by four tiny nails, one at each corner.

If your first inclination is to take those little nails out and start fixing the frame from scratch, don't. It's very hard to put those mitered joints back together. Just squirt a bit of glue into the space at those corner joints, and then tap the nails to drive them back into the wood. Put the frame on a flat surface while the glue dries. And make sure the angles are square. You can do this even if you don't have a carpenter's square by using four sheets of paper as guides. The paper has perfect right angles at each corner, so place a corner of one sheet of paper under each corner of the frame. Line up the sides and you can't go wrong.

Once the glue has hardened, the frame will be as steady and square as when new. Rebuild the worn corners by smoothing on a thin coat of gesso. Sand when dry and refinish the frame as you like.

At one time, one of the most common types of frame was the oval. Most families seem to have had at least two hanging in the parlor. One held an uncompromising photograph of Mother in her Sunday best, high-collared and proper, and gazing due south. The other frame had the companion photograph of Father in his black suit and walrus mustache, the picture of Victorian dignity, and *he* was staring due north. Have you ever wondered if it could have been the photographers of that day or the subjects who insisted on such grim poses?

Makers of these oval frames used cheap wood covered with gesso. You'll find them painted everything from bridal white to bordello red, but most often they're a dull brown with a darker glaze to simulate wood grain.

When you refinish an antique, you should try to simulate the original finish as closely as possible. This imitation wood is one exception. Some people see no virtue in trying to reproduce or save such a dreary finish and paint such frames in gold or the latest decorator colors.

Most of these oval frames with gesso overlay have a hard finish that does not take a stain well, so you have to repaint them. But you don't have to remove any old finish. Just sand it smooth. The chances are good, however, that you'll find cracks and nicks in the thin gesso. That old plaster is quite fragile, and time does take its toll.

You can use either Spackle or gesso to fill those cracks and holes. Spackle is more expensive, but it has the advantage of staying pliable in the can and ready for immediate use. It only takes a few seconds to open the can, fill a small crack, and put the can back on the shelf. There's no waste and no mess to clean up.

1. This garage-sale purchase showed evidence of a long life. Many cracks and chipped areas marred the gesso overlay.

2. To repair this tattered frame, fill damaged areas with Spackle.

3. Even sanded as smoothly as possible, the surface of the frame isn't flawless enough to take a coat of regular paint satisfactorily. A thin coat of flat white paint or undercoat paint helps to seal the surface.

4. Paint the repaired frame with a special gold-leaf paint, available at hardware stores and home-improvement centers.

5. The finished frame glistens with gold, and a vintage Kodak magazine advertisement fills it nicely.

Regardless of whether you use Spackle or gesso, fill all cracks and holes, sand smooth, and spray with a waterproof plastic finish or brush with shellac or polyurethane. You'll then be ready to paint.

The repaired surface of your gesso-covered frame must be free of imperfections for any painted finish to be acceptable. Otherwise the tiny cracks and mends will show through the paint and detract from the overall effect. If the frame has suffered so much from use and time that it's virtually impossible to make undetectable repairs, you can still try to save it. This solution is certainly not one a purist would recommend for most antiques, but it's the best one under the circumstances. To salvage such a frame, paint it and then brush on a light coat of antiquing glaze. (Complete directions for the antiquing process are in chapter 9.) The glaze tends to blend in the obvious repairs until they are almost unnoticeable. This frame will certainly not have the value of a lovely old rosewood or oak frame, nor will it have the value of a gesso-covered frame that has been expertly and perfectly repaired, but it will be pretty and quite charming. Frankly, I would rather antique such a frame and so let it offer more years of pleasure in a home than throw it away.

Most of these oval frames had curved glass to protect those original photographs. Rarely will you find one with that glass intact. Some large retail glass companies provide replacement curved glass on order. If your local glass firm doesn't have this service, ask it to cut a piece of regular glass to fit. Your antique frame will then be ready to display for fine needlepoint, a bouquet of preserved flowers, or a family portrait. Or consider having a mirror cut to fit.

REPAIRING WOOD FRAMES

Wood frames are among the most beautiful of all antiques. You can refinish and repair them using the techniques described for furniture in chapters 5 and 6 of this book.

MIRROR GLASS

Air pollution, time, and hard use combined take their toll on old mirrors. You'll seldom find a really old mirror that isn't discolored or damaged in some way. Many have deep scratches in the silvering or large patches where the silver is missing.

I've found very few mirrors more than a hundred years old in top condition. The ones that have survived nearly always have a backing of heavy cardboard or thin wood. The latter seems to be most effective in guarding mirror silvering from damage. A wooden backing is also a good indicator of the age and quality of the entire mirror and its frame, too.

What happens if you find a mirror whose silver is too badly damaged to use or sell in its current condition? Can such an old mirror be resilvered. The answer is no.

Resilvering an antique mirror is an expensive process done with sophisticated equipment by a few experts. If you live in New York City or another large metropolitan area, you probably can find such a company in the yellow pages. Most cities, however, don't have glass companies that offer this service.

You have two options when faced with a mirror whose silvering is so badly worn it can't be used.

First, you can begin by brushing a thick coat of paint remover on the silvering. Wait a few minutes, and then scrape if off with a razor blade. Some, but not all, of the old silvering will probably come off with the paint remover. You must scrape away the remaining silvering with more razor blades. *Warning:* You're in for a long and tedious job. It's really worth the effort only when the original glass is beveled and quite thick. Once the old silvering is removed, however, the glass will be sparkling clean.

Then have a new mirror cut to the exact dimensions of the old mirror. Place the original piece of glass, now clear, in the frame, and put the new mirror behind it. The result can be quite beautiful because you've actually increased the depth of the glass.

The second option is simply to discard the old mirror and replace it with a new one.

Before you take either of these paths, though, take a good look at the mirror. Is it really a total disaster? Or does it have just a few bare spots? Part of the beauty of an antique is that it has obviously been used for many, many years. An old mirror with a few blemishes is usually far more beautiful than a new one.

CHAPTER 9

RENOVATING OLD TRUNKS

Renovating old trunks can be even more addictive than refinishing antiques in general. Once you restore one you'll be on the lookout for another . . . then another . . . then another. Perhaps this is because few antiques have as much charm, color, clear evidence of historical value, and modern usefulness as an old trunk.

I became interested in old trunks when I noticed one out in front of a row house in Binghamton, New York. It seemed the family was holding an impromptu yard sale, so I stopped my car to get a closer look. Dirt, grime, and some rust covered the trunk, but its smaller size and rounded top said it offered some possibilities. I loaded the trunk into my car and headed home. Several days later, I hauled the dirty trunk into my driveway and began scrubbing its embossed tin surface. A package of steel wool, some dish detergent, and a lot of rubbing later, the original finish began to emerge. While rust had begun to eat into small portions of the tin surface, it wasn't that bad and could be removed using some Naval jelly.

The wooden slats were in fair condition, and even the hardware worked like new, after a few shots of lubricating spray. The interior paper, though faded, was still there. After refinishing, it now serves as storage and as a colorful accent in my den.

Don't be discouraged by the abominable condition of many trunks. Short of complete disintegration, almost every antique trunk can be restored with enough care. As soon as you bring a trunk home, open the lid and take a good whiff. Pretty musty, huh? That's probably because it has been sitting in a damp basement or airless attic for goodness knows how many years. You have to rid your trunk of that odor, so before you do anything else, you must give it a good cleaning. You may find the tattered remains of an old paper or cloth lining clinging to the interior sides. If so, scrape this off, retaining any picture or medallion on the inner lid if it is at all salvageable. Vacuum thoroughly, using the crevice attachment tool to reach into corners. After you have all the loose dirt and lining out, douse the interior of the trunk well with an insect spray such as Raid. Close the lid and allow the spray to work overnight. This will rid your trunk of any migrant silverfish, roaches, moths, earwigs, or other undesirable tenants. Do this fumigating outdoors to keep the insects from resettling in your closets.

The next day wash the entire trunk, inside and out, with your favorite cleaning solution. Use a commercial cleaner or pine oil. Finally, spray the interior of the trunk with a pleasantly scented room spray. You'll then have a clean, pest-free, fresh-smelling trunk to renovate.

While some old trunks were made solely of leather, most had a rough wooden framework on which the maker fastened some sort of outer covering. This covering can be leather, canvas, tin, or cabinet wood. Each type of exterior will require a different restoration method.

Regardless of which kind of covering your trunk has, the first thing you must do is turn it over. You may find a wooden bottom with small casters on each corner. Inspect the wood care-

fully. With luck, the wood will be fairly solid. The bottom doesn't have to be in perfect condition to be usable, but it does have to be firm enough to hold the screws from the casters and to serve as a base for the trunk.

If still there, the casters may be rusty and stiff. Clean them with a wire brush and hot, soapy water. Scrub away until you've removed the rust and the wheels roll easily. Spray the rollers with a good lubricant. If the original casters are missing, you can replace them with reproductions. A couple of good suppliers are listed at the back of this book.

The best remedy for a trunk whose bottom is unsightly and riddled with holes is to make a new bottom from plywood. Remove any remaining casters first. Cut a new base from ¼-inch plywood, using the same dimensions as the bottom of the trunk. Position this new base on the trunk and attach it with long screws at each corner. Make sure the screws go far enough into the corner posts to bite into firm wood. Sand the edges of the new base, and either paint or stain it in a color that will blend with the final color tone of your trunk. Then reattach the old casters or install new ones.

Repair the base, if necessary, and get the casters in good working order before repairing any other section of the trunk. Do this for two reasons: First, you will be moving that trunk around quite a bit as you work on it, and trunks are heavy. The smoothly rolling casters make the job much easier. Second, the casters raise the trunk a bit, leaving a half inch or so between its bottom and the surface of the worktable. This allows you to paint, polish, or do anything else to the lower edge of the trunk without that edge being jammed against the worktable.

Your next step will be to check the *stays,* those hinged supports attached to the sides of the trunk base and lid. They keep the lid from opening too far and tearing off its hinges. Often these stays are missing from an old trunk. If this is the case, and the hinges are so firmly attached you don't want to remove them, install a temporary stay. Use a sturdy shoelace, piece of twine, or flexible wire—anything that will hold the lid on securely while you're working on the trunk. Don't put new stays in yet. They may be installed after the new lining is in, and that's one of the last parts of the renovation. If the original stays are still firmly attached, just leave them on for now.

Next check the bolts or screws that secure the hinges to the back of the trunk. Many screws work loose from trunk hinges as the screw holes become enlarged with time and hard use. You have two options should you find bolts or screws loose or missing. The first is to remove any existing ones, separating the lid from the base. This allows you to work on the trunk in two sections. Many people prefer to work on a large trunk, especially, as two units instead of one. The only disadvantage occurs if you're painting the trunk. Since you paint the lid and base separately, you'll have to reassemble the trunk later on. The screws won't have been painted when you painted the lid and base, so you'll have to touch them up, adding a step to the refinishing process. This extra step is worth the convenience of working on the trunk in two sections instead of one.

Your second option is to replace the old screws with new ones right at the beginning.

Refer to chapter 5 for this information. You will have to work on the trunk with the lid attached, but you'll eliminate a little retouching at the end. The stays, whether temporary or permanent, must be firmly attached, though, if you go this route. Otherwise, even new screws can be jerked out of the wood should the top fall back suddenly.

Now take a look at the leather handles on the sides of the base. You'll rarely find a very old trunk with the original handles in good condition. Most are either missing, torn, or so brittle and misshapen that they're unusable. Trunk makers attached the original handles to their trunks with metal handle loops. Remove and save your handle loops, if they're still there, for later use. You can substitute reproduction ones if the old ones are missing.

Makers usually attached old metal handle loops to the trunk with short heavy nails. Use a tack hammer to lift the old nails, and release the loop from the body of the trunk. Place the slotted end of the hammer under the handle loop, and work it back and forth until the nail is loosened and the handle loop can be pulled off. Remove the remains of the old handle and fill in any resulting holes. On a wooden or canvas trunk, use wood putty to fill the holes. Use liquid steel on a metal trunk. Do nothing to the holes on leather trunks.

These handle loops fall into one of three designs. You'll find some that straddle the ends of a narrow handle that has holes cut into the leather near the ends. A sharp spike on the inside of the loop is driven through the hole and into the body of the trunk. This anchors the handle. A second type of loop uses the same type of leather handle, but instead of straddling that handle, the

One type of trunk handle loop straddles the leather handle. Brads driven through the loop and the handle secure it.

Another type of cloth handle loop encloses the ends of the handle, as shown here. This, too, is original hardware.

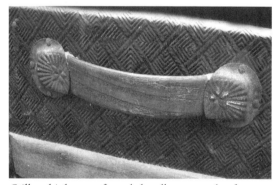

Still a third type of trunk handle was made of a bentwood strip, attached at both ends.

loop encloses the ends. This type of loop also has an inner spike that goes through the hole in the handle. The third type of loop is similar to the first mentioned, except it lacks the inner spike. It's meant to be used with a handle whose ends flare out in a fan shape. Trunk manufacturers placed the loop just inside the flared section of the handle to anchor the strap to the trunk. Replacement leather handles are available to fit any of these loops.

You can replace virtually any other piece of hardware on an old trunk, too, including the big center lock, clamps, corner protectors, drawbolts, dowels, glides, casters, hinges, and stays. All these parts are available in reproductions identical to century-old styles. The manufacturers' catalogs also list embossed wood and metal ornaments that you might want to use to enhance your trunk. Sometimes, you can use ornamental hardware to cover unsightly damage. A pair of plump cupids or a bevy of patriotic stars are great for disguising holes. A horizontal spray of bows and roses is a fine solution to a deep scratch, and at the same time adds a romantic touch of Victorian beauty to an old trunk. Attach the brass ornaments with tiny brass nails. You can install these at almost any stage of the trunk's renovation. Glue the wooden ornaments on before you oil or paint the trunk.

You can order these replacement parts from the suppliers listed at the back of this book.

The wooden bands or stays that encircle many old trunks may be so badly damaged that you can't repair them. Buy a wooden slat of a comparable wood at your lumber dealer. If the bands on your trunk aren't a standard size, ask the shop car-

This old trunk lacked its large lock. When replacing trunk hardware, you should do so last so that it doesn't get damaged in the refinishing process. You can also paint the hardware that's already on the trunk with either metallic paint or flat black rustproof enamel.

penter to plane and trim the slat to your requirements. This is a simple operation, and you may not be charged for it if you're a regular customer.

You'll need to distress this new wood with a hammer, deep and irregular sanding, or some other aging process. Otherwise, even though you finish it in the same manner as the rest of the wood on the trunk, the piece will look new.

You can even replace the curved bands that fit across the tops of many camel-backed trunks by using a jig to shape the slat, as described in chapter 5. An easier method for the simple shape of a trunk top is to make a rudimentary jig of six- or eight-penny nails and scrap lumber.

On paper, draw the arc you wish the slat to assume. Transfer this design to scrap wood. Hammer the nails on either side of the drawn line. Soak the slat at least an hour or two, then force it into the channel between the two lines of nails.

Allow to dry overnight. Once dry, the band will hold the new shape well enough for you to nail it to the trunk lid.

LEATHER TRUNKS

You'll find leather in reasonably good condition simple to renovate. Clean the leather thoroughly with saddle soap and allow it to dry. Dab on a generous coating of a silicone waterproofing liquid, then polish the leather to a soft gleam.

Most old leather trunks had heavy leather bindings around the outer edges. If only small sections of this binding are loose, you can repair them yourself. Work contact cement between the binding and the body of the trunk, and let it dry under pressure. If whole sections are badly torn or missing, you'll have to rely on your shoe-repair shop for help. The repairer can replace torn or missing sections with comparable leather and stitch them in a pattern that closely resembles the original stitching.

Some of the leather that formed the body of these old trunks was quite thin since the maker applied it over a sturdy wooden base. Time, sun, rain, and abuse have played havoc with much of this glove-thin leather, and some of these trunks aren't salvageable as leather trunks. If the trunk as such is unsalvageable, cut all the leather off and renovate the wooden base underneath. This base, although made of inexpensive wood, may have acquired a lovely patina. In such a case, refinish the trunk as described in the following section on wooden trunks.

If you come upon a leather-covered trunk, however, where only one or two small sections of the leather covering are in bad shape, you can replace those sections. Using an X-Acto knife, cut away the damaged leather at the nearest joining, be it at the edge binding, underneath a strap, or under a wooden slat. Make an exact pattern of the area from which you removed the damaged leather, and buy some leather of a similar color and origin from your shoe-repair shop or leather-crafts store. Cut a new piece to fit. Brush a coat of contact cement onto the wooden base, and carefully fit the new leather piece into place. Press with your fingers, then allow it to dry overnight. You'll undoubtedly have to dye the new leather to match the old. You can use commercial shoe dye or shoe polish. Just experiment on a scrap of leather until you get a color close to that of the old leather. Then polish the entire trunk with a protective finish.

WOODEN TRUNKS

Renovating an antique wooden trunk is similar to renovating a piece of antique wooden furniture. First check to see if all joints, slats, bands, and corners are solid. Any that aren't tight should be glued together and reinforced with recessed screws. Fill all holes and cracks with wood putty, then sand the trunk thoroughly. Polish the brass hardware with a good commercial polish, and replace any missing hardware with reproductions. Oil and varnish the trunk as described in chapter 6. The result will be a charming and distinctive accessory to complement your lovely antique furniture.

The exterior of this wooden trunk, shown at an antiques show, has been lovingly restored.

The interior of the same trunk has been completely reupholstered with appropriate fabric and contrasting upholstery trim.

CANVAS TRUNKS

Many old storage trunks started life with a sturdy canvas covering glued to a wooden base. Some very old canvas trunks have remained in remarkably good condition. If you should find an antique canvas trunk in good condition, your first step in refinishing it would be to scrub the entire surface thoroughly with a fiber brush and your favorite cleanser. Don't be too harsh with the brushing, because you could easily damage any loose canvas. When the canvas is dry, check it over, inch by inch, for small tears, worn spots, and loose areas. Glue these down to the base with a mixture of equal parts wood glue and water. (Undiluted glue would leave a thick, shiny buildup on the canvas.) Once you repair the small damaged areas, you'll hardly notice them. And a few worn spots will just attest to the authenticity of your trunk.

Oil any exposed wood and polish the brass hardware. Finish the entire trunk with a coat of polyurethane varnish.

METAL TRUNKS

Rust is the biggest enemy of metal trunks. It's quite rare to find one whose bottom and lower edges are in near-perfect condition.

Turn your metal trunk over and examine the bottom. Is it covered with tin? Trunk makers constructed many of their trunks with metal bottoms. If the bottom of your trunk is badly rusted, remove the casters, and with tin snips, cut the damaged metal to within an inch or so of the edge. Beneath the tin you will find a wooden base that may be in reasonably good condition. If so, use it as is. You should trim around the perimeter of the base, however, with some thin wooden stock to cover the sharp cut-metal edges. Reattach the casters and you're in business.

If the wooden base is full of holes from decay or termites, construct a new plywood bottom as described earlier in this chapter.

On a badly damaged trunk, the rust may have progressed past the bottom and started up the sides. If this is the case, buy some wooden stock wide enough to cover the damage, and then simply nail it over the rusted metal. If you repair the trunk in this way, be sure to distress the new wood a bit before you install it. Sand the edges well to eliminate the sharp edges. Then beat the wood up a little with a hammer. Inflict enough "wear" on it that, once painted or stained, the new wood will blend imperceptibly with the original wooden bands of the trunk.

One day you may come upon an old metal trunk that just tugs at your heart. Once beautiful, it has fallen on hard times; the poor thing has rusted *all over*. Turn and walk away. Unless you have access to metal putty, fiberglass filler, grinding machines, and the expertise to rebuild the damaged metal, you'll soon regret your decision to repair it. You'd spend far more money and effort trying to repair the trunk than it's worth.

You can *replace* damaged units of tin on an old metal trunk, however, by cutting away the old tin and nailing in new pieces. Plain, smooth tin can probably be found at a local sheet-metal shop. You'll find embossed tin, the kind used for trim on many old metal trunks, available from one of the suppliers listed at the back of this book.

Use liquid steel to fill any tiny holes in the trunk metal or to bridge the spaces between old tin and replacement sections.

This unrestored trunk came from a yard sale in Bing-hamton, New York.

Mask off the plain metal parts of the trunk before painting them a flat black. Paint them using a medium-bristle brush.

The interior, while dirty, contained its original paper lining, complete with nineteenth-century decorations.

Apply oil-stain finish to the wood trim and allow to dry. Afterwards, spray the embossed tin with protective clear coating so that it keeps its shine.

To clean the embossed tin surface, use medium-grade steel wool. Wash the wooden trim using the techniques described in chapter 6.

The completely restored trunk is now ready to be used to store winter blankets or sweaters.

You may want to paint your tin trunk, especially if you replace any damaged tin or add a new wooden band. This results in an attractive, colorful storage piece that can be an asset to any home. For an example of the restoration of a metal trunk, see the photos on page 138. You can also use the antiquing process described below.

THE ANTIQUED FINISH

Paint can hide a multitude of problems on an old trunk. For instance, if the hardware had been brass plated, but the finish is now in poor condition, you can paint it black. However, don't paint a trunk that has a mellow patina. Even more of a sacrilege would be painting a leather or canvas trunk. Each of these trunks would lose much of its personality if covered with paint. Such blasphemy would be tantamount to painting a lovely old cherrywood dining table avocado green to match the leaf pattern in the draperies!

However, painted trunks *do* have their place in the scheme of things. There's no reason why you shouldn't paint a metal trunk that has absolutely no distinguishing facets on the tin covering. You can even improve some wooden trunks with paint if they're made of ugly, mismatched boards that no amount of TLC can enhance. And painted trunks are most attractive when given an antiqued finish. This section will give you the simple directions to "antique" an antique trunk.

Working outdoors, remove the old paint or varnish with a good paint stripper. When stripping furniture, you must get every speck of paint out of every pore. When stripping a trunk to be antiqued, just get *most* of the paint off. You're going to cover the trunk with more paint any-

way, so a little color left on doesn't matter. Do try to eliminate any thick buildup of old paint, flaking paint, or loose areas, however.

When the trunk is relatively free of paint, sand it well. Brush a coat of rust-inhibiting primer/conditioner on a metal trunk. If your trunk has wooden bands, you may want to leave them their natural color to contrast with the painted sections. If so, cover the wood with paper and masking tape. Polish, then cover any hardware you plan to leave unpainted.

Antiquing is a two-step process. First paint on a base, and then wipe a glaze over that base. You can buy antiquing kits or paint and glaze especially for this purpose. Since not every paint store carries antiquing materials, you may have to shop around. You're looking for a low-luster latex enamel that will take the glaze well, and a colored glaze especially made for this purpose. Don't settle for substitutes. You may not be happy with the results.

When you find a paint store that carries antiquing materials, look at the color chart that illustrates the results of different shades of glaze over a variety of base colors. Don't be appalled by the bright colors of the base coat. These primary colors become subdued when used with the glaze.

After you've stripped and masked your trunk, you're ready to begin. Brush on a coat of the base color, beginning with the bottom of the trunk. When you turn the trunk upright, the casters will keep the bottom off the work table and allow the paint to dry without sticking. If you didn't remove the top from the base as suggested earlier, you'll have to prop it up to keep the upper and lower lips from touching as the base coat dries. Prop a board a few inches longer than the height of the trunk under the lid, making sure the board does not touch the front of the trunk. The extra length supports the top, preventing it from resting on the base.

Paint the outside of the top and the base, extending the paint a few inches to the inside at both lips. Paint the handle loops if you were able to save them. Allow the paint to dry overnight.

Many people like to decorate their antiqued trunks with hand-painted floral designs. If you're fortunate enough to possess this skill, just be sure to paint the designs over the base coat and before you apply the glaze.

The next day, remove any masking tape. If you leave the wood bands natural, brush some oil on them, as described in chapter 6, to preserve the wood and give it an attractive color.

You're now ready for the glazing process. The glaze must be brushed on and then wiped off. With some glazes, you paint the glaze on, then wipe immediately. With others, you allow the glaze to set for fifteen minutes or so before wiping. If you are using the first type, brush the glaze on in small sections; otherwise, the glaze becomes too thick before you can wipe it off. Test a section or two on the bottom of the trunk first. It will help you determine the correct length of time to leave the glaze on for the effect you want to achieve. Remember, the longer the glaze remains on the base coat, the darker and more opaque it becomes.

Remove the protective masking tape and brush the glaze sparingly over all painted surfaces and *very* sparingly on unpainted wooden surfaces and hardware. Don't forget the inside of the lips.

Once the glaze has set for the recommended time, go back and wipe it off with rags or crumpled paper towels. Gently wipe in smooth, even strokes from side to side. Do this carefully, since it is easy to eliminate the entire glazing step with too vigorous strokes.

The purpose of the glaze is to give that old, well-used appearance, so leave more of it in areas that would normally show the most wear. Think about the places furniture shows age most readily, the places it normally darkens with use. Most people get the best results when antiquing by leaving a thicker coat of glaze at the edges of the trunk and around the hardware. The glaze will naturally settle into dents and low spots. Allow it to stay there, since these areas would normally be dark on an old trunk.

Let the glaze dry overnight. If the color is too light or too bright, just repeat the glazing step.

When the entire trunk is dry, attach the handle loops and handles. Use new brass screws with new reproduction hardware. Any screws will do if you've saved and painted the original loops, since you'll want to retouch the screws with paint and glaze anyway.

Replace the hinges if you separated the top from the base. Retouch the screws with paint and glaze.

Give the entire trunk—painted sections, natural wooden trim, and hardware—a coat of polyurethane varnish. Protect the leather handles from the varnish with foil or plastic wrap. Apply a second coat if you plan to use your trunk in a child's room or as a coffee table.

Remember, any trunk you treat in the above manner will lose any value it had as an antique. Only when you restore it does a trunk retain its value.

INTERIOR TRAYS

Most old trunks had trays at one time. Occasionally you find one with the tray intact—often you don't. Use the tray if it's available. If it's missing, either discard the wooden tray supports from the inside of the trunk, if they're still there, and use the trunk without a tray, or just build a new one.

Should you decide to use a tray, you'll need tray supports on both sides of the trunk. Discard the old ones if they don't essentially meet the measurements and description listed here. You'll need two pieces of wood approximately 1 × 1 inch and ¼ inch shorter in length than the interior front-to-rear measurement of the trunk. Drill two or three evenly spaced pilot holes in each support. Measure the depth of your tray, and make a pencil line on each side of the trunk at the point you wish the tray to rest. This is the line you use to position the top of the tray support. Run a bead of wood glue on one long edge of one support. Place it against the side of the trunk with the upper edge against the pencil line. Using long thin screws, attach the tray support to the side of the trunk. The screws must be long enough to go through the tray support and well into the wooden framework of the trunk, but not thick enough to split the support. Repeat for the other side.

THE LINING

Remove any temporary or permanent stays for this final step in your trunk's renovation. But brace the lid by resting it on a chair seat or other support to prevent the lid from falling back and wrecking the hinges.

Originally, makers of trunks lined them with paper. As well as being the most authentic lining material, paper is also the least expensive and the easiest to install.

Buy a good-quality prepasted wallpaper with a small pattern you like. A small allover print is probably the best for your first attempt because you won't have to worry about aligning stripes or matching large patterns. On the other hand, you can create charming borders by cutting striped paper lengthwise. Be careful using vinyl-coated paper if you plan to use a border. You'll need to use special vinyl-to-vinyl glue so the border doesn't peel off.

Uncoated paper is best in this instance. Other than this, your main concern should be that both the color and pattern be compatible with the age of your trunk.

Wallpaper *can* be expensive if bought at its regular shelf price, so I watch for the "odds and ends" sales. These orphan rolls are useless to decorators and paper hangers, yet there's enough good paper in one roll to line two average-size trunks.

Working with the base of the trunk first, measure the sides from top to bottom and side to side. Add 2 inches to the side-to-side measurement. Add 5 inches to the top-to-bottom measurement if you plan to have a tray and only 1 inch if you don't.

Measure the back, bottom, and front of the base as one unit since you can line all three sections with one long piece of paper. Don't add any extra width or length to this long piece.

Working now with the lid of the trunk, measure its sides. Add 2 inches to the side-to-side measurement and 1 inch to the top-to-bottom measurement. Measure the back, top, and front as one unit.

Unroll the paper on the floor or on a large worktable. Keeping in mind that you want to center any pattern or space stripes evenly, transfer the measurements to the paper. Cut out the pieces with sharp scissors.

Now cut 1-inch slits every 3 to 4 inches into both sides and the bottoms of the two pieces cut for the sides of the base. Don't cut any slits on the top edges that will be at the top near the lip of the trunk. Don't cut any slits in the long piece that will form the base's back, bottom, and front. Repeat this process for the pieces for the lid. Cut 1-inch slits in the side pieces every 3 to 4 inches along the edges that will form the top and side edges. Don't cut any slits on the edge placed nearest the lip. Don't cut any slits on the long piece that will form the lid's back, top, and front.

Prepasted paper must be soaked in warm water to activate its glue. Some paper must be soaked longer than others. Carefully *read the manufacturer's instructions on the paper's plastic covering or insert.* Put a few inches of warm water in the bathtub, and lay one base side piece in the water. Swish it around for the required number of seconds or minutes. Lift, drain quickly, and carry to the trunk. Fit the piece in, allowing those slit edges to flare out onto the back, bottom, and front, making a flange.

If you're using tray supports, press the paper up, around, and over the supports. Using a soft cloth, go over the paper, smoothing out any wrinkles and bubbles. You'll find you have 1 inch of paper sticking out at each of the supports. Trim about half of it away, and notch the rest to elim-

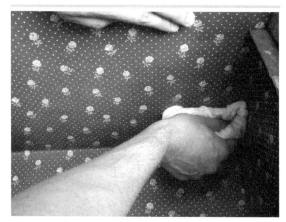

Use a cloth to smooth out the wallpaper, rubbing out any bubbles or wrinkles.

Paper around existing illustrations in your trunk's interior by cutting out the hole with an X-Acto knife.

inate some of the bulk. With a table knife, press this extra paper into the ⅛-inch space between the ends of the support and the front and back of the trunk. Repeat to cover the other side.

Next soak the long piece of paper, then press it into place on the trunk's back, bottom, and front. With your table knife, press the paper under the ends of the tray supports. No raw wood should show between the sides, the back, bottom, and front because of those side flanges. Glue and staple the top edges if they won't stick well. Repeat this process for the lid of the trunk.

Many old trunks had pictures or elaborate designs on the inside of the lids. These designs should be preserved whenever possible. Use an X-Acto knife to trim away any wallpaper that would cover such a design *before* you install it in the lid. Use the suggestions in chapter 4 for reinforcing old labels if your picture is in poor condition.

Measure the distance around your trunk, add 1 inch, and cut two pieces of decorative braid to that measurement. Lay a good bead of glue on the upper edge of the base and the lower edge of the lid. Press the braid onto the glue, working the glue well into the fabric with your fingers. Cut another piece of braid long enough to go around the picture, then trim it out the same way, notching the braid at the corners of the picture to eliminate bulk. Instead of braid, you can trim the edges with strips cut from the wallpaper.

Using the same techniques described above, line and cover your tray. If you feel the tray is too difficult to cover, considering the hand holes, lifts, and tiny compartments, paint the tray to blend with the lining paper's most dominant color. Or, make the tray, if you have to build a new one, of cedar, and leave it unfinished. The moths will hate you!

Your final step in renovating this now-beautiful old trunk is to reattach the side stays. Attach the upper edge of the stay to the lid with a sturdy new screw. Reproduction stays often come with brass brads, but sometimes these don't hold the stays securely. The wood framework in many antique trunks is sometimes less than solid from years of use and neglect. There's a possibility that these brads will pull out and the lid will fall back, damaging the hinges, so, you might want to use screws that will get a good bite even into old wood.

Open the stay. With the lid upright at a right angle to the base, mark the logical spot to attach the lower half of the stay. Again, with a sturdy screw, attach the stay to the side of the trunk.

Now, sit back, admire your lovely, restored antique trunk, and give yourself a well-deserved pat on the back.

CHAPTER 10

YES, YOU CAN MAKE MONEY IN ANTIQUES!

Sooner or later, almost everyone who loves antiques voices the wistful thought, "Wouldn't it be fun to sell antiques?" The lure of working with those beautiful objects can be very strong, but it can have its pitfalls.

Before you take the plunge, if at all possible you should work for at least a few months in someone else's antiques shop. The experience you gain there can be far more valuable than any general information in a book. Every town is different, and practices that would succeed famously in one town could fail miserably in another. A shop in a small town in Vermont would have to have a different personality, offer different services, and stock different types of antiques than one in downtown San Francisco. You'll be able to best gauge the needs of antiques collectors in *your* town by working with a dealer there.

Soon you'll learn the ropes of this business, and your chances for success will be far better.

You can sell your refinished antiques through antiques malls, co-ops, in-home shops, and shops in commercially rented space.

Regardless of which way you choose, you'll need to follow some basic guidelines.

Watch for trends in antiques. Trends develop in antiques just as they do in clothing or hairstyles. For instance, primitive furniture was a big seller in the 1980s. Of course, this changed, and for a while Art Deco pieces were all the rage in the early 1990s. Prices skyrocketed. Then, the bottom dropped out. Now, interest is renewing in primitive pieces once again. Dealers who can foresee such trends are the ones who make money.

How can you do the same? Read the articles in trade journals such as *Antique Trader, Antique Week,* and *Kovels' Antiques and Collectibles Newsletter.* Read the "wanted" ads in those papers. They tell you what professionals in the business are buying and therefore what will sell in today's market. Watch the "for sale" ads. They tell you what professionals are unloading—the items whose popularity is waning.

Go to all the antiques shows in your area. Talk with the dealers. Ask them what their biggest sellers are. Visit successful shops in your area and talk with the owners. People who deal in antiques love to talk about them, and these people can be a major source of information as to what's selling in your area.

Attending local antiques auctions is another excellent way to determine what is selling (and what's not). You'll get dramatic and fast proof of just what is "hot" in your area. All you have to do is watch the temperature level of the bidding. Popular items will be bid up to high prices, while the duds no one wants will go begging.

Because people settled this country in vastly different periods, the antiques available in one section simply don't exist in another, except in museums or high-priced shops.

In the Northeast, for example, history goes back more than 300 years. The people who live there are accustomed to seeing antiques that are very old. They favor styles common to the early years of this country and woods that were in use during the eighteenth and early nineteenth centuries.

In the Deep South, however, most people still prefer the romantic styles of the mid-Victorian era. They're especially fond of rosewood, walnut, and mahogany—woods that were popular during that era.

It wasn't until years later, though, that the West could boast much more than log cabins and soddies. Therefore, western antiques shops contain very little furniture that's much more than one hundred years old. Oak furniture filled western homes at the turn of the twentieth century, and it still remains the choice of most westerners today and is most common in the western antiques shops.

So what sells in one part of the country may not sell in another.

Recently, at an auction in Virginia an attractive oak buffet came up for bid. But there wasn't any interest in it. The auctioneer finally sold it for a paltry $85. Not long afterward, a walnut china cabinet came up, and the dealers present went crazy. After spirited bidding, the china cabinet sold for $470. In another part of the country, the buffet might have been the hot item, not the china cabinet.

The moral here for the novice in selling antiques: Study, study, study—then put your money in items that people in *your* area want to buy.

Pricing and Bargaining

One of the most satisfying aspects of the antiques business is that you have absolute control over your prices. No manufacturer can advertise a set price, and "fair trade" doesn't exist in this business. Also, each antique is unique, so your competition is unlikely to have an identical piece. You only have to be concerned with offering your customers good merchandise at a reasonable price, not the same price as other dealers.

This flexibility, coupled with your ability to buy antiques at low prices and refinish them yourself, gives you an opportunity to make some money. You'll discover, as you become knowledgeable about what and where to buy, that the profit potential in this business is as high or higher than it is in any other legitimate business around today. Where some high-volume stores delight in making 10 to 15 percent profit after expenses, yours can easily be many times that figure. Many antiques dealers regularly mark up their stock 200 or 300 percent over cost. As a refinisher and dealer, you may be able to top even that ratio.

When setting your prices, don't just take into consideration your cost of the antique and the refinishing materials used on it. You must consider a small margin to allow for markdowns. You also had to spend some of your time and gasoline to ferret out those antiques in the first place. Don't forget your acumen in finding the antiques and your skill in refinishing. These are worth something, too. A doctor or lawyer charges heavily for years spent learning the profession. You're entitled to the same consideration. Add up all these factors, and *then* tack on your profit.

You may have to allow for delivering some large items, too. Many shops will deliver any antique without charge to any address within the city limits. A dealer may even deliver an antique *anywhere* a truck can go, but then charge a set price per mile, one way, on all deliveries outside the city limits.

Should you set firm prices or be willing to negotiate? Some shop owners don't like to haggle over prices. To them it's undignified and unbusinesslike. They prefer to set what they consider a fair price and stick with it. Other dealers, knowing how many collectors delight in bargaining, routinely price their antiques about 10 percent above the figure they're willing to settle for. After a little polite and good-natured bargaining, they cheerfully drop the price; the customer says, "I'll take it" and leaves feeling he or she made a good deal. This is a good selling technique. Most customers cannot resist buying an antique they genuinely want if they can get it for less than the marked price.

Dealers almost universally give one another a 10 percent discount on antiques. And since it is assumed the antique is for resale, no sales tax is charged. Just be sure to note the dealer's sales-tax number on the sales slip for your own records. Your local tax department may require this information when you file your returns at the end of the year.

Whether discounting to customers or other dealers, make a policy on just how much you will lower any one item. Then stick with that decision. Better to miss a sale once in a while than to sell a good piece at such a low price you make no profit on it.

Keep a record to help you increase your profits in this business. It should be a detailed tally of each antique you buy to refinish. Note the purchase price, cost of refinishing materials, selling price, and profit. This record is kept in columns in a ledger so you can look down the sheets and tell at a glance, for instance, that your overall profit ratio on floor lamps and office chairs is higher than that on lamp tables and kitchen cabinets. This will help you know not to go overboard on buying lamp tables and kitchen cabinets because you make more money on lamps and office chairs.

This breakdown of costs and profits is in no way definitive, of course, since each antique will cost you a different amount, and some require much more refinishing than others. You might buy an office chair for $35 at auction, spend $50 on refinishing and hardware, and still get the same price for it that you get for one in which you have only $28 invested. But, *overall,* the cost breakdown will help you determine where your greatest profit lies.

Rotate your stock to keep it interesting. Many people who are furnishing a home or bed-and-breakfast inn—these can be some of your best customers—make a point of browsing through antiques shops every week. They may be looking for just the right mirror to go over a fireplace, a perfect rug for the hallway, or a charming high chair for the nursery. It doesn't take long for those regular customers to become tired of looking at your stock if you never rotate it.

Many successful dealers use a 120-day schedule. If a piece hasn't sold in 120 days, yet they feel it has potential, they remove it from the shop, store it, and fill the space with another item.

They bring that first piece back in a few months. When reintroduced to the sales floor, the antique will be new to many customers and probably forgotten by those who saw it the first time. Its chances of selling are then good, espe-

Item		Purchase Price	Refinishing Costs	Selling Price	Profit	
#212	Rocking chair	$70	$44	$265	$151	57%
#213	Round table	$230	$17	$425	$178	42%
#214	Single bed	$75	$30	$225	$115	51%
#215	Iron lamp	$15	$10	$125	$100	80%
#216	Hoosier cabinet	$325	$40	$455	$90	20%
#217	Small table	$50	$30	$225	$145	64%
#218	Office chair	$35	$30	$195	$130	67%
#219	Small desk	$55	$15	$245	$175	71%

As you can see in the above table, smaller items yield more profit. However, the profits listed above don't include the hours of labor needed to bring these pieces to a saleable state.

cially if you display it in a different place with different accessories. Generally, customers notice accessories first, then the piece of furniture. The concept is similar to that of a woman who can make the same dress look different by the way she accessorizes it.

Dealers in antiques also know that simply shifting stock from one side of a space to another, from one shelf to another, or from back to front can create new interest. Many times a dealer has an item—a teapot, for example—sit on a shelf for months with customers showing no interest. That same dealer might move it to another spot and sell it within three days.

On the other hand, if you find yourself stuck with an obvious mistake, reduce the price and get it out of the store. Better to take a loss than to have customers become bored looking at the same old merchandise.

A word or two about displaying your antiques. Most customers don't like to go into a shop or booth that's too crowded. They're afraid they'll stumble over or break something. So leave enough space around furniture for customers to examine it easily, and keep your shelves full but not jammed with merchandise.

Color is another big factor in sales. It has a psychology of its own that can actually attract or repulse customers. Red, for example, is exciting, sexy, and powerful, but used in excess it can be disturbing. Yellow is cheerful and happy, and, when combined with light green, makes customers think of spring. Green used alone symbolizes quiet forests and coolness. Blue almost universally gives an impression of serenity and peace, water and sky. Think carefully before using

a predominance of orange, purple, or gray in your displays. Many people dislike orange and purple, and gray can be depressing.

Pleasant background music can also help increase sales. While a radio tuned to a soft music station will work, an even better idea might be to play CDs of nineteenth- or early-twentieth-century music to complement your antiques and set the mood. Research has shown that shoppers will gear their own progress through a shop to that of the background music. If the tempo is too fast, they hurry through and make few or no purchases. Slow melodies, on the other hand, encourage them to amble from display to display, making them far more likely to stop and buy.

Granted, if the shop is full of customers chatting and asking questions, no one will hear the music. But on a quiet day soft music can give a shop a pleasant ambience that makes people feel comfortable and encourages them to stay and browse. Many people dislike entering a shop that's too quiet.

(You'll find a more complete discussion of these topics in *How to Start a Home-Based Antiques Business,* also published by The Globe Pequot Press.)

Regardless of how you choose to market your antiques, you'll probably discover that a distinct sales pattern evolves. Little serious antiques shopping goes on during the heat of summer, but fall's crisp weather inspires people to get out and begin prowling through the antiques shops again. Your biggest sales time, therefore, will be from Labor Day until Christmas.

As far as Christmas is concerned, not many people buy large, expensive antiques for Christmas gifts, so always stock a lot of small boxes, framed prints, lamps, mirrors, china, and colored glassware around the end of November. Also make gift certificates available for anyone who doesn't want to chance giving a church pew to his girlfriend when what she really wanted was a player piano.

Even during the balance of the year, from the end of the holiday buying season until Labor Day, you may notice a buying pattern among your customers. To help with your own buying, you'll want to keep a month-to-month record that will show you just what you sold throughout the year. If you find, for instance, that you sell more chairs in May than any other month, you'll know to increase your inventory of chairs in late April, although this may not always be the case. In any event, look for selling patterns and stock accordingly.

You may not want to make selling antiques your full-time occupation. Many of us have other jobs or simply don't want the responsibility of owning and managing a shop. In that case, your best bet is to rent space in a mall or join a co-op.

The Antiques Mall

The most popular concept in merchandising antiques today is for many dealers to rent spaces in a large mall that's managed by someone else. You'll find these establishments all over the country, and they offer you the most opportunity for profit with the least amount of time and financial investment.

Antiques malls work this way: Someone rents or buys a large building, renovates it to accommodate booths of varying sizes, and then subrents the booths out to individual dealers. You may be one of several hundred dealers renting space in a huge antiques mall. You'll find it a great way of having your antiques available to the public every day with virtually no responsibility on your part other than stocking your booth.

You'll pay a monthly rental based on the square footage of your space. In addition to the rent, you'll pay the owners of the mall commission—usually 10 percent—on all sales from your space.

At the end of the month, they give you a printout that lists your sales for the month, along with deductions for commissions and rent. Accompanying the printout is a check that reflects your net income for sales after those deductions.

Most mall dealers use standardized price tags, furnished by the owners. These tags have spaces for your dealer number, your inventory number for the antique to which you've attached it, and the price.

Keep an inventory notebook that lists every antique you place in the mall, the price you paid for it, and the price you place on it. When the item sells, mark it "sold" in the notebook, along with any discount given.

You may have literally hundreds of antiques in your space at any one time. So to make it easy to locate an item in the inventory book, use different categories and have separate pages for separate categories—*SS*, for example, means sterling silver; *G*, glassware; *K*, kitchen collectibles; *F*, furniture; *B*, books; and so on. The first piece of furniture you place in the mall should be listed as *F101*, the second as *F102*, and so forth.

This attractive themed booth in an antiques mall draws lots of customers.

Visit the mall once or twice a week to rearrange the stock, fill in empty places with new stock, and generally spruce things up. The owners of the mall, however, take care of all selling once you place an antique in your space.

Many people come into the mall every day, not to buy, but with antiques to *sell*. The owners of the mall keep a record of which dealers want to buy specific items for resale. If someone comes in with such antiques to sell, the owners will immediately call the dealer. Any negotiations, then, are strictly between the seller of the antiques and the dealer.

You might wonder whether you'd make more money by specializing in a specific type of antique (clocks, for example) or by dealing in a variety. According to the owners of most malls, it really doesn't seem to make much difference. The main caveat is to stock what the public wants to buy, not necessarily those for which *you* have a personal affinity.

The Co-op Antiques Shop

The co-op concept allows several dealers to share the financial and physical responsibilities of owning a shop. In most cases dealers have equal amounts of floor space in the building and pay equal portions of the rent and utilities. They share all other expenses, too—advertising, repairs, decorating, promotions, and so on.

Each dealer also takes a turn at "keeping the store." If six dealers own a co-op, then each works one day a week. If ten dealers own a shop, each works three days a month, with adjustments for February and months with thirty-one days. They usually agree to trade off with one another whenever it's advantageous to all concerned.

The biggest problem with co-op shops is trying to be fair about who works which days. Someone *has* to be there on Saturday, yet most people like to have weekends off to be with family and friends. The only really equitable way to handle this problem, unless one person in the group really wants to work Saturday, is to assign days on a revolving basis. A person would work Thursday one week, Friday the next week, Saturday the next, and so on.

While individual dealers are responsible for keeping their own spaces clean and attractive, the person who keeps the shop on any particular day is usually responsible for sweeping or vacuuming the floor and cleaning the bathroom. He or she also has to reconcile the accounts at closing time, make a bank deposit, and leave enough cash in the till for the start of business the next day.

Partners in a co-op also have to meet regularly to discuss business and any problems that arise. If one partner drops out, the others have to fill in with time and money until another suitable partner can be found. Since this is a cooperative venture, each existing partner should agree upon accepting the new one. There has to be agreement about the quality of antiques to be placed in the shop, the division of labor, the policy on discounts, and so forth. More than one co-op has failed because friction or genuine antagonism arose among members.

(*NOTE:* Some of the information in the following two sections applies to both a home and a commercial antiques shop.)

The In-Home Shop

You may want to turn your living and dining rooms, your lower floor, or your garage into an antiques shop. Fine, but be sure to check the local zoning laws first. Some residential neighborhoods have very strict laws about in-home businesses. You may not be allowed to operate *any* type of business that involves people coming to your home. Other areas will allow the business if you don't hang out a sign. Still others will allow the business and the sign as long as the sign is unobtrusive and the neighbors don't complain about too much traffic at your place.

If you're allowed to have the business but not the sign, you'll just have to attract customers through word-of-mouth recommendation. Many dealers who operate this way don't keep regular business hours. Known as "attic dealers," they're available to their customers by appointment only. While operating an antiques business as an attic dealer is fine for a part-time business, it naturally is seldom as profitable as managing a shop full-time. Many people who started selling

An in-home shop may be the best outlet for your antiques.

antiques as a hobby, however, used this method to "test the water" before going into the business on a larger scale.

The happy compromise between an unadvertised attic shop and commercially rented space is the full-time in-home shop with a sign out front. Who could ask for more? You have the chance to run a profitable business right from your own home, with none of the hassle of driving to work in bad weather and the trouble of maintaining two establishments. You make one mortgage or rent payment, pay one utility bill and one telephone bill, and can deduct a large portion of those bills from your income tax as legitimate business deductions. During slack times you can take care of household duties or work at refinishing stock for the shop. Women who run an in-home shop are there to supervise their children when the school bus unloads in the afternoon.

Your expenses will also be far less than those for

a shop in commercially rented space, enabling you to be more competitive in your pricing. Another advantage is that your customers will see your antiques displayed in a home environment. It'll be easy for a woman to visualize a dining table in her own dining room, for example, when she sees it displayed in what was once *your* dining room.

While dealing in antiques is certainly fun, one owner of an in-home shop warns, "Don't romanticize this business!" It's work and a full-time job. Barring genuine emergencies, your doors must be open for customers at regular hours on specific, stated days. And forget the forty-hour week! Even though your shop is only open four or five days a week, you'll undoubtedly find yourself working fifty, sixty, or more hours every week.

You may find, too, says the owner of one in-home shop, that shoppers won't always respect your posted hours. She says people have even beaten on her shop door at 10:00 P.M., knowing she was home upstairs. Their rationale? They were visitors passing through, had heard about the shop, and just wanted to browse before they drove on.

Another disadvantage of managing a full-time in-home shop is that it certainly can cause some disruption in the family routine. Children must be reasonably quiet while the shop is open, and a portion of the house is off-limits for family activities. Converting the rooms into a shop will cost something, and those expenses must come out of the first profits. These alterations may have to be torn out later, at more expense, if you should decide to abandon your home enterprise and move the shop to commercial space.

An in-home shop can be ideal under certain circumstances, however, and as a bridge between selling antiques as a hobby and selling them in a shop "downtown."

Before you take this step, give yourself a little test. The answers will show quickly just how practical an in-home antiques shop is *for you*.

First, you should ask yourself if you *really* want to take the leap into full-time management of your own business. Many people who genuinely love antiques and can see the profit potential in selling them aren't prepared to be self-employed on a full-time basis.

Take a few minutes to write down answers to the following questions. Be honest!

- Do you have a family background in small business?
- Do you enjoy making decisions?
- Have you served on committees at your church, synagogue, clubs, children's schools, etc.?
- Can you work alone without being lonely?
- Are you in good health?
- Can you plan ahead?
- Do you have (or can you get) any business training?
- Do you get things done on time?
- Are you a self-starter?
- Are you an organized person?
- Do you stick with projects until they're finished?
- Do you have a reputation for having a pleasing personality?

- Are you self-disciplined enough to work regular hours without someone else overseeing your schedule?

- Can you arrange your family and other responsibilities around the hours necessary to run your own business?

- Is your family agreeable to your running a business in the home?

- Will you have a problem with the neighbors?

While there isn't a right or wrong answer to any question, too many "no's" are a signal that you should rethink this important step.

Now, ask yourself about the economics of antiques shops in your area. Are existing ones doing well? If so, your shop would probably succeed, too. If there are no shops nearby, however, ask yourself the reason. Perhaps there isn't a large enough population base to support one. Again, honest answers can help you decide whether opening a shop is financially feasible.

We may live in the space age, but most people will travel to your shop by automobile, and they must have a place to park their cars. Can you provide parking—legally and physically—at your in-home shop? Ideally, this would be in a paved off-street area. Granted, there are probably two or three spaces at the curb in front of your house, but you don't own the street. Anyone has the right to park a car there, quite effectively usurping convenient access by your customers. If at all possible, plan for off-street parking on your premises. Your shop won't only look more businesslike if you do so, but you'll attract more customers.

If this is your first experience in self-employment, you should schedule an appointment with a representative of the Small Business Administration (www.sba.gov). The SBA is a government agency, and this service is free.

You'll probably meet with a retired executive who works with people just like you, advising them about opening and running businesses. While it is highly unlikely that the person you talk with has ever run an antiques shop in a home, he or she will be knowledgeable about the basics of business in your area.

Probably one of the first suggestions this person makes will be for you to write a business plan. This plan has two purposes for the home-based businessperson. It will force you to think through every aspect of your new business, and it will help you chart your progress in the months ahead.

Don't panic! This isn't as complicated as it sounds. You can request a booklet from the SBA that has all the information you'll need to write a good business plan. Your business plan won't be as complex as that of some other types of businesses. It will, however, contain certain items. Among them will be:

- Your business name. If you use any name other than your own, you must register it with your Secretary of State. "Mary Smith Antiques," for example, doesn't require registration. "Smith Antiques Ltd." or "Oak Street Antiques" does.

- A list of start-up costs: for remodeling the room or rooms to be used for your shop, shelving, signs, supplies, permits, subscriptions, advance advertising, etc.

- An advertising budget (usually 1 or 2 percent of projected sales).

- An analysis of paid advertising media (radio and newspapers) in your area to determine which will be the most cost effective for your shop.

- An analysis of the competition. Is it growing or declining? Why is it growing or declining? How will your business be better?

- Your arrangements for liability insurance and coverage on your stock.

- A statement of cash on hand or available.

Regarding that last item, most experts strongly discourage people from going into long-term debt—that is, taking out bank loans—to finance the start of a home-based business. Once you've been in business for a year or two and find a genuine need for expansion, you can then consider approaching your bank for a loan. Until then, pay-as-you-go is the sensible system.

One dealer who made a success of her in-home antiques shop has another wise suggestion. In addition to financing all start-up costs from cash on hand, you should also have in savings enough cash to carry your shop—and your personal expenses if this is your only income—for at least six months. It might take that long for you to establish yourself and begin making a profit.

If you don't already have an accountant and an attorney, make appointments with both to get counseling before you open for business. Many first-time business owners don't hire professionals to help them because they don't know how to choose good ones or how to value their services. There are times, though, when using an accountant and an attorney are critical.

The services of these professionals aren't inexpensive, but working without good ones can be costly in the long run. And if you have a list of questions or concerns *written out* and ready to discuss at your first meetings with them, you'll probably be able to wrap up all your preliminary needs in an hour.

Your accountant. CPAs (Certified Public Accountants) not only help you prepare your tax returns, they can also set up a bookkeeping system for you that's accurate and easy to maintain. They can advise you on a variety of financial matters. Your questions might concern incorporation, record keeping, allowable expenses, estimated tax payments, and so forth.

If you have a friend in business, he or she might be able to recommend a good CPA. CPAs are also listed in the yellow pages. One of the most important criteria in choosing a CPA, however, is that he or she has *extensive experience* working with small businesses. This is vital, because the needs of a small-business owner are quite different from those of an individual or a large corporation. Any CPA you interview should be able to give you references from other clients, and he or she should deal with you openly about fees. He or she should also be willing to come to your business occasionally if you feel you need on-site help.

Your attorney. An attorney can advise you about the legal aspects of operating a shop in your home or at a commercial location. If yours is to be a partnership, or if your accountant recommends incorporation, you should work out those details with an attorney. While the chances of any litigation are slender, it's always wise to have established a personal relationship with an attorney in advance.

Again, a recommendation from an existing client is by far the best way to choose and retain an attorney. Ask your banker, your CPA, or a friend who's in business for their recommendations. Your local Bar Association probably has a referral service, too. This number should be in the yellow pages. As with the CPA, the attorney you choose should specialize in working with small businesses.

Attorneys' fees vary widely, so don't hesitate to ask what the hourly rate is right up front. Attorneys who are associated with large firms usually charge the highest rates. They must support large staffs and expensive locations, and they usually deal with people whose legal needs are quite complicated. As a small businessperson with simple requirements, you'll probably find an attorney in a one- or two-person office a more affordable choice.

Your bank and banker. Your antiques shop may be just a converted garage or living room at first. You may have no employees and work with the simplest bookkeeping system. Even so, you should open a business checking account separate from your personal one. You'll find it infinitely easier to reconcile expenses and deposits that way.

You may already have a good working relationship with an officer at your current bank. If so, stick with that bank. But if for any reason you need to shop for bank services, I'd suggest checking out a small, locally owned bank. After unsatisfactory experiences with large national banks, many people switch to a small, locally owned one. Why? Because they're more friendly and you're not just an account number to them. This can be important to a small businessperson with limited funds and frequent financial needs. When you walk in, the tellers and officers smile and greet you warmly by your first name. They *call* you (instead of mailing a memo that could take days to be delivered) if something comes up you should take care of. If you need assistance in interpreting the phraseology in a contract or some other out-of-the-ordinary service, it's provided cheerfully and quickly.

Your initial banking requirements will be just an account for check writing and deposits. But someday you may need a loan for expansion. You'll get better, faster, and more personal service at an institution where the people know you by sight and name. You won't regret doing business with a small, locally owned bank.

Your insurance agent. You definitely need liability, theft, and fire coverage for your shop. Again, if you're satisfied with the agent who writes your automobile and home insurance, go to him or her first. Agents usually work with only one company, however, and not all companies provide all types of insurance.

If your own agent can't write policies for everything you need, shop around among the insurance brokers in your town. Brokers deal with many companies, not just one, and they'll search the entire industry until they can put together a package that gives you the coverage you need.

Commercially Rented Space

This will be your choice if you're ready to take the plunge and manage a shop in direct competition with other shops in your town.

Think long and hard before you decide just *where* to open this shop. Many businesspeople try to find a location where theirs will be the only department store, drugstore, hardware store, or whatever in the neighborhood. For many types of retailing, this is good business—but not with antiques. Competitive dealers find profits for all actually increase when they cluster their shops near one another.

The mystique of your antiques shop is magnified many times over when you locate it on a street or in a neighborhood with other antiques dealers. The dealers in those areas usually go all out to preserve or create an atmosphere of old-fashioned charm on the shop facades and the street itself. They use flickering gas lanterns, striped awnings, stained-glass transoms over doorways, potted plants on the sidewalk, old English lettering on their signs, used-brick and barnwood exteriors, and anything else within reason to maintain the atmosphere of "days gone by."

Those who love antiques thrive on this relief from the concrete, plate glass, and steel that dominate most architecture today and find any excuse to visit and linger in such a neighborhood. The same urge usually isn't triggered by the lone antiques shop incongruously squeezed in between a fifteen-story bank and Joe's Pizza Palace.

Antiques collectors are inveterate browsers, prowling from one store to another, sometimes for days or weeks, before finally making a purchase. You can see this for yourself by taking up a post in a neighborhood where antiques shops cluster. Stand on the sidewalk on a Saturday and watch the people weaving in and out of the shops, first on one side of the street and then on the other. Most will visit *every* shop in the neighborhood at least once before deciding to buy. This is commonly referred to as "going antiquing," a phenomenon not found in any other business. It's a quest—a concentrated search for that one item needed to fill out a collection. Or it can be a pleasant way to spend the afternoon.

Therefore, each one of the shops in the area has a chance to sell to virtually every person who is seriously interested in buying. The lone shop on the other side of town just isn't in the same ball game.

For example, an 84-square-mile area in the Catskills resort area of New York contains more than one hundred thriving antiques shops. Pine Street in Philadelphia offers several dozen dealers that have been there for decades. These are quite successful, largely because collectors *know* the areas by reputation and know they will have hundreds of thousands of antiques from which to choose there. Emulate their success when you open your shop. You'll never suffer by having your competition next door.

We can't always dictate our circumstance in life, though, and you may not be within reasonable distance of such a cluster of antiques shops. In that case, you must make your shop so desirable that people will drive miles out of their way to seek you out. You might offer the lowest prices in the county, have the largest selection of antiques or the most interesting collection, or specialize in a particular type of antique. And don't skimp on highway signs pointing the way to your shop. A large sign inviting motorists to TURN HERE TO GRANNY'S ATTIC ANTIQUES SHOPPE will entice curious buyers in your direction.

MERCHANDISING TECHNIQUES

You will probably want to be a step ahead of your competition in some way, especially when you first open your shop. Perhaps you can stay open until 5:30 P.M. when other shops close at 5:00. When other shopkeepers on the block shepherd their customers out at closing time, those same customers may gravitate to the one that's still open. And interestingly enough, these last few minutes of the sales day are often when many shops make the fastest sales. People have finished "looking" and are ready to buy, so the shop that's still open is the one most likely to make the sales.

Maybe you can devise some type of sales incentive that will make buying at your shop a little more attractive than at other shops. One dealer signed up with the local welcome service and offers a 10 percent discount on every new customer's purchase. You might price your antiques just a bit lower than the competition for the first few months, until you develop a following.

One good selling technique used by almost every successful antiques shop is a file of customer "wants." All this takes is a card file box and a supply of 3- x 5-inch cards. Whenever someone asks for an item you don't have in stock, just note the item and the person's name, address, and phone number on a card. File the card under the item, and then when you get one in, call the customer or drop him or her a note. Most people appreciate this personal touch, and you'll make many sales that would otherwise be lost.

Also, if you have a computer, ask your customers for their name, address, phone, and e-mail address. Prepare an e-mail group using the e-mail addresses from your customer contact list or a regular mailing list from their physical addresses. Once every two or three months, send out a list of new antique acquisitions, highlighting several special items. This will ensure that customers will keep coming back. And don't forget to note what type of items each customer collects under their name on your master list.

PUBLICIZING YOUR BUSINESS

Your budget must include a substantial sum for advertising, promotion, and publicity. Many newcomers to retailing may cringe at the thought of paying hard-earned dollars to advertise their businesses, especially when "everything is going out and nothing is coming in." Yet the fact remains, you must spend some money up front to attract the customers who will ensure the success of your shop.

One of this country's most successful businessmen had a motto he consistently reiterated to the men and women who bought franchises from him. It was, "Early to bed and early to rise, and *advertise, advertise, advertise!*" It's excellent advice.

Your grand opening is the first opportunity to make a big splash with the antiques lovers in your community. Play this for all it's worth. Place display ads in your local papers announcing the date and flagging some special inducement for customers to visit the store. This might be a 10 percent discount on every item purchased the first day, a drawing for a free gift certificate, refreshments, flowers for the first twenty customers who visit the store, or something of the sort.

A feature story about the shop in the local newspaper on the same day the ad appears will triple the impact of that ad, and the story is *free*. To get that feature story, make an appointment, a couple of weeks in advance, with the editor at the newspaper who handles stories about new businesses. Call the local newspaper to get this person's name.

Pull out all the stops when you sit down across the desk from this person. Appear enthusiastic, knowledgeable, and interesting. Hand the editor a typed press release that gives all the details about you, your shop, and the grand opening. Include the five *W*s of journalism—who, what, where, when, and why—in the release, and bring along a clear black-and-white glossy photograph of yourself taken at the shop. Ask a local advertising agency or a journalism student to prepare the release and photograph if you don't have expertise in those areas. Ask the editor to send a reporter to the shop if at all possible to get more information for the story.

Make your shop as festive as possible on the day of the grand opening. Place flowers near the cash register and at several other locations throughout the showroom. Play soft but lively music and station yourself near the front door to greet each person who enters. If the area's zoning code allows, you might place some type of attention-getting device on the outside of the building. This could be twinkling lights on a pair of potted trees or anything else that's in good taste yet will attract the attention of passersby.

After the grand opening keep up a small but steady advertising campaign. Most antiques shops don't run large, expensive display ads regularly. A small ad in the classified section under "Antiques" is usually enough, since most people who are searching for antiques will look there first. Change the ad weekly, featuring a half dozen or so different items each week. Make sure the name and address of your store is either in boldface type or capital letters.

Join the local merchants' association to take advantage of any group advertising and promotion possibilities.

Try to get your name and the name of the store in the news section of the newspaper occasionally, too. Perhaps you could dress in turn-of-the-twentieth-century clothing on the anniversary of your town's founding or some other date of local historical importance. You could offer to take pictures of each customer who visits the store dressed in period costume on that date. A local museum curator could judge the costumes, and you could give a prize for the one deemed most authentic. Arrange to display an especially valuable antique from the collection of a local person. Perhaps you could acquire an unusual antique to sell on consignment, one that would warrant a notice in the newspaper. Arrange for a well-known local historian to give a series of short talks at the shop. Perhaps he or she could give a walking tour of the neighborhood, beginning and ending at your shop. Above all, be creative.

DECORATING YOUR SHOP

Not very many years ago, antiques shops were often stodgy places decorated with crystal chandeliers and Oriental rugs. Antiques were for the rich, and the sales staff—men dressed in tailored suits and women in tailored dresses—acted like well-trained British butlers and maids. Many potential customers stayed away from these exclusive shops because they thought the prices would be out of their range—and they usually were. Also, they didn't want to seem ignorant to those who knew so much about the fine pieces they were selling.

At the other extreme were the dark, musty-smelling "Old Curiosity Shoppes," their goods piled high in a massive jumble. These appealed to people who liked to search through them for hidden treasures.

Today, all that's changed—thanks to the *Antiques Road Show,* hundreds of antiques books, and Web sites on the Internet that have educated the buying public. Sure, many high-end shops are just as formal, but their owners know that if they don't welcome everyone, they just might miss the sale of a lifetime from the person who looks down-and-out but who, in reality, is actually a millionaire. And those who still run junky antique shops know what every item is worth. In fact, they're often the worst places to shop because they seldom price their antiques. Instead, they wait for a not-so-knowledgeable customer to wander in and then decide what the price will be on the spot, depending on the person's appearance.

Things have taken a distinct turn for the better. Today's successful antiques shop is more likely to be a clean, warm, inviting store where the customer is welcomed in an atmosphere of down-home friendliness. Many store owners are "going natural" to reinforce this ambience, covering their shop walls with quaintly patterned wallpaper and old barn siding. They're using hanging plants and curtains in the windows. They're aiming for a sense of rustic warmth that encourages customers to enter and linger. Unless you plan to deal in only the most expensive and rare antiques, you should plan your store decor to follow the popular "country" theme.

Your storefront windows can be an excellent silent salesperson and attract many customers if you decorate them well. One dealer always features one or two real "crowd stoppers" in his front window. These might be an exceptionally lovely press-back rocking chair and chest of drawers or a charming child's high chair and cradle. These items are always in the middle price range and are clearly marked so the price is visible to casual passersby. He wants people to know that he has high-quality merchandise at a fair price. He usually has a colorful stained-glass piece hanging in the window, too. A permanent fixture in his tall window is a potted tree that adds color and graceful lines to the featured arrangement. You'll find, as he does, that well-decorated windows are well worth the time they take to prepare.

A lot of people who come into your shop will be browsers. They simply love antiques and want to enjoy looking at them. Many, however, will be searching for a specific item to fill a specific need. They may need a set of six mahogany chairs to complement their Duncan Phyfe table, a sturdy maple end table to hold the CD player in the living room, or a Victorian rosewood bed for a child's bedroom. You can help them envision your antiques filling those needs if you arrange your merchandise in room groupings rather than just line them up like boxes of cereal at the grocery store. This will help customers picture the way an antique would actually look in a home setting. You'll lose fewer sales because of that old "I wish I knew how it would look with my furniture."

Go another step toward more sales by using accessories that dramatize the beauty and usefulness of the antiques. Place attractive fresh or dried floral arrangements on some of the end tables, and accent the charm of others with a few old books. Put some nice antique china and crystal on the shelves of a glass-fronted china cabinet. Hang some pretty hand-embroidered linens on the upper bar of a washstand and drape a scarf or two over the hanging hooks of a hall tree. All of these small decorative touches will make the individual antiques more appealing as well as add color and pizzazz to the entire shop. Few things are as dull as a shop filled with brown furniture and no bright, colorful touches.

About once a week get to work early enough to rearrange most of the furniture. Switch groupings around so repeat customers don't see the same old arrangements every time they stop in. Sometimes an antique will look completely different in one setting than it does in another. This is one of the easiest ways to increase both interest in your stock, and sales. After you've finished moving the furniture, take another half hour or so to go over each piece with some good furniture polish. This one act, neglected by so many dealers, can go a long way toward increasing the desirability of your merchandise.

Plenty of good strong light is also necessary if customers are to see the beauty of the wood and the lovely lines of your stock. Track lights are useful to highlight walls, which may be too dark to show off your wares properly. Place several lamps, floor or table, throughout the store. Your cus-tomers will find their soft pools of golden light inviting, cheerful, and homelike.

Also, keep a few of those floor and table lamps lit at night. Many customers will come back during the day to inspect an antique they glimpsed while window shopping the night before.

STOCKING YOUR STORE

One of your biggest problems as the owner of an antiques shop may be developing and maintaining a reliable source of stock. You'll have filled your shop when you open, of course, but with any kind of luck, you'll begin selling quickly. Each piece you sell must soon be replaced with another or your shop will begin to look empty. This means you must have the time to find and refinish as necessary a continuous supply of antiques.

Most antiques shops are open about eight hours a day, six days a week. Will those nonworking evenings and days off be enough for you to get out and scout around for new stock? They may not be if you're trying to handle every aspect of the business alone. You shouldn't have any trouble hitting a few carefully selected garage sales on Saturday mornings before you open the shop, but what about the antiques and estate auctions on Saturday afternoons?

Assuming you hire part-time sales help so you can leave the shop occasionally on buying forays, will you have the time to refinish the antiques you do buy? Will you be willing to give up your free evening and Sunday hours for refinishing? This could quickly get to be a real drag. One dealer solved this problem by having his workshop in the back of his antiques shop. Actually, it was almost a part of the selling floor, with just a

Use accessories like these quilts and dolls to dramatize the antiques in your shop.

waist-high barrier separating the two. He did a great deal of his refinishing and repairing there during business hours while keeping an eye out for customers. He didn't do any stripping, sanding, or varnishing during business hours, however, because of the odor and noise.

This dealer managed to do an incredible amount of work on his antiques by utilizing slow hours in the shop. This meant he couldn't wear dress clothes to work. Jeans, a sturdy shirt, and casual shoes were the order of the day, but his customers didn't seem to mind the unconventional dress. In fact, his "regulars" actually looked forward to hanging over that barrier and chatting with him as he worked. They'd stop in just to see "what was cooking in the back room" and occasionally become so entranced with an antique in the works that they'd come back later and buy it. This dealer managed to keep his shop well stocked by combining these two facets of the business.

If you don't care to run your shop so casually, the solution might be to own your shop jointly with a partner who could share the buying, refinishing, and selling chores. A partner would also free you to make out-of-town buying trips to one of the several areas in the country where antiques are plentiful. Many dealers regularly take trucks to the Midwest and buy enough antiques to keep them in business for six months or more. Iowa seems to be a favorite spot, but some make wide-ranging forays that cover half the country. They attend country auctions, place "antiques-wanted" ads in small-town newspapers, and buy from wholesalers in many states.

These wholesalers run ads in the antiques-industry trade papers. Dealers contact them and examine their stock. They determine if the prices are compatible with making a profit "back home." If so, the dealer finalizes the deal and loads up the truck for the trek home. These wholesalers are especially valuable to the dealer who lives in an area particularly devoid of antiques.

While the antiques business isn't as faddish as some, trends *do* develop, and the wise dealer keeps on top of them. It will do no good, for instance, to have a shop full of beautifully refinished formal mahogany Chippendale- and Hepplewhite-style furniture if 90 percent of the people in your area are buying casual, turn-of-the-twentieth-century oak.

You should constantly research current information about your trade. You can keep up on *overall* trends in the antiques business by reading the half dozen or so excellent trade journals on the market. To judge local tastes, though, you can hardly do better than to attend local antiques auctions, as mentioned earlier in this chapter.

Many successful dealers follow the "rule of three" when stocking their shops. They try to have three of any one type of item—china cabinets, for instance. One china cabinet will be priced to sell quite low. Another might have curved glass and claw feet and be priced in the middle range. The third will be a real bell-ringer with a beveled mirror, lovely carved trim, and stained-glass inserts, and with a correspondingly high price tag. This gives customers a good selection without overwhelming them with too many options. If you had only one china cabinet, the customer might understandably think, "This is nice, but I really should shop around before I buy." By offering three cabinets in a range of styles and prices, you have a much better chance of making a sale before the customer leaves your shop.

Be cautious about investing in any antique, no matter how beautiful, that won't fit into the average home or apartment. Some dealers fall into that trap and live to regret it. One dealer bought a magnificent secretary that he was sure would sell right away. It was truly beautiful and the most imposing he had ever seen. That was the trouble, though. Counting the lovely carved "bonnet" at the top, the secretary stood 9 feet tall. Most ceilings today are 8 feet high. Many customers admired the piece, but it took eighteen months before someone came along who had not only the money to purchase such a beauty, but the 10-foot ceilings to accommodate it. Fortunately, this was the only "dog" in his shop, because no dealer can make it with such a slow turnover of stock.

One way to survive the inevitable slow periods is to have a good supply of inexpensive antiques that will sell readily. It's usually far easier, for instance, to sell four Art Nouveau lamps at $95 than one bookcase at $395. Many dealers, therefore, keep plenty of framed prints, small mirrors, lamps, and "collectibles" on hand. Some go much further and handle a wide variety of small nonfurniture items—sterling silver souvenir spoons, china cups and saucers, dolls, crystal stemware, embroidered linens, and so forth. These can be sold for anywhere from a couple of dollars to $30 or $40—the price range many people seek when buying gifts.

Also, it takes much less time and materials to refinish, say, a small storage cabinet or a wooden clock case than it does an armoire, bed, or sideboard. You'll also find that you can charge more for the smaller items because of their high demand as gifts than you can for larger pieces, thus increasing your profit on each piece.

You might also consider carrying a line of fine furniture polish. One dealer keeps a few bottles of an excellent polish, especially made for antiques, near the cash register. When the customer asks him, "How shall I care for my antique?" he has a ready answer. He suggests a bottle of the polish, and the customer invariably buys one. The dealer makes a couple of dollars' profit on the polish, and the customer is delighted to have this high-quality product to care for the antique.

Some dealers also add to their profit potential, as well as add color to their shops, by selling hand-crafted, old-fashioned-looking accessories on consignment. These could include pieced and quilted pillows, needlepoint pictures, embroidered aprons and linens, or any other type of high-quality gift item. The dealer takes a 10 or 15 percent commission on the selling price in exchange for handling the sale. Just be careful that you don't go overboard with the artsy-craftsy things. One dealer so loaded her shop down with pot holders, quilts, stuffed dolls, and linens that customers could hardly find the antiques! She eventually went out of business, even though three other antiques shops on the block thrived.

You'll almost surely have to have some sort of layaway plan. Be prepared with a rubber stamp that details the terms of the agreement, and then imprint this stamp on the face of the sales receipt. The stamp should state the number of days the item will be held. Most stores allow ninety days

Household and kitchen items make great inexpensive items to sell that can also accessorize the antiques in your booth or shop.

for an item to be paid off and picked up. Ask for a 25 or 30 percent down payment and the balance in weekly or monthly installments.

Sometimes a purchase will have to remain in the store for days, weeks, or even months after the sale until the buyer has a place for it or until it is paid for. If you're crowded for space and have antiques waiting to be brought out onto the sales floor, you'll probably want to move the sold piece into the storeroom or closet. If you have the space to spare, however, you can subtly advertise the fact that your antiques sell well by using some distinctive red cards printed with SOLD in bold black letters. Place one of these on every antique that's sold but waiting for pickup or delivery. The cumulative effect of a few of these cards on a customer is undeniably, "This is a successful shop where sales happen fast. If I see something here I want, I'd better buy it because it may not be here long."

A useful, attractive, and reasonably priced antique will sometimes sell itself, especially if the customer makes several return visits to the store to examine it. You'll make many more sales, however, and more often on the customer's first visit, if you use some of the proven techniques of selling these luxury items. Many consider antiques, like diamonds, to be luxury items as well as excellent investments.

You'll find the following three methods to be particularly useful when showing an antique to a customer. First, demonstrate the beauty of the wood's patina and the sturdiness of the construction. Explain that the craftsmen who made furniture years ago took a great deal of pride in their work. Each piece was lovingly manufactured and finished with an eye to lasting through many generations. Such isn't the case with most modern furniture.

Second, explain the investment potential of an antique. Quality antiques increase in value every year. Barring a major depression, experts see no reason for this trend not to continue. At the same time, a piece of modern furniture, regardless of its original value, can lose up to 80 percent of the selling price as soon as it leaves the store. It immediately becomes just used furniture.

Third, try to find some interesting tidbit of information you can give the customer about the particular antique under consideration. You might tell about the people who would have used such a piece and why it was popular at a particular period. This is where a good background in the history of antique furniture can be invaluable. A dealer had a pretty little mahogany table once that usually attracted only casual attention. It was only when she told some customers that the table was a lady's writing desk circa 1865 that they became really entranced with the graceful lines and color of the wood. Suddenly they could visualize a hoop-skirted belle sitting there as she penned letters to a beau at some far-off military post. Because of her anecdote, the table developed a personality of its own. Before that it was just a table.

Don't hover over your customers with a constant stream of chatter. Many people like to inspect an antique, go away, think about it, and then come back to buy. You can irritate and alienate customers by being *too* enthusiastic.

Once your shop is in operation, you can increase your sales volume immensely by forming an alliance with the interior decorators in your town. Decorators often have a free hand in decorating the homes and offices of well-to-do clients, and they usually don't quibble about prices. You'll find working with them an excellent way to place your most expensive pieces. You might invite all the decorators in town to a festive after-hours wine-and-cheese party at the shop. This would give you a chance to show off your antiques in a relaxed, social atmosphere.

Running an antiques shop successfully means you must be a good businessperson, of course. You should have a flair for merchandising, know how to promote your business, and be able to get along with customers. Even more important, according to many studies, you must have a thorough knowledge of antiques. If you know and love antiques and can discuss them with enthusiasm, your customers will have confidence in you as a dealer.

Increase a customer's knowledge of antiques by cheerfully sharing your own, and you'll make friends with everyone. They'll come back to you as a dealer because they'll have confidence in your expertise and because they, too, want to become more knowledgeable about antiques.

Many, many antique dealers had absolutely no prior experience at retailing before they opened their own shops. But the vast majority of those antiques shops are successes today, mainly because practically no one goes into this business unless he or she really loves antiques. Add some basic knowledge to this love and good merchandising, and you have a winning combination that's hard to beat.

The preceding pages can only give you a brief explanation of the many factors involved in owning an antiques shop. If you're serious about opening your own shop, read *How to Start a Home-Based Antiques Business* (also published by The Globe Pequot Press), which details valuable information you should have before venturing into business as the operator of an antiques shop, whether home-based or in commercially rented space.

CHAPTER 11

OTHER WAYS TO MAKE MONEY WITH YOUR ANTIQUES

You may become seriously involved in restoring antiques and want to start making a profit on your "hobby," an avocation more accurately described by longtime buffs as an "obsession" and a "disease." Yet you may not have the desire or time to manage an antiques shop or even rent space in an antiques mall. However, several other options are open to you.

SELLING ON CONSIGNMENT

One answer is to sell on consignment through other people's shops. Hundreds of antiques dealers sell their wares this way, and it could well be the most satisfactory method for you, too.

Consignment selling is quite simple. In return for certain services, you give the shop owner a commission of a certain percentage on each sale. This percentage varies from community to community but averages between 15 and 30 percent of the sales price. However, this percentage is often negotiable.

One woman placed her antiques in several shops at several different commission rates. The terms depended on the services she received and the shop owner's enthusiasm about having her merchandise in the store. Sometimes, if you find just the right situation, you can pay a commission as low as 10 percent. You can seldom work out such a deal, however, unless antiques are *not* the shop's main source of revenue. Many merchants today realize that a few pieces of antique furniture add a touch of elegance to their places, in addition to being excellent for displaying merchandise. An owner of a small gift shop had hundreds of charming stuffed animals, pot holders, quilts, wood carvings, wall plaques, and door decorations. Each item in her shop was on consignment from one of dozens of creative men and women. The shop owner had nice merchandise but rather poor display methods, so a friend, who refinished antique furniture, approached her with the idea of putting a couple of small tables and a few chairs in her shop. The idea delighted her since her merchandise would be far more attractive when displayed on antique pieces. The understanding was that each of her friend's antiques would be plainly marked with a sales price.

This worked out quite well, since her license specifically covered consignment merchandise. Thus, she had no legal or contractual problems in selling her friend's antiques. She just sent her friend a check, minus her 10 percent commission, each month to cover sales. She collected the tax and included it with her own reports.

Another deal, with a prestigious men's clothing shop, was a bit different. The store, tastefully decorated in a Victorian motif with stained-glass chandeliers and thick carpets, with classical music playing in the background, seemed like the ideal place for antiques. Though putting some antiques in his shop, not only for display but also to carry out the old-fashioned theme, interested the owner, his business license didn't cover consignments, so he couldn't sell antiques. But this turned out to be no real problem. Whenever a customer showed an interest in one of the antiques, the shop owner just gave him one of the refinisher's business cards and asked him to get in touch with him personally. The customer and the refinisher worked out the sales arrangements between themselves. The shop owner never handled any money or collected any taxes for the refinisher, but the refinisher did give him a 10 percent "finder's fee" on each sale from his shop.

Most antiques consignment deals, however, are with the owners of antiques shops. And on the whole, this is where you'll have the best luck with consignment selling.

Placing antiques on consignment is also an excellent way to help you decide whether you really want to get into this business before you rent mall space, join a co-op, or open a shop. You can place a few items on consignment with the owner of a shop, then sit back and see if you feel your profits are high enough to justify the time and effort involved in locating and restoring them.

You can also use this method if you move to a part of the country where you know little about what will sell there and how much people will pay for antiques. In this case, approach the owner of the best antiques shop in town and ask if she'd take a few things on consignment. If she agrees, bring in a few of your best pieces—perhaps a small table, a nineteenth-century fireplace screen, and a small dresser. Pay attention to what sells and what doesn't and adjust your consignments accordingly.

Disadvantages as well as advantages do exist, of course, with consignment selling, and you should understand them before going into any such arrangement with another dealer.

Some of the advantages are:

- You gain excellent and continuous exposure for your antiques in the ideal showcase—a shop where people come specifically to browse and/or buy antiques.

- Shop owners who have the space usually are quite happy to work with you as a consignor, since they risk none of their own capital yet have an opportunity to make a profit on your antiques.

- You don't have to manage a shop and deal with customers. Someone else handles sales and gets the merchandise out the door.

- You usually develop a close friendship with the store owner. This is valuable in helping you learn more about the business of buying and selling antiques.

Some disadvantages of consignment selling are:

- You must pay the consignee a substantial commission for displaying and selling your antiques.

- You can't control all circumstances regarding your antiques while they are in the shop (theft, fire, damage) since they aren't in your physical possession.

- You can't control the way your antiques are displayed. Many retailers give the best selling spots to their own merchandise rather than to consignment items.

- Any retailer, given a choice between pushing his or her own merchandise or yours to a customer, will quite naturally choose the former.

Your relationship with the store owner is called an *agency relationship*. This means he or she never takes title to the merchandise but acts only as your agent in passing title to the buyer. Therefore, since the consignee never *owns* the merchandise, any liability for loss remains with you. You may be able to make an agreement with a consignee to share any loss, but in the absence of such an agreement, you're responsible for any loss involved.

You need to be aware of other legal implications of consignment selling. First, you should have a contract with the consignee that stipulates exactly what the terms of the agreement might be. This can be a quite simple document as long as you spell out all the facets of the relationship. The terms should include such items as which of you picks up and delivers the antiques to the shop, the amount of the commission the consignor pays the consignee, and the length of time the consignee will keep the antiques in the shop. You should specify which of you has the final say on pricing and that no price (once decided upon) will be reduced without your knowledge. You should have a clear statement of how and when payment will be made to you for those antiques that sell.

By and large, the following is an accurate statement of the status of a consignment agreement, based on many court decisions:

- The consignor may demand return of the merchandise at any time.

- The title rests with the consignor until the merchandise is sold. At that point, the title moves directly to the buyer and never passes through the consignee.

- The consignee may return unsold goods at will and without obligation.

- The consignee is authorized to sell the goods only at the specified price or not less than the agreed-upon price.
- The consignee must forward proceeds of any sale immediately to the consignor or deposit them in a special account.

Don't be frightened away from consignment selling by all this legal talk. If you have any doubts, consult your attorney. Thousands of antiques are sold this way every year, quite to the satisfaction of everyone involved.

SELLING FROM YOUR HOME

Another way you can run a part-time antiques business is by selling from your home. The nice thing about this is that you have absolute control over the date, time, location, and items involved in the sale.

You can sell one or two antiques at a time if you like. Look in the classified section of your daily newspaper under the "Antiques" listing. You'll probably see a few ads offering buffets, tables, dressers, or whatever. Some of these ads, of course, were placed by people who simply want to sell the antique because they have no use for it. A few, however, will probably be placed by people who sell antiques regularly as a part-time business. They find this method of advertising to be highly effective and quite economical.

You'll increase your ratio of sales if you have *several* of the same type of item to sell each time you run an ad, but you actually only list *one* of them. For instance, your ad might read:

Antique rocking chair, completely refinished, excellent condition. $275. 555–8233.

Now, you might actually have three rocking chairs of different descriptions and selling for different prices. So when the phone calls start coming in, you just describe all *three* rocking chairs to each caller. The chances are at least one of your descriptions will intrigue each caller, and he or she will be interested enough to come by your home. When the first rocker sells, you just describe the two remaining rockers to the next callers. When another sells, you describe the third and last rocker to the callers. You could, of course, describe all three rocking chairs in the ad, but that would make it quite long and expensive. This little trick can save you many dollars in advertising costs.

If you have several types of antiques to sell at one time, you should list each one. You might run an ad that says:

ANTIQUES *for sale! Oak princess dresser, $195; mahogany dining table, $650; walnut Victorian bed, $350; matching commode, $225. All completely refinished. 555–6655.*

Don't use such terms as *much more* to indicate additional items. Most people who are looking for a specific piece of furniture won't respond to an ad unless that item is listed. Including your cell phone number, if you have one, in your ad will allow you to go about your business without being tied to your home or business phone.

An easier and more effective way to sell from your home is to have one big sale a year. Set aside one Saturday and plan to do nothing else that day except show and sell your antiques. You'll save time, and you'll draw a large crowd of buyers who may come for one item but actually end up buying more.

An ad for this type of sale might read:

BIG ANTIQUES SALE!
Library table, marble-topped lamp table,
set of four chairs, odd side chairs, rocking chairs,
fern stand, fainting couch,
pine commode, dressers, china cabinet,
floor lamps, frames, mirrors.

Saturday, June 14, 8:00 A.M. to 4:00 P.M.
123 McKinley Drive

I guarantee such an ad will draw a crowd! Notice that you don't list your phone number in this ad. You don't want to spend time on the phone describing all those pieces of furniture. And you don't want to give people a chance to wheedle you into showing them your wares at another time than that stated for your sale day.

One word of caution about such a sale: You should check local zoning laws to make sure such a sale is legal in your neighborhood. This is really not a garage sale, and you might be bending some regulations about in-home businesses. In any event, I would advise you to charge sales tax on every sale *if* you have applied for and received a license as a legitimate dealer. Most communities regard any sale made by a dealer to be taxable, whether that sale is made in a shop, in a home, at a show, or wherever.

General Hints on Advertising

Regardless of the kind of sale you plan, you should know a few basic rules of effective news-paper advertising. Follow these guidelines, and you can hardly go wrong:

- Catch the reader's attention in some way. Often this will be by having the word *antiques* in uppercase letters as the first word in the ad. Use large-size type and don't crowd it. White space may cost you more money, but it's a good way to make your ad stand out in those long columns of closely set type. If your newspaper offers such a service, you might set your ad off with a star or check mark. These are good attention getters.

- Include the price of each item if that's practical. Most readers like to know the price of something before they inquire about it. You won't be able to do this if you have a long list of antiques that includes several similar items with different prices.

- Use simple words and short sentences. Don't use meaningless phrases such as *priced to sell.* Why else would you be running the ad if you hadn't priced the things to sell? Make every word a selling word. Use descriptive adjectives so people will be intrigued about the item. *Curved-glass oak bookcase secretary with beveled mirror* would be better than *oak secretary,* for instance.

- Avoid abbreviations. Make it easy for readers to understand and respond to your ad. Don't make them wade through underbrush such as *rosewd. Q. Anne din. tabl., 6 chrs., perf. cond.*

- Run the ad long enough for it to be seen by a large number of people. Not everyone reads the paper every day. It's usually less expensive day for day to contract for a seven-day rate than a three day rate, for instance. You can always cancel the ad if the item sells the first day or so, then get a refund on the unused time.

- If your paper has a "bargain box" section in the classified pages, be sure to use it. This section, which lists only items under a certain price, is often the first read by many people. Some local papers, for instance, list items for $500 and less in this section. The fee for listing an item in this section is very low. Use this section whenever you have something you can sell for a low price and still make a profit.

- Take advantage of the expertise of the ad writers at the paper. They're trained to write "selling" ads and can help you word yours for the best effect.

SELLING AT ANTIQUES SHOWS

There isn't any other way to expose your antiques to more people in less time with less effort than by "working the shows," as it's known in the trade. If you've never attended an antiques show, be sure to go to the next one in your area. You'll be amazed at the amount of buying and selling going on. Instead of waiting for the customers to come to them, the dealers at these shows have, essentially, gone to where the buyers congregate. These buyers come looking for good merchandise, and they're willing to pay a reasonable price for their purchases.

The beauty of this type of selling is that an antiques show attracts so *many* of those buyers. Literally thousands of potential customers walk through the aisles of most shows—collectors, dealers, and casual buyers. For this reason, renting a booth at a good antiques show can return more profit per hour than any other form of selling antiques. To make this profit, however, you must have a good stock of those antiques that are most in demand.

As with selling from the home, selling at a show also allows you control over your time. While some of the larger shows may go on for a week or two, most smaller ones are held on weekends, so the part-time antiques dealer can easily work the schedule around other commitments. Most part-time antiques dealers work one or two shows a year in their own towns, in contrast to the full-time dealers who set up a circuit that may include twenty or more shows across the country a year.

How do you get involved in working the shows? Start by attending every one within reasonable driving distance of your home. You'll find they come in all sizes. Some of the smaller ones may have space for only twenty or thirty exhibitors, while the real "biggies" in cities such as New York, San Francisco, Denver, and Philadelphia may attract hundreds of dealers.

Each show will be staged by a promoter of one kind or another. Frequently, the promoter will be a nonprofit organization such as a church or service club. These people are raising operating capital for their organizations through booth rental and entrance fees. Other shows will be organized by regular professional promoters who also work the show circuit, holding shows in many cities across the nation. They, of course, are in business, and all the profit after expenses goes to them. The professionals may sometimes have a bit of an edge over the nonprofit folks when it comes to sophistication, but that isn't always the case. Enthusiasm for their cause can make real go-getters of the volunteers when it comes to putting on a good show.

Each promoter will arrange for preshow publicity in the media. This is vitally important since it's the only way most buyers know about the show. So, judge for yourself the effectiveness of that publicity. Are press releases in the local paper backed up with spots on radio? Did the promoter put flyers in each antiques shop in town and any other spots likely to attract the attention of antiques buyers? Is there a large, attention-getting banner outside the hall where the show is held? These are the types of things that will bring eager buyers to the show and money into your pocket.

At each show you should wander around and get a feeling for the likely success of the affair. Is the building large enough to hold the dealers' booths and still allow plenty of room for customers to walk around with ease? Is the room well lit? Are there adequate parking facilities for customers? Is some sort of food and drink available for customers? A good promoter looks to all facets of the show, not just to getting the dealers in.

Then make another round of the room or rooms and look at the antiques on display. How do they stack up for quality? Would you be proud to show your things alongside the ones in the show? Is every booth filled? Empty booths might indicate poor management on the part of the promoter.

Talk with the dealers. Explain that you're thinking of signing up for the next show. Ask if they're happy with the show's promotion and management. Are they selling enough to justify the trouble and cost of entering the show? Ask if they've shown in that particular show before. People don't rent space a second time in a poorly run or unproductive show.

You might think the dealers would tell you to buzz off and mind your own business after being asked such personal questions. Not likely. All antiques dealers are antiques lovers at heart and like nothing better than to talk about their obsession. To them every acquisition is a conquest and every sale a way of sharing the beauty of their wares. They'll gladly talk with you and advise you about their successes and failures.

If you like all you see and hear at a show, then scout around until you find the promoter. Explain that you're a new dealer and would like to rent space in the next show. You might be surprised to hear that all booths have been rented in advance for the next *two years*. Frankly, there's more competition for space than you realize.

However, you may not have any trouble getting into the next scheduled show, arranged by another promoter. This may lead to referrals to other promoters looking to mount new shows, giving you additional opportunities to sell your pieces.

The procedure for renting space in an antiques show is pretty much the same everywhere. Once you decide on the show you like, and assuming the space is available, you'll be asked to sign a contract. This contract will state the place, time, and date of the next show. It will spell out the promoter's obligations as to advertising, promotion, facilities, etc. It will probably have a blank line where you fill in the type of antiques you will be bringing to the show. And it will list the price you will be charged for booth rental. This could be anywhere from $150 to $200 for a small show to several thousand dollars for one of the glittering events in a major city. You will probably be expected to pay half the rental fee upon signing the contract. The other half is due the first day of the show.

Let's say you've decided on a weekend show that will run from 10:00 A.M. to 9:00 P.M. on a Saturday and from 11:00 A.M. to 5:00 P.M. on Sunday. Usually, you'll be allowed to bring your antiques in on Friday afternoon and evening. The building will be locked and guarded during the nights, so you don't have to worry about theft. You'll set up your display on Friday evening and then arrive an hour or so early on Saturday morning to touch up.

Plan to allow some time for preopening shopping around at the other dealers' displays before the doors open to customers. You can study the other dealers' stocks and check your prices against theirs. Perhaps you'll even find the gateleg table or pier mirror you need for your own collection! Actually, an amazing amount of buying, selling, and trading goes on in that hour before the doors open. As mentioned earlier, you should give a 10 percent discount off your marked prices to other dealers as a courtesy. This is also your chance to get to know your fellow dealers and make some fine friends. They can help you understand trends and marketing of antiques at shows. So be sure to take advantage of this hour before the show actually starts.

Booth size in the average antiques show probably averages about 10 X 20 feet. Imagine such an area, and you can see that it takes a great deal of stock to fill it. You may not have that many antiques to sell at one time. It takes quite a bit of time and capital to acquire and refinish some twenty to twenty-five major pieces of furniture. This doesn't mean you can't have the fun and profit of participating in an antiques show, however. The answer is to share the space and rental fee with another dealer.

Two friends did this for two shows a year. Neither sold antiques full-time at that time, so neither had enough stock to fill a booth, but each could easily manage half the space. Each paid half the rental fee, which made their up-front costs less and their profits higher. One dealt primarily in fine cut glass and the other dealt primarily in furniture, so the first used the second's furniture to display her cut glass. This turned out to be a beautiful arrangement for both of them. Not only did it cut their expenses and make for a full and inviting booth, but antiques shows are more fun when you share it with a friend.

When setting up your booth, always have a few showstoppers to bring the customers in. These pieces should be unique in some way, whether in style, color, or size. Place one or two deep in your booth at the back and another out near the aisle. Generally, you should place larger pieces, such as tall chests or armoires, toward the back so that they don't block the view into your booth. Let's say you have a rustic pine turn-of-the-twentieth-century armoire. You might want to place it at the rear and a set of balloon-back Victorian Rococo Revival side chairs up front. You also have a Victorian Eastlake marble-topped side table, which you place in the center. The

When you rent a booth for an antiques show, to draw in customers try to provide a real showstopper placed near the front, such as this child's pony cart, and a couple placed toward the rear of the booth, such as the nineteenth-century blanket chest and primitive yellow pine sideboard in the background. Place one near the aisle and the other two, which should be larger, toward the back of your booth.

marble-topped table sells within an hour of the show's opening, and the armoire that afternoon. But the side chairs, as beautiful as they are, just sit there. They bring a lot of browsers into your booth, but no one takes the bait. However, all three items, even the armoire with its SOLD sign on the door, attract customers who linger long enough to buy other smaller pieces. So you cart the side chairs back home and display them at a

second show several months later. They sell almost immediately.

Remember, you have to be patient in the antiques business. It's not like you're selling a whole line of side chairs, just two matching ones. And the right customer has got to come along to buy them. However, if the armoire hadn't sold, and you had to cart that around from show to show, it might possibly get damaged—and that's not counting the expense of renting a larger truck to get it to each show. So while it may be a show-stopper, its size and extra expense both in refinishing and delivery can make it a much less profitable item. You might even be forced to lower its price just so you don't have to take it back home.

A popular variation of the traveling or seasonal antiques show is the indoor flea market. Sometimes, these are just tables set up in rows in a firehouse social hall, and sometimes they're a bit more elaborate. But the promoters of these events usually advertise heavily locally, plus, because they're held on the same day of the month or several times each year, they gain a following. Dealers sign up in advance for the 3- x 8-foot tables provided by the promoter, paying him from $10 to $15 for each table they use or a flat amount, say $25 for a space with two tables in it. Sometimes, promoters sell the space and dealers have to bring their own tables. Dealers cover these tables with odd sheets and fabric remnants, then display their glassware, china, and jewelry on them. If the promoter limits space to tables only, you'll have a problem displaying any type of furniture, except perhaps a small child's chair, boxes, table book racks, or a small cabinet. So this type of "show" isn't so good if you're refinishing furniture to sell.

The best type of antiques show for the beginner is a local one, held perhaps twice a year. These are smaller affairs—usually with fifty or sixty dealers. The quality of goods is quite high, but the prices are reasonable, which makes them excellent selling shows. Customers come to them knowing they'll be able to afford the items. It's not uncommon to see happy showgoers carrying out all sorts of items. If the promoter does his job right, there will be good mix of dealers—furniture, memorabilia, china, glass, linens, and so on—so competition won't be as keen. This means you'll be able to ask decent prices for your items and make a profit. Lastly, the biggest advantage to this type of show is the somewhat lower booth rental.

SELLING ON EBAY

It seems that people are selling just about anything on eBay these days—and that includes antiques. This might be the perfect selling venue for you, especially if you're just starting out. While you're not limited to the size of items you sell, you'll have to factor in the delivery cost when you price them. Obviously, smaller items such as wooden boxes, little cabinets, and frames would be better for this market.

Though you need to register before you can sell on eBay, there's no fee. However, you'll have to pay a 2–5 percent commission. Simple directions appear at their main page online (www.ebay.com). EBay offers you millions of registered customers. After registering, you can list one or a dozen items at any one time. In fact, if sales go well for you, you may want to set up an eBay antiques "store." With this arrangement, you can sell some items for auction, soliciting bids from customers, or you can offer them as "Buy It Now" items, in which case you set a price that the customer can pay at any time.

To successfully sell on eBay, you'll need to purchase a digital camera—a three-megapixel model will do just fine—so you can take photos of your pieces. Be sure to keep the backgrounds simple, using sheets as backdrops. To keep the lighting relatively even, shoot in the shade outdoors for larger pieces or purchase photo lights on stands from a photographic supply house such as B&H Photo Video in New York (see the listing at the back of this book). These aren't very expensive and will provide even cross lighting for your smaller objects.

It's also important to describe the object in detail—especially its condition. Too many people have gotten scammed on eBay when sellers show one thing and it turns out to be another. (You'll find additional information about selling on the Internet in *How to Start a Home-Based Antiques Business,* also from The Globe Pequot Press.)

APPENDIX

CAUTIONS

Prevent problems when repairing or refinishing furniture by following these simple precautions:

1. Be extra careful with fumes in your work area. While water-based strippers aren't nearly as powerful as their oil-based cousins, breathing the fumes they create when they react with paint and varnish can make you light-headed and produce headaches. If you begin to feel sick or faint, leave your work immediately and go outdoors for fresh air. Aim a fan at an open window to ventilate your work area. If at all possible, work outdoors so the wind blows the fumes away from you.

2. To avoid breathing in toxic fumes, wear a respirator with an organic-vapor filter. For dusty work, make sure it has a dust filter.

3. *Do not* use any type of bleaching solution indoors without adequate ventilation. And be sure not to use it in combination with other chemicals, such as ammonia or stripper. The combination can produce lethal fumes.

4. Be sure to wear protective clothing—a long-sleeved shirt and pants—when working with chemicals that may harm your skin. Wear protective gloves when working with harsh chemicals such as strippers and bleach.

5. *Always* wear safety goggles or glasses when working with chemicals to prevent any from splashing in your eyes.

6. Throw paint- or chemical-soaked rags away immediately after use. A bag of rags is cheap and safer than trying to be thrifty.

7. Protect all work surfaces with plenty of newspaper, an old sheet, or a shower curtain.

8. Follow the manufacturer's instructions on refinishing products. Pay special attention to the hazard warnings.

9. Keep all tools and dangerous chemicals out of the reach of children and pets. If either ingests chemicals, contact your local poison control center immediately. To be on the safe side, post the number of the poison control center by your phone—even better, add it to your speed dial list.

10. Be sure to store all your refinishing chemicals in a cool, dark place. If you plan to store any unused chemicals or glazes, be sure to label the container accordingly.

11. *Do not* pour old or unused chemicals down any house drain. Dispose of them correctly through your local recycling center. Or call your local government office to find out where to do so.

12. *Do not* drink alcoholic beverages while inhaling potentially toxic fumes. The combination will make you sick.

TIPS FOR MAINTAINING ANTIQUE FURNITURE

The key to maintaining antique furniture is keeping it clean. The following tips will help you do just that without damaging it:

1. Avoid using any of the popular spray dusting helpers. These tend to leave a nasty buildup on furniture that's hard to remove later on. Instead, use a soft cloth to gently wipe away the dust. You can also slightly dampen the cloth with liquid glass cleaner.

2. Avoid using any of the popular oil-based liquid furniture polishers. These leave an oily residue that attracts dust. Lemon oil is one of the worst because it doesn't sink into the wood like commonly thought but lays on the surface, acting as a dust magnet.

3. If there's oily dirt or grease, such as may get on pieces in a kitchen, remove it with a mild dish detergent and water solution. Work on small areas at a time and dry immediately with a soft cloth.

4. Be extra careful when cleaning any wood that has been gilded. The gilt is usually applied with a water-soluble adhesive that can be removed by detergent cleaners.

5. To clean uneven or carved surfaces, use a soft-bristled brush or your vacuum cleaner with the brush attachment. Be careful not to hit the furniture in any way with the vacuum cleaner itself.

6. *Do not* use feather dusters. They move the dust around and can scratch the surface.

7. Before using any cleaner on the surface of your furniture, test an inconspicuous area toward the back first.

8. Always avoid using too much liquid directly on your furniture's surface.

9. You can get long-term protection by using a good paste wax, such as Minwax. This is a petroleum-based product that comes in both natural and dark shades for light- and dark-stained furniture, respectively. The hard surface it produces can be dusted more easily and without the danger of scratching because it's smoother. Waxing once or twice a

year is sufficient for tabletops and chair arms. For less used areas of furniture, such as chair legs and case pieces, wax only every four years.

10. Try not to polish hardware while it's attached to the furniture. The polish will damage the furniture's finish. Instead, remove the hardware and polish separately, being sure to rinse or wipe it thoroughly before reattaching it to your pieces. If you can't remove the hardware from your piece, be sure to mask it from the furniture's surface to prevent damage. For ornate hardware use a cotton swab dipped in the detergent solution.

11. *Do not* polish ormolu, which really isn't brass but bronze. Instead, wash it with a soft cloth soaked with a mild dish detergent.

12. To freshen up your antique furniture, you can use Wood Sheen, a rubbing oil stain and finish made by Minwax that combines tung oil with a coloring agent, available at many hardware stores and home-improvement centers. This product comes in a variety of wood stain colors to match most types of wood. Before use, be sure to dust your furniture with a soft cloth dampened with plain water, then go over the surface again with a dry cloth. Afterward, go over the piece lightly with a pad of extra-fine (0000) steel wool. Wipe the surface again with a damp cloth. Apply a thin coat of Wood Sheen using an old sock and let it dry for an hour or two. *Do not* do this more than once every year or so.

13. To remove the musty odor from an antique cabinet or drawers of a chest, spray with Febreze and let dry. To keep it fresh, place a new dryer sheet inside each cabinet or drawer.

14. If mold or mildew forms on a piece of antique furniture, dampen a soft cloth with a very mild bleach solution (two tablespoons of bleach to a quart of water) and wipe the affected area. Dry immediately with a soft cloth, then wax as stated above.

15. Heat dries out the wood of antique furniture, loosening joints. Keep your house at a comfortable level but not excessively hot in the winter. If you must keep the temperature up, put pans of water around to humidify the air or use a humidifier. The air will be healthier for you, too.

GLOSSARY

Acanthus A graceful leaf design used on all types of furniture, home accessories, and architectural details.

Angel-bed An open bedstead without posts.

Apron The flat horizontal section that separates the top of a table, desk, or chair from the legs.

Armoire A wardrobe for hanging clothing.

Bag sewing table A sewing table that originally had a fabric bag suspended below the drawer to hold work in progress. Popular during the first half of the nineteenth century.

Balloon back A favorite Victorian-style chair back, resembling an inflated balloon.

Baluster The leg of a piece of furniture, often a central column on a table. Usually has bulbous sections alternating with smaller turned sections.

Balustrade A series of balusters supporting a rail.

Banding A thin strip of veneer used to decorate the top or edge of a piece of furniture; always of a different type of wood from the body of the piece.

Banister A slender baluster.

Baroque A fanciful, ornate style of decoration using many extravagant curves and much deep carving.

Beading A narrow wooden molding used by furniture makers as a decorative finish to their pieces.

Bedstead The frame of a bed, including posts, headboard, and footboard.

Bentwood Round pieces of wood bent by steam and formed to serve as the supporting members of furniture. Often used on Victorian rocking chairs.

Bevel The slanting edge of a surface, such as a mirror or tabletop.

Bib box A wooden box used to hold books and valuable papers.

Binder cane The strips of cane used to edge and finish off hand caning on a chair.

Block-front design A style in which the front of a case piece is formed with alternating blocks, the outer ones usually being extended and the center one recessed.

Bombé A style often used on chests of drawers, characterized by a serpentine horizontal line, with the vertical line swelling out at the bottom.

Bonnet The upper, often elaborate, section of a cabinet or clock.

Bowing A warping in wood that results in a bend along the grain.

Bracket A projecting support or ornament, used between the top of a table or another piece of furniture and its legs or base.

Brass or brazen foot Ornamental brass castings made to enclose the ends of furniture legs.

Breakfront A style of bookcase or sideboard in which the continuity of the front surface is broken by a projecting or receding middle section.

Broken pediment A triangular pediment with the central upper portion cut away.

Buffet A sideboard used to store linens and china and to hold serving pieces during a meal.

Bunfoot A common foot style used on furniture primarily during the William and Mary period; shaped like a bread bun.

Bungee cord A strong elastic cord with hooks at either end.

Bureau Synonymous term for chest of drawers.

Cabriole leg A furniture leg based on the cyma curve.

Cameo carving Carving resembling delicate raised cameo cutting.

Cant A sloping or angled surface or edge.

Carcass The foundation frame of a piece of furniture.

Card table A table for four, used for card playing. The top usually has narrow side leaves or folds over itself. Popular from the William and Mary period through the Victorian period.

Carpet cutter An early form of rocking chair in which the rockers were very narrow—usually less than an inch thick. The rockers extended up into the chair's legs rather than being attached to the ends.

Cartouche An ornament applied to case pieces, in the form of a shield or scroll.

Carver The larger chair in a set of six dining chairs, usually with arms. Some sets have two carver chairs.

Caryatides Figures of women, usually in classical form, used in place of columns or legs on furniture.

Case furniture Furniture made to enclose or store items; i.e., chests, cabinets, desks, and so forth.

Casket box A small wooden or leather box used to hold jewelry and valuables.

Caster The small wheels on the base of furniture legs. Early ones were of wood, later ones of metal or porcelain.

Caul A strip of wood used to protect other wood from damage due to the pressure of metal clamps.

Chaise longue An upholstered couch, often backless, with one end resembling the back of a chair.

Chamfered corner A corner that has been cut

or planed to eliminate the sharp right angle, and in so doing forms another, wider angle.

Chest-on-chest A tall case piece consisting of a smaller chest of drawers attached to the top of a larger chest of drawers.

Chest-on-frame A chest of drawers or cabinet mounted upon a matching framework or desk. Made as two separate pieces.

Chest table The lower section or frame of a chest-on-frame.

Chiffonier A delicately designed sideboard popular during the Victorian period. Narrower than the usual sideboard, it has a shelf or two at the top and enclosed shelves below. The lower cupboard doors often have gathered silk inserts.

Circa "About" or "around" in terms of time. Abbreviated *c.*

Classic styles Styles in emulation of the ancient Greek or Roman styles.

Claw and ball foot A carved animal or bird's claw grasping a ball, used as the terminus of a leg or post.

Claw foot A foot shaped like an animal's paw.

Commode A small, low chest of drawers.

Console A small table with three legs, two at the back and one in the front. The back of the table is flat to fit against a wall, the front usually being a half circle.

Corner chair A chair with a back and one arm, designed to fit into a corner.

Cornice A horizontal molding crowning a case piece.

Court cupboard An ornate open cupboard, usually of oak, designed to store household linens and to display treasures.

Cyma A double curve in which a convex curve and a concave curve are joined as one.

Diaperwork A repeating pattern of diamonds.

Dovetail A joint formed from two interlocking wedge-shaped parts, usually used on drawer sides.

Dowel A wooden pin, usually round, used in place of nails on antique furniture.

Drop-front desk A desk with the writing surface on hinges. This surface is supported by chains while in use as a desk. When not in use, the writing surface is raised, becomes a lid, and is secured with a clasp.

Ebonizing A finish on wood that imitates ebony.

Escutcheon A wooden or brass ornamental plate surrounding a keyhole.

Etagère A highly ornamented whatnot used for the display of decorative objects.

Festoon A garland of fruits, flowers, or leaves suspended from two points—most often carved on furniture.

Field bed A bed with four high posts and a domed, framed canopy.

Finial A decorative terminal part that projects upward from the top of a case piece, lamp, clock, or frame.

Fluting Long, rounded grooves carved into wood, usually in a series of four or more.

French polish A mixture of shellac and alcohol used by furniture refinishers to produce a clear, glossy finish.

Fretwork Ornamental wooden trim consisting of interlaced straight and curved lines.

Frieze A horizontal band of decorations.

Gadrooning A continuous band of parallel, narrow, bulging oval forms.

Gesso A mixture of plaster of paris and water used to surface and make trims for architectural and decorative articles.

Gilding Gold leaf applied to a surface, directly on wood or on a plaster of paris decoration.

Gimp A decorative braid used to trim upholstery.

Gothic A style emulating medieval architecture, characterized by the pointed arch.

Hall stand A tall wooden stand with a mirror, pegs or hooks for hanging hats and scarves, and perhaps an umbrella stand.

Harlequin Furniture that contains secret compartments, usually revealed by touching hidden springs.

Highboy A tall case piece consisting of a chest of drawers placed on a matching frame, which usually has drawers.

Hoof foot A table or chair foot in the shape of an animal hoof.

Hoosier cabinet A freestanding kitchen cabinet, usually consisting of shelves behind doors in the upper section, a flat work surface, and drawers or flour bins in the lower section. Frequently, the upper section contains a flour sifter.

Incised carving Carving in which the design is cut into and below the surface.

Inlay Pieces of wood, metal, shell, ivory, and other materials set into the surface of wood to form pictures or decorative motifs.

Key To roughen the surface of a piece of furniture before painting or staining and varnishing.

Knee The projecting, curved part of a chair or table leg.

Knife box A pierced and slotted box made to hold cutlery.

Ladder-back chair A style characterized by a series of three or more horizontal slats set into upright side posts.

Love seat A small couch intended to seat two people.

Lyre A graceful design used for the ends of tables and backs of chairs, named for the musical instrument of the harp family that it resembles.

Marquetry Decorative inlay work composed of small pieces of veneer of various woods, arranged to form a design against a background of a contrasting-color wood.

Marriage The joining of two or more major parts of as many antiques to form one piece.

Mortise and tenon An especially strong wood joint consisting of a hole cut into one section with a related projection in the other. The two fit closely together when joined.

Ogee curve A cyma curve constructed with the convex portion above and the concave portion below, as in the letter s.

Ormolu A bronze mount with gilding; found on mostly French furniture.

Ovals The generic term used to describe the popular, plain oval frames (often with curved glass) of the nineteenth century.

Parquetry A veneer arranged in a geometric pattern.

Patina A characteristic deep soft glow on wood that comes with years of use and polishing.

Pediment A triangular or curved ornamental top for a case piece.

Pembroke table A small breakfast table with drop leaves and, usually, X-crossed stretchers.

Piecrust-edge table A table with three legs whose top is carved from a solid piece with a raised and fluted edge.

Pier mirror A tall, narrow mirror, often placed above a low table.

Pier table A low table made to stand between two long windows.

Pole bed A bed placed lengthwise against a wall. Midway between foot and head, a tall pole supports drapery, which extends to the head and foot.

Quarter-sawing A form of sawing, now outmoded, in which logs are sawn first into quarters, then into boards. The purpose is to expose a distinct grain.

Quartetto tables Set of four tables that nest one under the other.

Rail The horizontal members of a chair, table, or other type of furniture frame.

Raised carving Carving in which the raised surface varies to different planes.

Relief carving Carving in which the raised design height is fairly uniform above the surface.

Reproduction A modern copy of an antique.

Rococo A style of decoration, developed in France, characterized by elaborate and profuse flowing curves and motifs, often with deeply carved designs imitating foliage, shells, scrolls, and so forth.

Sawbuck table Swedish-inspired table with a top supported at either end by X-shaped members joined by a long stretcher.

Scroll feet Furniture feet that resemble rolled-up scrolls.

Secretary A drop-front desk surmounted by a bookcase top. Also, a side-by-side arrangement with a glass-fronted bookcase alongside the desk.

Serpentine A style usually used on dressers or chests of drawers, in which the front is curved, usually with two outer convex curves and one inner concave curve.

Settee A small sofa.

Settle A primitive form of seat—essentially a long chest with a lid—having a high back and low arms.

Sewing rocker A low, armless rocking chair.

Shield-back chair A chair in which the back fans out in an oval shape.

Shim A thin, wedge-shaped piece of wood or metal used to fill a space (n.); to fit with a shim (v.).

Sideboard A large cabinet made especially for the dining room, usually filled with drawers and cupboards for storing flatware, dinner china, and table linens.

Side chair A chair without arms.

Skirt A vertical band of wood on a table, just below the top.

Slant-top desk Similar to a drop-front desk, with the lid forming an angle when closed. Sometimes supported when open with pulls rather than chains.

Sleigh bed A bedstead with a high headboard and footboard, each rolled outward.

Slipper chair A low chair with short legs, originally used by women to change their shoes.

Splat A flat board that extends from the top rail to the seat in chair backs.

Spline Thin pieces of cane that hold sheet cane in chair grooves.

Split spindle A spindle split lengthwise into two parts. Applied as ornament to case pieces.

Spoon-back chair A chair whose back is formed to fit the contours of the human spine.

Stretcher The horizontal members that brace and join the legs of a piece of furniture.

Tambour Narrow strips of wood glued and nailed to cloth. Used to close rolltop desks, Hoosier cabinets, and so forth.

Tester The fabric covering for a framework that tops the four tall posts of a bed.

Tilt-top table A small table or candle stand constructed so that the top can be tilted up on a hinge and locked in place.

Transitional A term used to describe any piece of furniture that transcends two or more styles and contains elements of each.

Tripod tables Three-legged tables whose legs slope outward from top to base.

Trundle bed A small bed on casters that rolls underneath a regular bed when not in use.

Veneer Thin cabinet wood used to top wood of lesser quality.

Washstand A small table, sometimes with drawers and/or compartments, made to hold a basin and pitcher.

Whatnot A set of open shelves used to display china, books, pictures, and so on.

Windsor chair Any of several styles of chair, all with slender spindles rising from a wooden seat.

Wire brads Small nails of a uniform thickness, often used to attach trims and moldings.

SUGGESTED READING

The following publications are both interesting and valuable for anyone interested in antiquing as a hobby or second career:

Books

Fake, Fraud, or Genuine?: Identifying Authentic American Antique Furniture, Myrna Kaye, Bulfinch, 1991

Field Guide to American Antique Furniture, Joseph T. Butler, Owl Books, 1986

George Michael's Treasury of Federal Antiques, George Michael, Hawthorn Books, 1972

How to Make $20,000 a Year in Antiques and Collectibles Without Leaving Your Job, Bruce E. Johnson, Ballantine Books, 1987

How to Start a Home-Based Antiques Business, Bob Brooke, Globe Pequot Press, 2005

Kovels' Guide to Selling Your Antiques & Collectibles, Ralph and Terry Kovel, Crown Publishing Group, 1990

The Lyle Official Antiques Review 2004, Anthony Curtis, Perigee Books, 2003

Pictorial Price Guide to American Antiques 2005–2006, Dorothy Hammond, Antique Collectors' Club, 2005

Refurbishing Antiques, Rosemary Ratcliff, Pelham, 1971

Schroeder's Antiques Price Guide 2007, Schroeder Publishing (editor), Collector Books (division of Schroeder Publishing Company), 2006

Shaker: A Collector's Source Book II, Don and Carol Raycraft, Wallace-Homestead Book Company, 1985

The Treasury of New England Antiques, George Michael, Galahad Books, 1969

Weekend Refinisher, Bruce E. Johnson, Ballantine Books, 1989

Magazines

American Antiquities Journal
126 East High Street
Springfield, OH 45502
(937) 322–6281
www.americanantiquities.com/journal.html

Antique Trader Weekly & Price Guide
700 East State Street
Iola, WI 54990-0001
(800) 258–0929
www.antiquetrader.com

Antique Week
27 North Jefferson
Knightstown, IN 46148
(317) 345–5133
www.antiqueweek.com

Antiques and the Arts Weekly
The Bee Publishing Co., Inc.
5 Church Hill Road
Newtown, CT 06470-5503
(203) 426–8036
www.antiquesandthearts.com

Antiques & Auction News
1425 West Main Street
West Mount Joy, PA 17552
(717) 653–1833

Antiques & Collecting Hobbies
1006 South Michigan Avenue
Chicago, IL 60605
(312) 939–4767

Antiques Journal
92 Main Street
Ware, MA 01082
(413) 967–3505

Antiques Magazine
980 Madison Avenue
New York, NY 10021
(212) 734–9797
www.antiquesmag.com

Antiquing USA
Route 2, Box 11
Fontanell, IA 50846–9702

Art & Antiques
89 Fifth Avenue
New York, NY 10003
(212) 206–7050
www.artandantiques.net

Coastal Antiques & Art
P.O. Box 1088
Savannah, GA 31402
(912) 652–0487
www.coastalantiques.com

Collectors News
506 Second Street
Grundy Center, IA 50638
(319) 824–6981

Maine Antique Digest
911 Main Street
Waldoboro, ME 04572
(207) 832–7534
www.maineantiquedigest.com

New York Antique Almanac
P.O. Box 335
Lawrence, NY 11559
(914) 371–3300

Renninger's Antique Guide
P.O. Box 495
Lafayette Hill, PA 19444
(800) 827–6392
www.renningers.com

Southeastern Antiquing & Collecting Magazine
P.O. Box 510
Acworth, GA 30101
(888) 358–7827
www.go-star.com/antiquing

West Coast Peddler
P.O. Box 5134
Whittier, CA 90607
(562) 698–1718
www.westcoastpeddler.com

RESOURCES

The following list includes some of the firms that provide supplies for refinishing and restoring antique furniture. For a small fee, most of the companies will send catalogs describing their products, or you can visit their Web sites to order their products.

STAINS, FINISHES, AND WAXES ARE
AVAILABLE AT ALL HARDWARE AND
PAINT STORES.

Antique Trunk Company
3706 West 169th Street
Cleveland, OH 44111
(216) 941–8618
(Trunk hardware)

The Arden Forge
301 Brinton's Bridge Road
West Chester, PA 19382
(215) 399–1530
(Antique hardware)

B&B Rare Woods
4581 South Queen Street
Littleton, CO 80127
(303) 986–2585
www.wood-veneers.com
(Wood veneers)

B&H Photo Video
420 Ninth Avenue
New York, NY 10001
(800) 606–6969
www.bhphotovideo.com
(Photographic supplies)

Ball and Ball
463 West Lincoln Highway
Exton, PA 19341
(800) 257–3711
www.ballandball-us.com
(Reproduction hardware)

Barewood LLC
106 Ferris Street
Brooklyn, NY 11231
(718) 875–9037
(Antique hardware)

Blenko Glass Company
P.O. Box 167
Milton, WV 25541
(304) 743–9081
(Antique glass)

The Caning Shop
926 Gilman Street
Berkeley, CA 94710
(800) 544–3373
www.caningshop.com
(Caning supplies)

Charlotte Ford Trunks
P.O. Box 536
Spearman, TX 79081
(806) 659–3027
(Trunk hardware)

Doug's Supply Co.
144 Sheldon
Climax, MI 49034
(269) 746–4104
www.doug-supplies.com
(Brass reproduction hardware and casters)

The Faux Shop
301 South Main Street
Poplar Bluff, MO 63901
(573) 778–9967
www.fauxshop.com/wax.htm
(Metallic waxes)

Frank's Cane & Rush Supply
7244 Heil Avenue
Huntington Beach, CA 92647
(714) 847–0707
(Caning supplies and tools)

Furniture Knowledge
17012 Dwyer Road
Bonner Springs, KS 66012
(888) 498–4345
www.furnitureknowledge.com
(Furniture repair parts, wood care supplies, trunk hardware)

Horton Brasses
Nook's Hill Road #95
Cromwell, CT 06416
(860) 635–4400
www.horton-brasses.com
(Antique hardware)

Merritt's
1860 Weavertown Road
Douglasville, PA 19518
(610) 689–9541
www.merritts.com
(Clock-related parts, supplies, and clock glass)

The Old Fashioned Milk Paint Co.
436 Main Street
Groton, MA 01450-0222
(978) 448–6336
www.milkpaint.com
(Milk paint powders)

Paxton Hardware Company
7818 Bradshaw Road
Upper Falls, MD 21156
(410) 592–8505
(Lamp hardware)

Renovator's Supply Inc.
Renovator's Old Mill
Bridge Street
Miller's Falls, MA 01349
(413) 659–2241
www.rensup.com
(Reproduction hardware)

Restoration Hardware
417 Second Street
Eureka, CA 95501
(707) 443–3152
(Reproduction hardware)

Rockler Woodworking & Hardware
4365 Willow Drive
Medina, MN 55340
(800) 279–4411
www.rockler.com
(Darkening solution, brass cleaner)

S. LaRose, Inc.
3223 Yanceyville Street
P.O. Box 212038
Greensboro, NC 27420
(910) 621–1936
(Clock repair supplies)

Van Dyke's Restorers
P.O. Box 278
39771 S.D. Highway 34
Woonsocket, SD 57385
(605) 796–4425
www.vandykes.com
(Replacement chair seats)

Williamsburg Blacksmiths
Goshen Road
Williamsburg, MA 01096
(413) 268–3206
www.williamsburgblacksmiths.com
(Reproduction hardware)

Woodbury Blacksmith & Forge
Main Street South
Woodbury, CT 06798
(203) 263–5737
(Reproduction hardware)

INDEX

Runners, 26-27

The late **JACQUELYN PEAKE** discovered a badly neglected antique at a garage sale more than thirty years ago. By the time she had refinished it, she was firmly launched into a lifelong hobby of discovering and refinishing antiques. An avid writer and lecturer, she spent many hours sharing her wealth of antiquing knowledge with enthusiasts across the country.

As an avid collector of a variety of antiques and collectibles for the last twenty years, **BOB BROOKE** knows what he's writing about. Besides writing about antiques, Brooke conducts seminars on antiques for various organizations, including the Smithsonian Institution in Washington, D.C. In addition, he has also sold in flea markets and shops. His antiques articles have appeared in many antiques and consumer publications, including *British Heritage, AntiqueWeek, American Antiquities Journal, Southeastern Antiquing and Collecting Magazine, History Magazine,* and many others. To read more of his articles, visit his main Web site, Writing at Its Best (www.bobbrooke.com) or his specialty antiques site, the Antiques Almanac (www.theantiquesalmanac.com).